SO-ABB-713

Contents at a Glance

BONUS CONTENT ON THE WEB
Visit www.samspublishing.com/register to register your book and gain access to the following exclusive bonus content:

Roxio®
Easy Media Creator™ 8

Lisa DaNae Dayley

SAMS
Teach
Yourself

Sams Publishing, 800 East 96th Street, Indianapolis, Indiana 46240 USA

Roxio® Easy Media Creator™ 8 In a Snap

Copyright © 2006 by Sams Publishing

International Standard Book Number: 0-672-32865-8

Library of Congress Catalog Card Number: 2005934723

Printed in the United States of America

First Printing: February 2006

09   08   07   06   4   3   2

Trademarks

Warning and Disclaimer

Bulk Sales

Sams Publishing offers excellent discounts on this book when ordered in quantity for bulk purchases or special sales. For more information, please contact

> **U.S. Corporate and Government Sales**
> **1-800-382-3419**
> corpsales@pearsontechgroup.com

For sales outside of the U.S., please contact

> **International Sales**
> international@pearsoned.com

Senior Acquisitions Editor
Linda Harrison

Development Editor
Jon Steever

Managing Editor
Charlotte Clapp

Project Editor
Seth Kerney

Production Editor
Heather Wilkins

Indexer
Ken Johnson

Proofreader
Juli Cook

Technical Editor
Stephen Nathans

Publishing Coordinator
Vanessa Evans

Interior Designer
Gary Adair

About the Author

Lisa DaNae Dayley was in two clubs in high school: the writing club and the computer club. She graduated from Brigham Young University with a bachelor's degree in advertising and has pursued those interests ever since. She has owned her own media creation business for 11 years. When she isn't on the computer, she can be found trying to round up her four sons or in the great outdoors, preferably in a Jeep. She is married to Brad Dayley, who is, of course, a software engineer and a writer.

Dedication

To Brad, with all my love, A & F

To my mother, who always believed in me.

Acknowledgments

This book was a collaboration of several incredible talents. My name is the only one on the front because there simply wasn't room for everyone. So for all of you who have made this work possible, here's your name in print!

A big thanks to Linda Harrison who put a lot of faith in me and was there every time I needed her. It was a great experience working with you!

Thank you, Stephen Nathans, for a great tech edit. You shared some of my same frustrations and provided invaluable information and insight.

Thanks to Jon Steever and Heather Wilkins for cleaning up my messes and helping me to create a polished finished product.

Thanks to Seth Kerney, who is most certainly an expert in translation! Anyone who can read and clean up that final draft has my admiration.

Becky Johnson, you've been a great friend! You have been my domestic support and really made this book possible by helping me with my home-front emergencies.

A huge thanks goes to my two oldest sons, Brendan and Caleb, who took a lot of extra responsibility on their shoulders so I could write. Thanks for not complaining and for being proud of me.

And finally, all my love and thanks to the man that believed in me, supported me, and even pushed me at times—my husband, Brad. Without him, this work would still be a dream on my part.

We Want to Hear from You!

As the reader of this book, *you* are our most important critic and commentator. We value your opinion and want to know what we're doing right, what we could do better, what areas you'd like to see us publish in, and any other words of wisdom you're willing to pass our way.

You can email or write me directly to let me know what you did or didn't like about this book—as well as what we can do to make our books stronger.

Please note that I cannot help you with technical problems related to the topic of this book, and that due to the high volume of mail I receive, I might not be able to reply to every message.

When you write, please be sure to include this book's title and author as well as your name and phone or email address. I will carefully review your comments and share them with the author and editors who worked on the book.

Email: consumer@samspublishing.com

Mail: Mark Taber
         Associate Publisher
         Sams Publishing
         800 East 96th Street
         Indianapolis, IN 46240 USA

Reader Services

For more information about this book or another Sams title, visit our website at www.samspublishing.com. Type the ISBN (excluding hyphens) or the title of a book in the Search field to find the page you're looking for.

✔ Start Here

Roxio Easy Media Creator 8 is actually a suite of more than 25 different applications, most of them designed to do widely different tasks. That's why it is important to understand these applications and how they work together to give you a complete media toolbox.

Getting to Know the Roxio Creator 8 Suite Home Page

The first step in understanding how the applications work together is to understand Roxio Creator 8 Suite Home. The **Home** page is divided into the **Project** window, the **project** pane, and the **Control** panel.

Project Window

The **Project** window displays whatever is selected in the **project** pane. For instance, if you have the **Audio** menu selected, the **Project** window automatically displays the **Audio Guide**. A few applications, such as **Jukebox Disc**, run from the **Project** window.

Project Pane

Project Window

The Roxio Easy Media Creator 8 **Home** *page.*

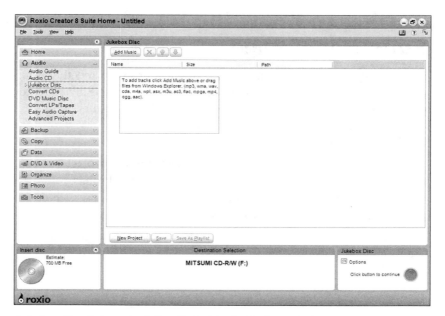

Jukebox Disc *is launched directly inside the* **Project** *window.*

Project Pane

+ MEDIA & DEVICES

The **project** pane effectively divides the applications into nine categories: **Home, Audio, Backup, Copy, Data, DVD & Video, Organize, Photo,** and **Tools.** Some of these categories have several applications, and some of them have only one or two. Easy Media Creator has attempted to make the menus more user-friendly by naming the tasks rather than creating a list of the applications. This works just fine when you are aware of the applications that are brought up by clicking on each task and what your other options are.

If you want to create a label for your disc, for instance, you would look under the **Tools** menu and click on **Label Disc.** When you do this, you are bringing up **Express Labeler,** a step-by-step wizard that walks you through each step of creating your label. If you are unfamiliar with the label-creating process, this wizard is great for introducing you to the basic concepts of label creation and even gives you the option of exporting your project into **Label Creator,** the full-fledged application, when you are finished with the steps of the process.

Launching Express Labeler

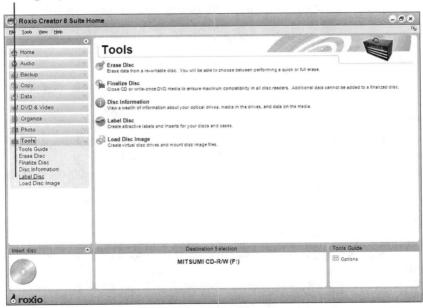

Express Labeler is launched from the Tools menu.

Launching Label Creator

*Launch **Label Creator** from a list of applications.*

But if you are familiar with **Label Creator**, you will probably find that creating just the right label is actually faster if you don't use **Express Labeler**. But how do you launch **Label Creator** without going through **Express Labeler** first? This is where the **Home** menu comes into play. If you choose the **Home** menu, one of the options you have is **Applications**. When you click on **Applications**, a list of applications comes up in the **Project** window. This list is nowhere near comprehensive, but it contains many applications that you can't find under the project menus, including **Label Creator**.

▶ NOTE

One other option you have for starting applications in the Easy Media Creator Suite is to choose **Roxio Easy Media Creator 8** from the **Start, Programs** menu. Under the Roxio Easy Media Creator 8 heading, you find eight project folders labeled **Audio, Backup, Copy,** and so forth. Each folder has a list of applications that apply to that particular project type. You select these applications by clicking on the application name rather than the type of task, as on the Roxio **Home** page. After you become familiar with the names of each application and what it can be used for, using the **Start** menu to open them will probably become the easiest option.

*Launching applications from the **Start** menu.*

Although you can't find all the applications in any one menu, you can find the same application in different menus. For instance, **Media Import** launches from the **Photo** menu if you click **Import Photos** and from the **DVD & Video** menu if you click **Capture**.

The final thing that you should be aware of concerning the applications is that sometimes the same, or essentially the same, application launches under different headings and sometimes different formats. The most notable is **Media Manager**, which is discussed later in the chapter, but there are also other applications to which this applies. **Easy Audio Capture**, for instance, comes up if you choose it out of the **Audio** menu. You will also find the exact same elements in the first step of the **LP and Tape Assistant** as well as in the audio tab in **Media Import**. As long as you are familiar with the basic elements in these applications, you will have no problem using the different versions of them.

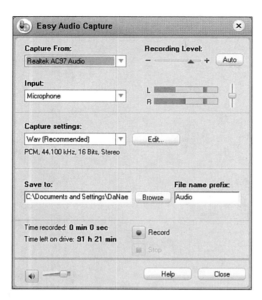

Easy Audio Capture.

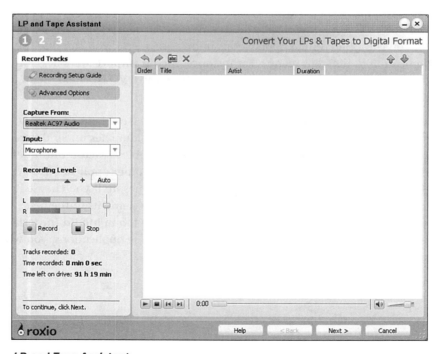

LP and Tape Assistant.

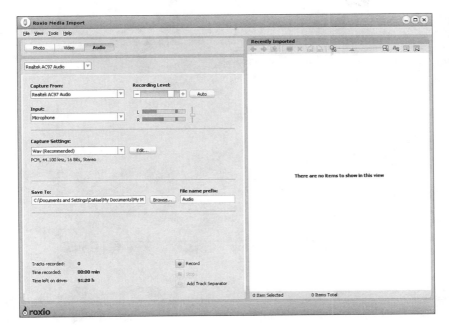

Media Import.

Control Panel

The **Control** panel in the Easy Media Creator **Home** page is fairly self explanatory. It contains three elements:

- The **Media Information Display** shows the information about the disc or hard drive that is the destination of your project.

- The **Input** panel displays several things, depending on your project. The destination drive, a progress indicator, and playback controls are among them.

- The **Action** area contains an **Options** icon that you can click on to change the settings of a particular project. It can also display a **Continue** button.

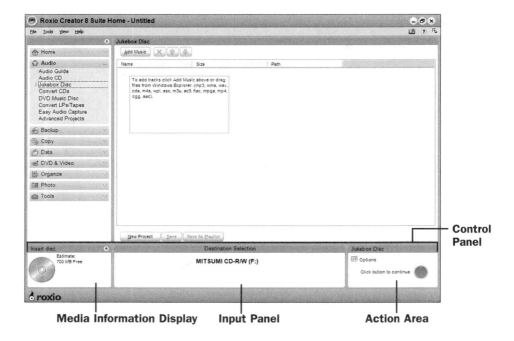

Media Information Display   Input Panel   Action Area

About Storage Media

Storage media are devices you can use to store your computer files. While you are using Easy Media Creator, you need to use storage media for various tasks such as saving files you import into the computer, saving projects you are working on, backing up your data, and creating portable copies of your files.

Storage media devices are given a letter designator on your computer that allows you to identify them. For instance, if you start **Windows Explorer** and look under **My Computer**, you should at least see one drive with the designator C:.

The following sections discuss the different types of storage media that you will be using as you import files and create projects in the Easy Media Creator suite.

Hard Drives

Hard drives are the main type of storage for your computers. Almost all computers have at least one internal hard drive with the C: letter designator. You can add additional hard drives by adding an internal hard drive inside your computer case. There are also external hard drives that plug into the computer using a USB or FireWire port. As you add additional drives they are given their own drive letter designator. Your computer might also have a partitioned hard drive that is segmented to store different types of data, such as applications and files, on different sections of the hard drive. If you have a hard drive with partitions, it appears in My Computer with two drive-letter designators, such as C: or D:.

When you can, use your hard drives to store the files with which you are working. The hard drive is much faster than any other storage media. Hard drives also can contain much more data, upwards of 500GB per disk.

CD-R

CD-R media are recordable CDs that allow you to write files onto them. The CD-burner drive, used to write files to disc, has its own drive letter designator, just like a hard drive. You use this designator to identify the drive when burning data and to access the data on discs that have been written.

You can use CD-Rs to create music discs, to make portable copies of your files to take to other locations, or to back up your PC. However, a CD-R disc only holds about 700MB of data, so space is limited.

There are also CD-RW discs that allow you to erase and then rewrite files onto them. CD-RW discs are more expensive than the CD-Rs and there are a limited number of times they can be rewritten before they must be replaced. Also, if you create an audio CD using a CD-RW disc, many CD players won't recognize the disc. CD-RW discs are also written more slowly than CD-Rs. For those reasons, CD-Rs are still more popular.

DVD±R

DVD±R media are recordable DVDs similar to the CD-R media. The biggest difference is that a DVD±R disc contains about 4.7GB of space. If you have large amounts of data you need to put on a disc, this is the best choice. You also use the DVD±R media to create DVDs that can be played in a standard player.

Recordable DVD media comes in two flavors: DVD-R and DVD+R. The only difference between + and – discs is that different manufacturers own the patents on them. Otherwise, they are identical, and if you bought your DVD burner in the past three years, it will burn both types of discs. Both DVD+R and DVD-R discs play in most, but not all, DVD players. If you burn a DVD that your player does not recognize, try another brand.

Several companies have also started manufacturing DVD±R DL discs. The DL stands for dual-layer. DL discs can store 8.5GB of data because they have two layers of storage on the recordable side of the disc. Creator can handle DL recording, but many burners cannot record these discs. The discs are expensive, the technology is still fairly new, and many players won't play DL discs, so you're better off sticking with regular 4.7GB DVD±R.

There are also rewritable DVD discs called DVD±RW. They have the same advantages and disadvantages of CD-RWs. Unless you plan on doing a lot of erasing and rewriting, DVD±R is a more reliable choice.

USB Disks

USB disks are similar to the external hard drives mentioned earlier. They connect to the computer using the USB port. The big difference is that they are much smaller, about the size of a finger, and only hold up to 1 or 2GB of data. When you connect a USB disk to the computer, it is given its own drive letter designator to access it.

Flash Memory

Flash memory are small cards that act like tiny hard drives. They are called flash memory cards because their memory can quickly be erased and replaced by new data. These cards are used to store data for numerous electronic devices, such as pictures taken by digital cameras.

A card reader must be used to read flash memory cards on the computer. Some computers come with built-in card readers, or you might need an external card reader that connects to the computer using the USB port.

There are seven types of flash memory media cards. The most popular are Secure Digital (SD), MemoryStick, and Compact Flash. They vary in size and appearance. However, many card readers now are able to read most or all of them.

To use a flash memory card, simply insert it into the card reader and a new drive letter for it is added. You can then access the card just like a hard drive.

Hard/USB Disks

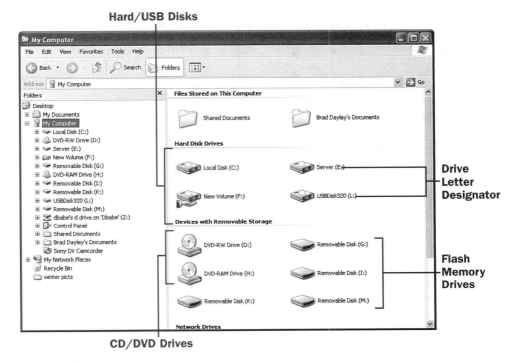

CD/DVD Drives

Hard drive variations.

About Media Files

As you begin to use Easy Media Creator to import photos, audio, and video, you will be confronted with some file type choices. This section will help you understand the different media file types so it will be easier for you to know which type to use and when to use it.

Audio Files

Audio files are any type of file that stores sound. When you import music from a CD or record a voice from a microphone or music from a record player, the sound is stored in an audio file. The following are the three main types of audio file you should know about.

MP3

MP3 files are audio files that are compressed. Compressing the files makes them much smaller so they are easier to transfer and you can fit more of them on a disk. However, compressing the audio results in a slight quality loss.

The most common use of MP3 file is for portable MP3 players, allowing people to have literally hundreds of songs at their fingertips at any time. Easy Media Creator allows you to capture MP3 files and add them to DVDs and MP3 CDs.

WAV

WAV files are audio files that are not compressed. They take up considerably more space. However, WAV files retain the full audio quality of an audio CD. If you are working with high quality audio or are using an application that does not accept MP3 files as audio, you need to use WAV files.

WMA

WMA files are smaller than WAV files. They are typically used as streaming audio for the Internet and are a good way to transfer audio through email because most Windows applications can access them.

Image/Photo Files

One of the best features in Easy Media Creator Suite is the ability to import, edit, and use images for a variety of projects. Image files can be photos that you import or graphic files that you create and save using applications on the computer. The following are the five main types of image files you should know about.

JPG

JPG (Joint Photographic Experts Group) files are compressed image files. The compression makes them much smaller and easier to use than uncompressed image files with only a slight loss of quality. For images that will only be displayed on the computer screen, JPG is definitely the way to go. JPG is also the standard format for most digital cameras, so the photos you copy from your camera to the computer are in JPG format already. JPG is usually a high enough quality to print photos to photo paper on a home printer.

TIFF

TIFF (Tagged Image File Format) is a high-quality image file format. TIFF files are used by professional photo studios that need the highest quality to have the ability to create large photo prints.

BMP

BMP (bitmap) is the standard graphic format for Microsoft Windows. This format is used to display windows and applications. The files are full quality and very large, similar to TIFF files.

GIF

GIF (Graphics Interchange Format) files are typically used as graphic files for web pages. They are compressed, so they take up less space. GIF files include two channels which allow them to be animated and have transparent backgrounds. Most GIF files are not typically good enough quality for printing photos to photo paper on a home printer.

PNG

The PNG (Portable Network Graphic) file format was designed to replace GIF as the web graphic format. It is also compressed and supports transparency.

▶ TIP

Just as when you copy a paper on a Xerox machine or duplicate a VHS tape, you lose quality every time you convert a file to a compressed format such as MPEG-2 for a video file or JPG for a photo file. As you edit these files, keep them in the highest quality format possible and try not to convert them more than necessary.

Video Files

Easy Media Creator Suite includes several utilities that allow you to capture, edit, and output video files. A video file is a file that usually contains both video and audio streams.

You can save your home movies as video files on the computer and then use those video files, as well as audio files and photo files, to create home video productions. The following are the main types of video files you need to know about.

MPEG-2

MPEG-2 is the compressed video format used on DVDs. It is not the highest quality, but it's obviously good enough for the current entertainment systems. You use this format to create DVDs.

▶ TIP

If the Easy Media Creator application uses only MPG or MPEG, it is referring to the MPEG-2 format.

MPEG-4

MPEG-4 is compressed even more than MPEG-2, which makes it smaller than MPEG-2 but reduces the quality. Although MPEG-4 is not compatible with the DVD format required by DVD players, it is perfect for sharing on computers or across the Internet.

DivX

DivX is based on the MPEG-4 file format. It is also compressed and is designed for use on the Internet. This format is becoming very popular on web pages for streaming video.

DV

DV is the high-quality video format used by most digital camcorders. It is full quality, but takes up much more space than the MPEG formats.

AVI

AVI is the computer equivalent of the DV format. AVI files take up much more disk space per minute of video than MPEG-2, but they are much higher quality. Most video-editing applications, including **VideoWave**, work natively in the AVI file format.

▶ **TIP**

If you are capturing video that you want to edit and use to create a video production, capture the video in AVI format. The video-editing applications will be faster because they do not have to convert from MPG to AVI.

Understanding Files and Folders

Capturing, importing, manipulating, saving, and viewing files on your computer is a major part of working with Easy Media Creator. Managing files and folders can be difficult and confusing if you are not familiar with the concept. If you are familiar with creating and managing folders and files, this section is a no-brainer, so feel free to skip it.

Because understanding how files and folders work is imperative to make the most of Easy Media Creator, this section discusses files and how to keep track of and manage them by creating folders.

Files

A *file* is simply a single data entity, for example, a photo, letter, video, or song that is stored on the computer in digital format. As you begin to use Easy Media Creator, you use files in one of three basic ways.

The first way that you will likely start using files is as a media file. A *media file* is created when you capture audio, video, or photos on the computer. For instance, if you capture video from a camcorder, that video is stored on the computer as a video file. Media files can be viewed on the computer or used by applications to create some kind of finished product. For instance, you could use several video, audio, and photo files to create a home movie and put it on a DVD.

The next way you will be using files is as a saved project file. As you create a project such as greeting card, DVD, and so on, you can save the settings and changes in a project file. The project file can be reloaded later, even if the computer has been rebooted, and all your settings and changes are restored. Almost all applications have **Save** and **Save As** options that allow you to save your settings to a file.

The final type of file that you will be using is the finished product files you output from your projects. For example, if you take photo files and use **Slideshow Assistant** to create a slideshow, you could save the finished slideshow as a video file. Another example is if you create a data CD project and output the finished project to a disc image file.

What you need to understand when creating or saving files is that you are creating individual items on the computer. You should give the file a name that is meaningful to you and can be used to recognize it later.

Folders

Now that you understand what files you will be working with, you need to know how to organize them. Imagine if all the files on the computer were stored in the same place. There would be literally hundreds of thousands of files all together. It would be a nightmare trying to find just one specific file.

You should create folders on your computer disks to store the files in separate locations. A *folder* is storage location on disk that can contain files as well as other folders. You can organize your files to make them easier to find and manage by creating folders and *subfolders* (a folder contained in another folder) with meaningful names to keep track of your files.

For example, if you are going to import a few thousand photos into your computer, you could create a folder with the name of each year that the photos were taken and then store the appropriate photos in the appropriate folders. If one particular year had many photos, you could create subfolders named for each month under the folder of that year. Then organize the photo files for that year by placing them in the appropriate month subfolder.

Another example of using folders to organize your files is to create a folder for each person that uses the computer. That way each person could save her own files in her own folder and always know where to find them.

Creating a folder is very easy; select a drive or a subfolder in Windows Explorer and select **File**, **New**, **Folder** from the main menu, and then type in the name of the folder. Before you begin using Easy Media Creator, you should get used to creating folders to organize your files. This helps you keep track of the files you import and save.

▶ **TIP**

If you save your files to a different disk than the C: drive, it can speed up your applications. Windows and applications use the C: drive to store temporary files, so you get better performance if your files are on a different disk.

Disk Drives
Main Menu

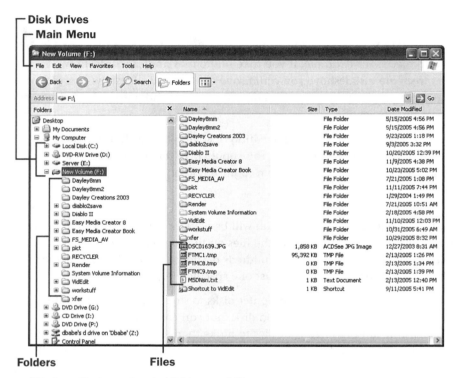

Folders   **Files**

Windows Explorer showing folders and files.

Understanding Media Manager

Media Manager is a superb organizational tool within the Roxio Easy Media Creator Suite. It allows you to store several links to your media files so you can find them by date, subject, or file type. You can also look at the files you have recently imported or most recently used.

In addition, you can create your own albums to customize your organization if you want. Because the files you store in your albums are only links to the actual file rather than a copy of the file, you can store your photos in as many albums as you like without using a significant amount of memory. For instance, you might want to create an album for each member of your family, an album for family vacations, and an album for each month. A picture of the family taken in Yellowstone in July of 2005 can be stored in all of these albums.

Understanding **Media Manager** is essential to every aspect of Easy Media Creator. Every time you add a file to a project, **Media Manager** opens to allow you to select that file. **Media Manager** comes up in essentially the same format, but under several names. **Media Selector**, **Add Photos**, and **Insert Photos/Videos** are a few examples.

If you have already created your own albums, or if you have folders that you have set up for your specific media files, you are much better prepared to use **Media Manager** to import your files into your projects.

▶ TIP

If you have yet to import any media files, please take the time to set up folders to store them in so you can find them whenever you want. You can use the Windows default, which is **My Documents**. **My Documents** is divided into **My Photos**, **My Videos**, **My Music**, and so forth. Or you can create your own folders wherever and however you choose. The important thing is to know where they are and to use them consistently.

Understanding the Browse Area

When you launch **Media Manager** from the **Organize** menu in the Easy Media Creator **Home** page, you get the works. **Media Manager** is not only an organizer, but it contains several fun tools that enhance your viewing and sharing experience. Take a look at Chapter 16, "Media Manager Tools," to get a run-down on how to watch an impromptu slideshow, email your photos, or share your media files over a network or the Internet.

Here, we are going to focus on organizing your files and using the pared-down version of **Media Manager** that pops up anytime you want to add a file to a project. Specifically, we are going to focus on the **Browse** area of the **Media Manager** window.

Browse Area

Media Manager.

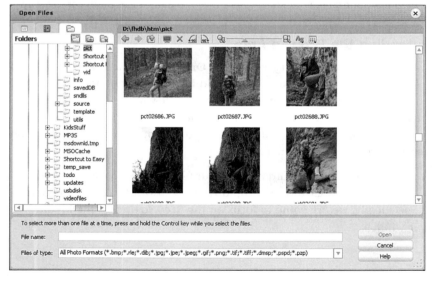

Media Manager when used to import a photo into PhotoSuite.

The **Browse** area contains four tabs: the **My Media** tab, the **My Albums** tab, the **Folders** tab, and the **My MediaSpace** tab. MediaSpace is covered in **126** **Share Media Files on Your Home or Business Network with MediaSpace** (on the Web), so only the first three are discussed here.

My Media
  My Albums
    Folders
      My MediaSpace

The four tabs of the **Browse** *area.*

My Media View

As you import files with Easy Media Creator, whether you use **Media Manager** or another application, a link to them is automatically stored within the **My Media** area. The **My Media** area is categorized into media types such as **All Photos** or **All Videos**. Clicking on any one of these options places all of the files in the area into the **File View**. This is perfect if you have very few files to choose from and you want to see them all. But if you have many files, you are going to want to narrow your choices to make the process of choosing a file a bit easier. By clicking on the **Plus** icon next to each one of these objects, you can bring up the following subcategories:

How would you like to sort your photos?

- **Date**—You can choose to look at the files by the date they were created. The menu starts with a list of years, and after you've clicked on the year, it then narrows it down to months.

▶ **NOTE**

Be aware that sorting your files by date can be deceptive in some cases. For instance, a photo that has been scanned is sorted by the date that it was scanned because there is no other way for Easy Media Creator to assign a date to it. If you want your files to be sorted by the date that they were actually created, you can create custom albums for each date and sort them yourself.

- **Recently Imported**—If you click on the **Recently Imported** option, **Media Manager** brings up a preview of the files that you have most recently imported into Easy Media Creator. This is the fastest way to add the files you have most recently imported into a new project.

- **Most Recently Used**—You can also sort the files by most recently used. This brings up a view of the files you have used most recently in an application in Easy Media Creator.

- **Rating**—As you view your files in **Media Manager**, you can rate them from one to five stars. You can use the rating system any way you like. Use it the conventional way and rate the files by your personal preference, or you can devise your own system. For instance, you could rate files that you know you want to use frequently as five stars. However you decide to rate them, you can sort them by their rating by clicking on the rating option.

- **Custom View**—You can create a your own custom views into which to sort your files. First you need to perform a search. Type your search criteria in the search box in the **File View** taskbar, or click on the **More** button to bring up your **Search** options. Choose your search criteria and perform the search. When the search is finished, you are given the option to create a new album or a custom view. Click on **Create a New Custom View** and give your custom view a name. It is added to the **Media** options.

My Albums View

The albums in **Media Manager** are completely customized by you. Unlike the **Media** options, the albums are not filled automatically, and you need to add your files to the albums. You can create as many albums as you want, and it is relatively easy to drag and drop your files into any or all of them. Albums act just exactly like folders.

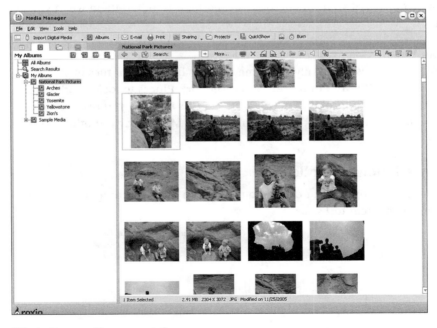

What albums will you create?

▶ **NOTE**

Remember that you are only creating a link to your file when you drag and drop it into an album. Don't worry about placing your file into as many albums as you like—the links do not take up a significant amount of hard disk space.

Start by clicking the **My Albums** tab at the top of the **Browse** window. This shows the **My Albums** view. There are a few prenamed albums in this area—you can use them or create your own.

To create your own album, simply click on the **New Album** icon in the **My Albums** options menu. This creates a new album with the name highlighted so you can type in a customized name.

At this point you are going to want to split the view so you can easily drag and drop files into your new album. In the **Media Manager** taskbar, click on the **Split View** icon. This divides the **Browse** and **Preview** areas into an upper and lower section. In the upper section, browse to the location of the files you want to add to your album. In the lower section, open your new album. Drag and drop files from the upper window into the lower window to fill your album. It's that easy.

Create as many albums as you like and add links to as many files as you like. The more organized your files become, the easier it is to find them when you need them.

Folders View

The **Folders** view is essentially the same thing as browsing for files in Windows Explorer. Start with **My Computer** or **My Network Places** to look for files you have stored on your local and network drives. This is where you need to start because until you have imported files into **Media Manager**, your other views are empty.

Advanced Viewing Options

You have several options for changing the view in **Media Manager**. Different views make different tasks easier.

Split View Icon   Sort Icon
                                                   View As Icon

Filter Icon

Click an icon to change the view.

View As

Select the **View as** icon from the **File View** taskbar to see a list of options for viewing each file. The default view is **Thumbnails**. You can add the file names to the thumbnails by choosing the **Thumbnails with text** option. The **Details** option shrinks the thumbnails significantly and displays more information about each, such as the file size, date, and rating.

► **TIP**

Choosing the **Details** view is probably the easiest way to rate your files. The **Details** menu shows several files at once, along with their ratings. You can quickly add or change any of these ratings by clicking on the desired star.

To get the details of your photo and a full thumbnail, choose the **Information** view. Last, if you would like to see as many files as possible (easier for dragging and dropping purposes), choose the **List** view to show a small thumbnail with the file name only.

Sort

Select the **Sort** icon in the **File View** taskbar to sort your files by name, size, date created, date modified, type, or rating.

Filter

In the **My Albums** view, you can filter your files by type. This is very useful if you are looking for video files to add to a **VideoWave** project, for instance. Click on the **Filter** icon in the **File View** taskbar to see a list of file types.

Split View

The **Split** view is almost necessary when moving files from one location to another. The **Split** view splits the **Browse** and **File** views into two sections so you can view two locations. You can use the first location to find the files you want to move and the second to browse for the location into which you would like to drop the files (such as a new album). When both destinations are set, simply drag the files from the top view and drop them into the bottom view.

Tagging Files

You can add tags to your files by adding keywords, comments, and sounds. You can also rate each file from one to five stars. Later, you are able to sort through your files using these tags.

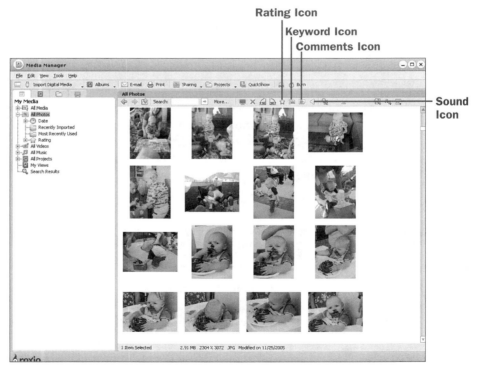

Make sorting your photos easier by tagging them.

Keywords

Add keywords to your files so you can search for the files using the keywords. Click on the **Keywords** icon in the **File View** taskbar to bring up a list of keywords. You can choose several files at a time and add as many appropriate keywords as you would like to the files.

Comments

Select the **Comments** icon in the **File View** taskbar to add any appropriate comments to your files. A comment area appears above your file listing and you can add comments to each file in turn by selecting it.

Sounds

You can narrate your picture or add sound effects by clicking on the **Sounds** icon in the **File View** taskbar. You are able to select an audio file to add to the selected file or record a narration or audio note.

Ratings

You can rate any file by selecting it and clicking on one to five stars to set the rating.

2

Importing Audio

IN THIS CHAPTER:

1. Capture Music Tracks from a CD
2. Extract Audio Tracks from a DVD
3. About Audio Capture Hardware
4. Capture Audio Using Easy Audio Capture
5. Capture Audio Using LP and Tape Assistant

Importing audio files in Roxio Easy Media Creator 8 is one of the most popular and wide-ranging uses for the product. You might want to import many types of audio. Probably the easiest and most common import is *ripping tracks* from your music CDs, but there are many other ways to import audio. You can extract the audio from a DVD, record a phone conversation, use a microphone to import live audio, or capture streaming audio from the Internet. Use the line-in option to digitize old tapes or LPs or to extract audio from VHS tapes. The best way of preserving and sharing your audio data is to have it on your computer (as well as several backups, of course).

▶ KEY TERMS

Rip—To extract a track from a CD or DVD and import it into your computer.

Track—One continuous line of data on a CD or DVD. On an audio CD this equates to one song, on a DVD each chapter or movie file is its own track, and one track is created for each burn session on a data disc.

If you are using some of the other aspects of Easy Media Creator, such as creating a slideshow or editing a video, *capturing* audio is an important first step to creating a fun, finished product. You can add any of the audio you have captured to your slideshows, videos, and even a DVD menu.

▶ KEY TERM

Capture—To convert audio, photos, and video to files that can be read and duplicated by your computer.

Easy Media Creator uses several interfaces for capturing audio. Ripping tracks from a CD and extracting audio from a DVD are handled in their unique venues. All other audio capture options are handled in one of two applications. **Easy Audio Capture** is a streamlined and efficient way of capturing audio from several input devices and saving it to a file for later use. **LP and Tape Assistant** is a complete audio capture, edit, and burn wizard. It captures audio from the same input devices and with the same settings as **Easy Audio Capture**, but adds continuing steps to allow you to immediately edit the audio you have captured and then export it to whatever source you choose. The application you use depends solely on your individual requirements. Review the steps for each application and choose which one will be best for you.

1 Capture Music Tracks from a CD

✔ BEFORE YOU BEGIN	→ SEE ALSO
Chapter 1, "Start Here" (Review information about audio file types)	**17** Burn Audio Files to an Audio CD **18** Create a Jukebox Disc

It is becoming more popular to have music on your computer in addition to CDs. There are many advantages to this. You can create playlists or sort your music by group, album, genre, or any other criteria that suits your fancy. You can also create CD mixes and burn them to a new CD for your CD player or car stereo. Or you can convert your WAV files to MP3 files so you can use them on your digital media player. Before you do any of this, you need to be able to import your music from your CD collection. This is one of the more popular uses of Easy Media Creator.

1 Select Audio from the Project Pane

Select the **Audio** button in the **project** pane to open the **Audio** menu.

2 Select Convert CDs

Selecting the **Convert CDs** option displays the **Convert CDs Wizard**. You will use this wizard to determine what audio tracks you would like to convert, from what source, and where you will save them.

3 Select the Source Drive

You need to specify which CD or DVD drive to use as a source to convert the audio tracks. Click the down arrow on the right of the **Source** drop-down menu and select the drive.

4 Insert the Audio CD into Your CD Drive

After you have the source drive selected, you need to insert the audio CD into the drive. You can click on the eject symbol to the left of the **Source** drop-down menu as well as using the eject button on the drive itself.

5 Select the Tracks to Convert

After you have inserted the CD, you will hear the drive spin up and read the track information. The track numbers and lengths should appear in the track list and, if Easy Media Creator is able to find the CD information from an Internet music database, the album title and the track titles are listed.

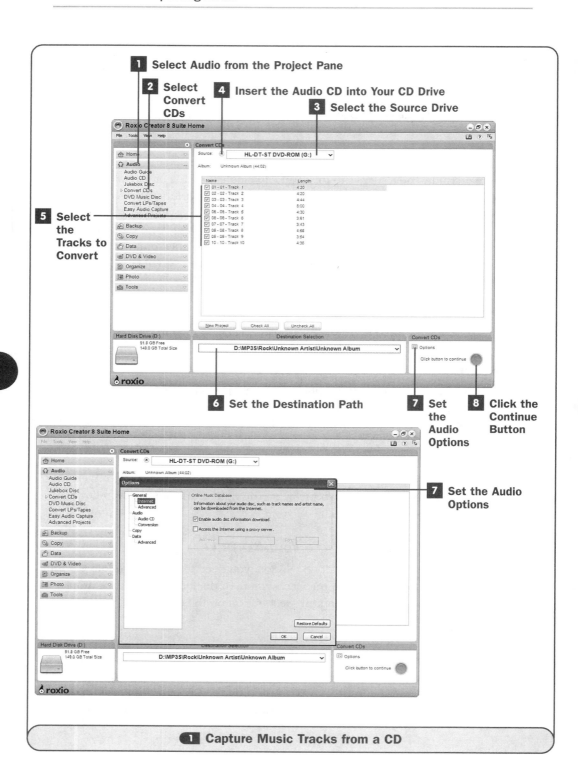

1 Select Audio from the Project Pane

2 Select Convert CDs

4 Insert the Audio CD into Your CD Drive

3 Select the Source Drive

5 Select the Tracks to Convert

6 Set the Destination Path

7 Set the Audio Options

8 Click the Continue Button

7 Set the Audio Options

1 Capture Music Tracks from a CD

After the tracks are listed, select the tracks you want to convert. By default, Easy Media Creator selects all tracks. Select or deselect the track by clicking on the check box next to the track number. A green check means that the track is selected. You can use the **Check All** or **Uncheck All** buttons to respectively select or deselect all tracks.

6 Set the Destination Path

After you have selected tracks to convert, you need to specify a destination path on your computer to save the converted tracks into digital audio files. The destination path is a location on a hard disk or any directly writable device, such as a SD card, Memory Stick, and so forth.

Select the destination path by clicking the down arrow to open the drop-down list in the **Destination Selection** option. From the drop-down list, select **Browse** and use the browser to navigate to the path to which you want to save the converted files.

▶ TIPS

Check the amount of free space available on the hard disk on which you are saving the converted audio files to make certain there is enough available space. For WAV files, you need about 10 megabytes (MB) of space per minute of audio; for MP3 files, 1–2MB, depending on quality.

Take some time to organize folders on your computer to save your converted files to so they will be easy to find and use later. Use descriptive names for folders.

7 Set the Audio Options

After you have specified the destination path to store the audio files to, you might want to take some time to review and alter the options available to convert your audio files. The options that are applicable to capturing audio from a CD are

- **Internet**—Enable Easy Media Creator to search Internet databases for the album and track titles of your CD.

- **Audio**—Enable the warning that once burned, an audio CD cannot be added to.

- **Audio CD**—Enable *normalization* of your audio tracks and reduce background noise. Normalizing your audio ensures that all your tracks have the same peak volume level.

1

- **Conversion**—Allows you to choose the file format to which you would like the tracks ripped. The file format you choose is determined by what kind of project you are planning and the amount of disk space you have available. A WAV file is the highest quality file available. It is also the best option if you are planning to edit the audio file in any way. You will be able to convert the file to a different file format after you have edited it. An MP3 or a WMA file is the popular choice for use with your computer or digital media player. They take up a significantly smaller amount of space but can still be very good quality. Either one is a good choice; it just depends on your preference. If you are limited on space and don't mind giving up quality, choose the lower quality settings.

▶ NOTE

Even though a WAV file is necessary to play a CD on your CD player or car stereo, there is no need to store your files as WAV files. Easy Media Creator automatically converts them back to WAV files when you burn an audio CD. This doesn't give you back any quality that you sacrificed when you compressed the file, but it does make the tracks CD compatible.

▶ TIP

The **General Internet** options in the **CD converter utility** allow you to enable the audio disc information download. This feature, enabled by default, is a real time saver because it searches Internet music databases and automatically fills in the album and track titles of your CD.

8 Click the Continue Button

After you have configured the audio options, you are ready to convert the audio CD into digital files. Click the red button on the **Convert CDs** option to begin converting the audio files. After the audio conversion is complete, select the **Done** button to return to the **Convert CDs** project.

2 Extract Audio Tracks from a DVD

✔ BEFORE YOU BEGIN	→ SEE ALSO
Chapter 1, "Start Here" (Review information about audio file types)	69 Import Video from a DVD

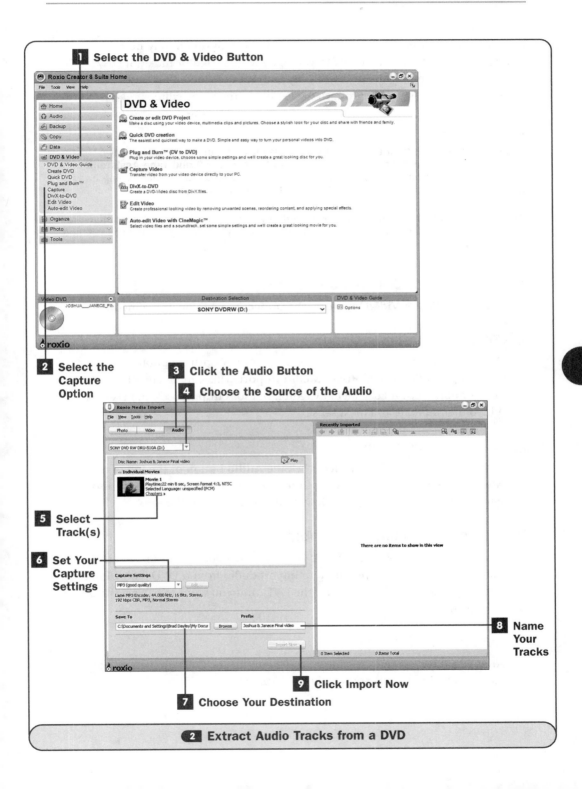

1 Select the DVD & Video Button

2 Select the Capture Option

3 Click the Audio Button

4 Choose the Source of the Audio

5 Select Track(s)

6 Set Your Capture Settings

7 Choose Your Destination

8 Name Your Tracks

9 Click Import Now

2 Extract Audio Tracks from a DVD

Importing audio from DVD to use in your projects adds an entirely new dimension to the audio that is available to you. Easy Media Creator makes it easy because you can import the audio directly without the video. This saves multiple steps in extracting the audio from the video file in the video editor.

▶ NOTES

If you would like to extract audio from video files on your computer, you have two options: You can record the audio in **Easy Audio Capture** or **LP and Tape Assistant**, or you can extract the audio using **VideoWave**. See tasks **4** Capture Audio Using Easy Audio Capture and **5** Capture Audio Using LP and Tape Assistant.

Of course, you would never import copyrighted material from a licensed DVD, but just in case you were thinking of it, be aware that most of them are encrypted and you will find it impossible.

1 Select the DVD & Video Button

Select the **DVD & Video** button in the **project** pane to open the menu.

2 Select the Capture Option

After the **DVD & Video** menu is open, select the **Capture** option. This opens a new application called **Roxio Media Import**. This can be done from multiple locations within Easy Media Creator, but for our purposes, the **DVD & Video** menu makes the most sense.

3 Click the Audio Button

After **Media Import** has opened, click the **Audio** button at the top of the **Media Import** window. This opens the **Audio Import** view. You can also change the view by using the **View** drop-down menu at the top.

4 Choose the Source of the Audio

When you have chosen the **Audio Import** view, choose the source of the audio. Because you are planning to import audio from a DVD, you will be selecting your DVD drive. Be sure the DVD that you want to extract the audio from is in the drive.

5 Select Track(s)

After you have selected the source, the menu for the DVD appears in the view. Select the track(s) you would like to extract by browsing through the menu.

6 Set Your Capture Settings

After you have selected the tracks you want, set your **Capture settings** by choosing from the drop-down menu. Your capture settings are determined by what kind of project you are planning and the amount of disk space you have available. A WAV file is the highest quality file available. It is also the best option if you are planning to edit the audio file in any way. You can convert the file to a different file format after you have edited it. An MP3 or WMA file is the popular choice for use with your computer or digital media player. It takes up a significantly smaller amount of space but can still be very good quality. Either one is a good choice; it just depends on your preference. If you are limited on space and don't mind giving up quality, choose the lower quality settings.

For the advanced user, you can also customize your audio. This option enables you to apply your own combination of settings, including an alternative file format, encoder type, bit rate, and file location. To define custom settings, click the **Edit** button to the right of the **Capture settings** menu.

7 Choose Your Destination

When you have decided on your capture settings, choose the location to which you would like the file saved. Make this a folder that is conveniently accessible and easy to remember. When it comes time to add these tracks to a project, you'll want to be able to find them again.

8 Name Your Tracks

After you've decided where to save your file(s), you need to name your track(s). You can enter a name in the **File name prefix** text box. **Media Import** uses the text you enter to begin the filename for each recorded file. For example, if you are recording several audio files and enter **Extracted Audio**, the recorded files are named Extracted Audio 00000, Extracted Audio 00001, and so on.

9 Click Import Now

To finish the extraction process, click the **Import Now** button in the lower-right corner. Your tracks appear in the right window as they are imported where you can preview them, sort them, or change the view.

3   About Audio Capture Hardware

→ SEE ALSO

4 Capture Audio Using Easy Audio Capture

5 Capture Audio Using LP and Tape Assistant

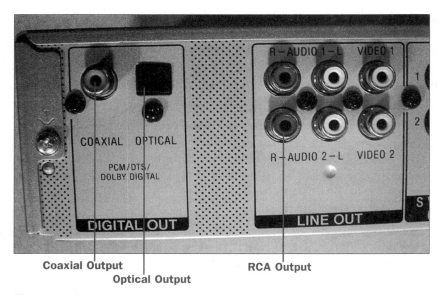

Coaxial Output
Optical Output
RCA Output

The out ports on a computer.

The ability to import audio from a variety of sources is one of the most useful features of Easy Media Creator. The best place to start when learning how to import audio is to understand the hardware components that are involved and how to connect them properly. This task focuses on helping you understand the types of hardware that audio can be captured from and how to connect them to your computer so audio can be imported into Easy Media Creator.

Three basic types of hardware are involved when capturing audio. The first is the audio output device, the second is the audio input device, and the third is the audio cable.

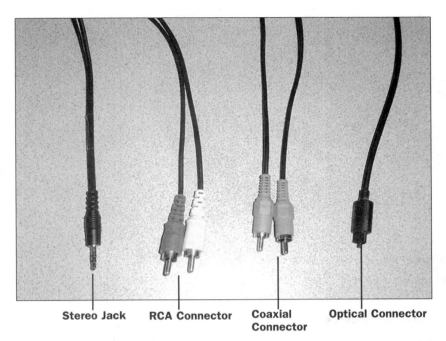

Stereo Jack   RCA Connector   Coaxial Connector   Optical Connector

Audio cables and connectors.

3

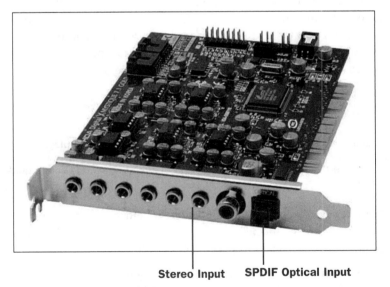

Stereo Input   SPDIF Optical Input

The input ports on a computer.

SPDIF Coaxial Input   SPDIF RCA Input

More input ports on a computer.

Audio Output Devices

An *audio output device* is literally any device that outputs sound.

The most common audio that is imported into the computer is music from a CD player, LP player, cassette tape player, or stereo. These devices need to have some type of audio-out port for you to be able to import the audio in a digital format using the computer. Most of these devices have RCA connectors on the back that allow you plug them into a home theater system. You can use these ports to connect these devices directly into your computer.

▶ **TIP**

Some old LP and tape players do not have audio-out ports on them. If your player has only stereo speaker-out ports and you have no other option, you can still play the LP or tape to speakers and use the microphone to import the audio; however, the sound quality will be greatly diminished.

Another audio output device you should know about is your home telephone. If you have your telephone line connected to your computer through a modem, you can record telephone conversations using Easy Media Creator.

In addition to the standard audio equipment and telephone, you can use any device that has an audio output on it, even if it is just a headphone output. Such devices might be digital audio recorders, palm devices, cell phones, and so on. For example, if you used your digital audio recorder to record notes for a college class, you could import that audio using your computer, store it to review later, and free up the recording room on the digital audio recorder.

The final output device is the microphone. The microphone is typically used for recording your own voice onto the computer.

▶ **TIP**

If you are going to use microphone very often to narrate audio or video, get a good-quality microphone. Many computers come with small microphones that work pretty well, but the sound is really not good enough to be in a video production.

Audio Input Devices

Audio input devices are the hardware devices that allow your computer to capture sound.

The most common audio input device is the computer sound card. Virtually every computer comes with at least a basic sound card of some sort built in. The sound card is simply a set of computer chips connected to an audio port that allow the computer system to input from and output to audio devices. Some sound cards are built into the computer's motherboard while others are push-in cards that can be added to or removed from the computer.

▶ **TIP**

If you intend to import audio a lot and are concerned with the quality, consider installing an after-market audio card in your computer that has either RCA or optical ports on it. Creative Labs makes several high-quality sound cards that are reasonably priced and easy to install.

A basic sound card has three audio ports on it: line-in, speaker-out, and mic-in. The ports on a basic sound card are typically stereo mini-jacks, discussed in the next section, "Audio Cables and Ports." More robust, after-market sound cards might include several ports such as auxiliary line-in, optical line-in, and Sony Phillips Digital Interface (SPDIF), also discussed in the next section. These ports provide a higher quality interface to import audio into the computer.

In addition to sound cards, other audio import devices are available for the computer. For example, there are simple devices, such as USB microphones, as well as expensive audio-processing equipment and cards for professional sound editing.

Audio Cables and Ports

Audio cables and ports are the hardware that is used to connect the audio output devices to the audio input device in your computer.

This is usually the most difficult-to-understand part of importing audio. Most people know which audio output device to use based on what they want to import, but are not certain exactly what to use to connect that device to the computer.

The biggest problem is that several types of audio cables can be used to connect audio equipment to the sound card. This can be confusing. To make it easier, just remember that the cable is simply a wire with a special type of connector on each end. After you understand the types of ports and know what ports are on your audio input and output devices, choosing which cable to use is pretty simple.

The following is a list of ports that you might be dealing with when connecting audio devices to your computer:

- **Stereo jack**—The stereo jack is the standard port in most sound cards for the line-in, the speaker out, and the microphone. This port does not provide as good a quality as the other ports, but it is used in most sound cards because it is small.

- **RCA**—The SPDIF RCA port is the standard port used on most stereo equipment. Some sound cards have RCA ports. The RCA port provides a better quality than the stereo jack.

- **Coaxial**—The SPDIF coaxial ports look exactly like the RCA ports; the only way to tell the difference is to read the documentation specifications on your audio equipment. These specifications can usually be found in the front or back of the user manual. The coaxial port provides a slight improvement over RCA ports.

▶ **TIP**

RCA and coaxial cables are the exact same size and can be interchanged with each other. The only difference is that the coaxial cable has additional shielding that allows it to run at a higher frequency, which reduces interference from external sources. If you have a device that has coaxial outputs and the cables need to be longer than 10 feet, try to use coaxial cables.

- **Optical**—The SPDIF optical port provides the highest quality audio. Instead of metal ports and wire cables, the optical port uses light to transmit digital audio over a fiber optic cable.

Now that you understand the types of ports, determining which cable to use to connect your audio equipment to your PC should be a simple process. Compare the ports on your sound card and your audio output device. Pick the best quality port that is available on each and select one of the following cables that match the ports on your sound card and audio device:

- **Stereo jack to stereo jack**—Use this cable to connect some of the alternative audio output devices that only have a headphone audio-out port.

- **Stereo jack to RCA**—Use this cable to connect your stereo equipment to basic sound cards.

- **RCA to RCA**—Use this cable if you have a sound card that has RCA or coaxial SPDIF ports.

- **Coaxial to coaxial**—You can use this cable if you have a sound card that has coaxial SPDIF and your audio output device has a coaxial port as well.

- **Optical to optical**—You can use this cable if you have a sound card that has optical SPDIF and your audio output device has an optical port as well.

▶ **TIP**

Make sure that you connect the cables to the output ports on the audio output device and the input ports on your sound card. The most common mistake when importing audio is to connect the cable to the wrong port.

4	**Capture Audio Using Easy Audio Capture**
✔ **BEFORE YOU BEGIN**	→ **SEE ALSO**
Chapter 1, "Start Here" (Review information about audio file types) **3** About Audio Capture Hardware	**5** Capture Audio Using LP and Tape Assistant **17** Burn Audio Files to an Audio CD **18** Create a Jukebox Disc

Easy Audio Capture is its own application within Easy Media Creator. Although the interface is a simple one, the capabilities are powerful. **Easy Audio Capture** allows you to capture almost every kind of audio in almost any way you can imagine, recording it and saving it to an audio file that you can edit and use at any time. This is an excellent way to digitize and preserve all your stored recordings, whether they are on LPs, tapes, or even 8-tracks. (Although it goes without saying that if you still have your music on 8-tracks, you prefer it that way.)

1 Select the Audio Button

Select the **Audio** button in the **project** pane to open the **Audio** menu.

2 Select Easy Audio Capture

After the **Audio** menu is open, select **Easy Audio Capture** to start this application.

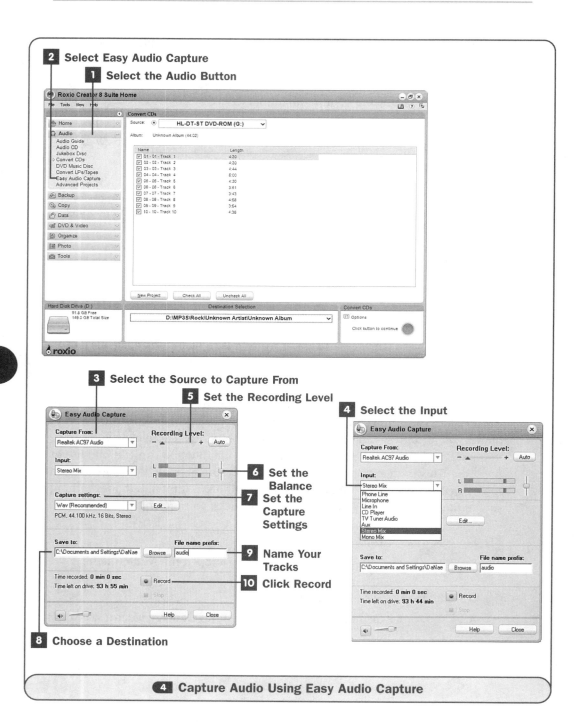

3 Select the Source to Capture From

After **Easy Audio Capture** has launched, you need to navigate the **Capture From** drop-down menu to choose the hardware device that will capture your sound. Commonly your sound card is the only device listed here. If you have a *USB* input device, this is also listed. Choose which source you will be using.

▶ KEY TERM

USB—A port on the computer that allows you to connect peripheral devices such as cameras, hard drives, MP3 players, and so forth.

4 Select the Input

After you have chosen what you will capture from, select your input device. This step requires that you have correctly set up the required hardware for the input device you would like to use. You can learn more about this in
3 About Audio Capture Hardware.

Several input devices are listed, so let's take a look at each one:

- **Phone Line**—Choose this option and you can record a phone conversation through a phone line connected to your modem.

- **Microphone**—Record live audio through a microphone by choosing this option.

- **Line In**—This option is for any device plugged into your sound card or a USB input device. For example, you would choose this option if you had a stereo hooked up to your computer in order to input LPs or tapes.

- **CD Player**—Use this option if you have a CD player or other digital input device plugged in to your line-in port on your sound card.

- **TV Tuner Audio**—If you have a TV tuner connected to your computer, you can capture the audio from your TV programs by choosing this option.

- **Aux**—If you have a device plugged into your auxiliary line-in port in your sound card, choose this option.

- **Stereo Mix and Mono Mix**—These are options for capturing streaming audio. A stereo mix gives you two channels of audio, while a mono mix gives you just one.

- **SPDIF**—This option appears in your menu if your sound card has RCA, coaxial, or optical ports. If you have these ports and the cables to use them, they are the best quality choice.

4

▶ **NOTE**

Your audio doesn't have to be streaming from the Internet for you to record it. You can also capture any audio your computer happens to be playing. You can extract audio from a video file this way.

5 **Set the Recording Level**

After you have set your input, drag the **recording level slider** to the desired position. You want your recording level to be as high as possible without creating distortion. Set your levels until the left and right meter indicators below the slider are in approximately the center of the meter. As your recording progresses, make sure that they rarely, if ever, reach the top of the meter. This keeps your recording free of distortion. You can also click the **Auto** button next to the recording level slide. You need to do this while your audio is being played so **Easy Audio Capture** can monitor the levels. **Easy Audio Capture** automatically tracks the levels of the meter in order to use the highest possible recording level.

6 **Set the Balance**

After you have set your recording level, drag the **balance slider** to balance the audio level between the left and right channels.

7 **Set the Capture Settings**

After you have selected the tracks you want, set your capture settings by choosing from the **Capture settings** drop-down menu. Your capture settings are determined by what kind of project you are planning and the amount of disk space you have available. A WAV file is the highest quality file available. It is also the best option if you are planning to edit the audio file in any way. You can convert the file to a different file format after you have edited it. An MP3 or WMA file is the popular choice for use with your computer or digital media player. It can still be very good quality, and it takes up a significantly smaller amount of space. Either one is a good choice; it just depends on your preference. If you are limited on space and don't mind giving up quality, choose the lower quality settings.

For the advanced user, you can also customize your audio. This option enables you to apply your own combination of settings, including an alternative file format, encoder type, bit rate, and file location. To define custom settings, click the **Edit** button to the right of the **Capture settings** menu.

8 Choose a Destination

When you have decided on your capture settings, choose the location to which you would like to save the file. Make this a folder that is conveniently accessible and easy to remember. When it comes time to add these tracks to a project, you'll want to be able to find them again.

9 Name Your Tracks

After you've determined where to save your file(s), you need to name your tracks. You can enter a name in the **File name prefix** text box. Media Import uses the text you enter to begin the file name for each recorded file. For example, if you are recording several audio files and enter **Audio**, the recorded files are named Audio_1, Audio_2, and so on.

10 Click Record

When you are sure that all your settings are correct, click the **Record** button. After you have clicked the **Record** button, start the audio that you are capturing. This ensures that no clipping occurs. When you are done recording, click the **Stop** button.

---

5 Capture Audio Using LP and Tape Assistant

✔ **BEFORE YOU BEGIN**	→ **SEE ALSO**
Chapter 1, "Start Here" (Review information about audio file types)	**4** Capture Audio Using Easy Audio Capture
3 About Audio Capture Hardware	**17** Burn Audio Files to an Audio CD
	18 Create a Jukebox Disc

The **Convert LPs/Tapes** option has many of the same features of **Easy Audio Capture**. After you are familiar with **Easy Audio Capture**, you will also be able to easily use **LP and Tape Assistant**. **LP and Tape Assistant** adds the further steps of being able to add tags and edit the audio that you have just captured, as well as allowing you to export it.

1 Click the Audio Button

Click the **Audio** button in the **project** pane to open the **Audio** menu.

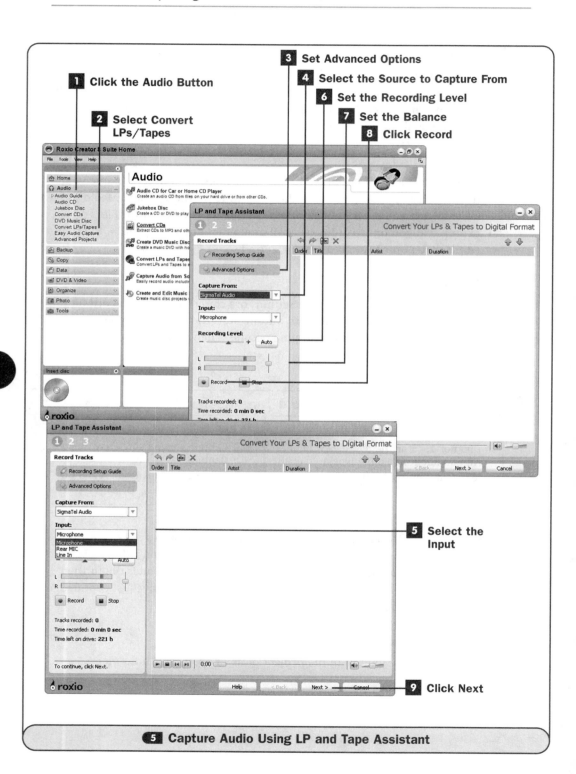

1 Click the Audio Button

2 Select Convert LPs/Tapes

3 Set Advanced Options

4 Select the Source to Capture From

6 Set the Recording Level

7 Set the Balance

8 Click Record

5 Select the Input

9 Click Next

5 Capture Audio Using LP and Tape Assistant

2 Select Convert LPs/Tapes

After the **Audio** menu is open, select **Convert LPs/Tapes** to launch **LP and Tape Assistant**. A button for a Recording Setup Guide is in the upper-left corner and if you have any questions about the hardware setup for a line-in option, this will probably answer those questions. You can also read more about hardware in task **3** **About Audio Capture Hardware**.

3 Set Advanced Options

After you have launched **LP and Tape Assistant**, take a look at your advanced options. Although the term *advanced* implies that only advanced users would want to set these options, this isn't true in all cases.

In the **General** window, you'll find that you can set a specific length of time to record as well as set an auto pause in case the recording goes silent for a specified amount of time. More importantly, you can choose the location to which you would like to save the file. Make this a folder that is conveniently accessible and easy to remember. When it comes time to add these tracks to a project, you'll want to be able to find them again. After you've determined where to save your file, you need to name your track. You can enter a name in the **File name prefix** text box. **LP and Tape Assistant** uses the text you enter to begin the file name for each recorded file. For example, if you are recording several audio files and enter **Audio**, the recorded files are named Audio_1, Audio_2, and so on.

In the **File Format** window, there are basic as well as advanced capture settings for the file format you would like to use. Your capture settings are determined by what kind of project you are planning and the amount of disk space you have available. A WAV file is the highest quality file available. It is also the best option if you are planning to edit the audio file in any way. You can convert the file to a different file format after you have edited it. An MP3 or WMA file is the popular choice for use with your computer or digital media player. It can still be very good quality, and it takes up a significantly smaller amount of space. Either one is a good choice; it just depends on your preference. If you are limited on space and don't mind giving up quality, choose the lower quality settings.

For the advanced user, you can also customize your audio. This option enables you to apply your own combination of settings, including an alternative file format, encoder type, bit rate, and file location. To define custom settings, click the **Edit** button to the right of the **Capture settings** menu.

In the **Track Detection** window, you can set up options that create a new track whenever a pause is encountered. This is handy if you are capturing

5

several audio tracks in one stream. For example, you could automatically create a new track for each song if you were capturing streaming radio from the Internet, a tape, or an LP.

▶ TIP

You want to enable Track Detection if you are recording a stream of several tracks. For instance, if you are recording radio off the Internet and don't want to monitor each song, the track detection feature automatically creates a new track for you at each specified pause.

4 Select the Source to Capture From

After you have set your advanced options, you need to navigate the **Capture From** drop-down menu to choose the hardware device that will capture your sound. Commonly your sound card is the only device listed here. If you have a USB input device, this is also listed. Choose which source you will be using.

5 Select the Input

After you have chosen what you will capture from, select your input device. This step requires that you have correctly set up the required hardware for the input device you would like to use. You can learn more about this in 3 **About Audio Capture Hardware**.

Several input devices are listed, so let's take a look at each one:

- **Phone Line**—Choose this option and you can record a phone conversation through a phone line connected to your modem.

- **Microphone**—Record live audio through a microphone using this option.

- **Line In**—This option is for any device plugged into your sound card or a USB input device. For example, you would choose this option if you had a stereo hooked up to your computer in order to input LPs or tapes.

- **CD Player**—This is simply another capture option for inputting audio from your CD or DVD drive.

- **TV Tuner Audio**—If you have a TV tuner connected to your computer, you can capture the audio from your TV programs by choosing this option.

- **Aux**—If you have a device plugged into your auxiliary line-in port in your sound card, choose this option.

- **Stereo Mix and Mono Mix**—These are options for capturing Internet streaming audio. A stereo mix gives you two channels of audio, while a mono mix gives you just one.

- **SPDIF**—This option appears in your menu if your sound card has RCA, coaxial, or optical ports. If you have these ports and the cables to use them, they are the best quality choice.

6 Set the Recording Level

After you have set your input, drag the **recording level slider** to the desired position. You want your recording level to be as high as possible without creating distortion. Set your levels until the left and right meter indicators below the recording level slider are in approximately the center of the meter. As your recording progresses, make sure that they rarely, if ever, reach the top of the meter. This keeps your recording free of distortion. You can also click the **Auto** button next to the recording level slide. You need to do this while your audio is being played so that **LP and Tape Assistant** can monitor the levels. **LP and Tape Assistant** automatically tracks the levels of the meter in order to use the highest possible recording level.

7 Set the Balance

After you have set your recording level, drag the **balance slider** to balance the audio level between the left and right channels.

8 Click Record

When you are sure that all your settings are correct, click the **Record** button. After you have clicked the **Record** button, start the audio that you are capturing. This ensures that no clipping occurs. When you are done recording, click the **Stop** button.

9 Click Next

When you are finished recording your audio with **LP and Tape Assistant**, click **Next**. This takes you to the next step, editing your newly captured audio. This is covered in **7** **Convert Audio File Formats**.

5

3

Editing Audio

IN THIS CHAPTER:

Besides being able to capture audio, Roxio Easy Media Creator 8 provides powerful audio-editing capabilities and several interfaces in which to edit audio. **LP and Tape Assistant** and **Quick Sound Editor** are abbreviated versions of **Sound Editor**, Easy Media Creator's full-fledged audio-editing application.

LP and Tape Assistant is a capture, edit, and export wizard that allows you to quickly process the audio you want to capture. The wizard gives you the option to export your audio to **Sound Editor** if you need more editing capabilities.

Quick Sound Editor can be launched from most of the audio project interfaces within Easy Media Creator. It has the fewest audio-editing capabilities, but is good for a quick clean up. Although it is not addressed individually within this chapter, all of its capabilities are found within **Sound Editor**.

6 Use LP and Tape Assistant to Edit Newly Captured Audio

✔ BEFORE YOU BEGIN

Chapter 1, "Start Here" (Review information about audio file types)
5 Capture Audio Using LP and Tape Assistant

→ SEE ALSO

9 Add Tracks to Sound Editor
10 Split, Crop, and Join Tracks
11 Fade Volume of an Audio Track
12 Set the Right and Left Audio Track
13 Clean, Enhance, and Equalize an Audio Track
14 Add Effects to an Audio Track
15 Mix Multiple Audio Tracks
16 Export Audio

LP and Tape Assistant is a complete capture, edit, and exporting wizard. It's useful if you would like to immediately edit the audio you have captured and then export it to whatever application or format you choose. If you are not familiar with the steps to capture audio in the assistant, refer to 5 **Capture Audio Using LP and Tape Assistant**.

LP and Tape Assistant is a simplified version of **Sound Editor**, a full-fledged audio-editing application. Most of the tasks in this chapter focus on editing your audio within **Sound Editor**. If you would like to use the advanced editing power of **Sound Editor**, you can either launch **Sound Editor** instead of **LP and Tape Assistant** or you can export your captured audio to **Sound Editor** in the last step of **LP and Tape Assistant**.

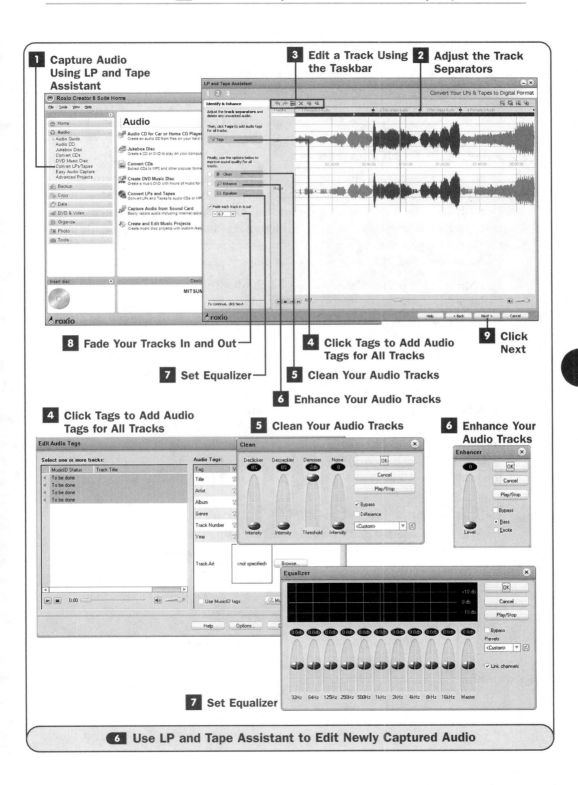

1 Capture Audio Using LP and Tape Assistant

3 Edit a Track Using the Taskbar

2 Adjust the Track Separators

8 Fade Your Tracks In and Out

9 Click Next

4 Click Tags to Add Audio Tags for All Tracks

7 Set Equalizer

5 Clean Your Audio Tracks

6 Enhance Your Audio Tracks

4 Click Tags to Add Audio Tags for All Tracks

5 Clean Your Audio Tracks

6 Enhance Your Audio Tracks

7 Set Equalizer

6 Use LP and Tape Assistant to Edit Newly Captured Audio

1 Capture Audio Using LP and Tape Assistant

In the Roxio Creator Suite 8 **Home** page, launch **LP and Tape Assistant** from the **project** pane under the **Audio** heading by selecting **Convert LPs/Tapes**. Follow the steps to capture your audio and click **Next**. If you are unfamiliar with this process, refer to **5 Capture Audio Using LP and Tape Assistant**.

2 Adjust the Track Separators

Here's your chance to really play with the tracks you've imported. Above your tracks is a header that labels each track you've recorded; in this case, **1 Recorded Audio**, **2 Recorded Audio**, and so forth. A line separates each track you've recorded. By holding your left mouse button and dragging those lines around, you can change the definition of the track boundaries. You can merge two or more tracks (or parts of tracks) or create a new clip entirely.

You can select any one of these tracks by highlighting the header. Or, by clicking anywhere inside the tracks, you can create a new selection line. You can leave it as a line in order to create a separator, or you can drag it to your preferred end point to highlight a larger selection. At any time you can preview your recorded audio by clicking the **Play** button at the bottom left of the screen to make sure you've selected the portion of the audio clip you want.

You can create a marker by right-clicking inside the track and choosing **Add/Remove Marker** from the context menu that appears. You can also do this by holding down the **Control** key and then clicking inside the audio. You create a new separator while leaving a marker in the place of your last separator. The marker appears as a little blue tab inside the dark upper border of the track view.

3 Edit a Track Using the Taskbar

You can edit a selected portion of the track by using the buttons on the top left of the **LP and Tape Assistant** window (called the *taskbar*). Listed in order, these buttons are

- **Undo**—Undo the last change you've made to the tracks
- **Redo**—Redo the last undone change
- **Rename**—Allows you to rename the selected track
- **Delete**—Allows you to delete a selected portion of the track

• **Add Track Separator**—Allows you to divide or crop tracks by adding a track separator

• **Delete Track Separator**—Allows you to combine tracks by deleting their separators

▶ KEY TERM

Taskbar—A group of icons that usually appears at the top of any application you are using, although it is also very common to see them down one side. These icons make it convenient to complete tasks just by pointing and clicking. A taskbar is sometimes called a toolbar or toolbox.

▶ TIPS

Right-clicking inside of the track gives you several options for more precisely selecting or moving around inside the tracks. You can also insert a silence of the duration of your choice by choosing the appropriate option from the context menu that appears.

Any time you have a portion of an audio clip selected, you can zoom to that selection by using the zoom tools in the upper right of your view or by right-clicking on the selection and choosing **Zoom to Selection**. When you are done editing your particular selection, you can zoom back to your full view by right-clicking and choosing **Zoom out Full**.

4 Click Tags to Add Audio Tags for All Tracks

After you have made your changes, click on the **Tags** button to add audio tags to your tracks. You can select any or all of your tracks and change their name, artist, album, genre, track number, and year. You can also assign track art. The **MusicID** button allows you to search the online database for your track information. This works if your tracks have been recorded in their entirety and you haven't made any major changes to them.

5 Clean Your Audio Tracks

When you have named your tracks, select the portion of the audio clip that you want to clean and click the **Clean** button on the **Clip Editor** toolbar. In the **Clean** dialog that opens, you can declick, decrackle, denoise, or add noise manually by selecting **Custom** (the default) at the bottom right of the pane and adjusting the sliders for each function until the cleaning effect is properly applied. You can also have the effect applied via **LP and Tape Assistant** presets by choosing a low, medium, or high setting from the bottom-right drop-down menu. Play the track that you are cleaning to hear the effect as you adjust it.

▶ **TIP**

Because the cleaning effects are layered on top of each other as you apply them, you should add the effects one at a time, adjusting each as necessary.

6 Enhance Your Audio Tracks

After you have cleaned your audio, you can enhance it by selecting the **Enhance** button. You can choose to enhance the **Bass**, or make your audio brighter by enhancing the **Excite**. There are no presets for either enhance function, so you'll need to adjust the effects manually with the slider provided.

7 Set Equalizer

When you are satisfied with the enhancement settings of your audio, click the **Equalizer** button to use Easy Media Creator's 10-band equalizer to change the levels of your audio track. You can use the presets or customize your settings by adjusting the levels manually. Customizing your settings is mostly a trial-and-error process, so change one setting at a time and preview your track to monitor the differences. There is a left and right channel indicator for each band. You can adjust each channel separately by deselecting the **Link Channels** option.

8 Fade Your Tracks In and Out

After you have set the equalizer, you have the option to fade your tracks. Selecting the **Fade each track in & out** option fades the beginning and ending of each track within the editor for the specified amount of time. Use the + and – buttons to increase and decrease the duration of the fade, or type your preferred time in the box provided.

9 Click Next

After you have completed your edits, click **Next**. This takes you to the final step within **LP and Tape Assistant**, where you have the option to burn your audio to CD or export it to a file on your hard disk. You are also given the option to continue editing your audio using the more advanced **Sound Editor** or to export the track to **Music Disc Creator** so it can be added to a project. For more information on exporting your audio, see **16 Export Audio**.

▶ **TIP**

You can preview your audio by using the play buttons on the bottom left of **LP and Tape Assistant**. Use the slider to choose where you would like to begin the playback, and use the volume indicator to mute (by clicking on the speaker icon) or change your volume.

▶ NOTE

As you add effects to your audio, you will notice **Bypass** and **Difference** check boxes in the effect adjustment windows. As you preview your audio, you can select **Bypass** to listen to your audio without the effect, or **Difference** to hear the difference the effect is having on the audio without the rest of the audio. Note that only the **Clean** dialog includes both a **Bypass** and a **Difference** check box. You can achieve the same effect as clicking **Difference** by simply deselecting **Bypass** when working in the other effects windows.

---

7 Convert Audio File Formats

✔ BEFORE YOU BEGIN	→ SEE ALSO
Chapter 1, "Start Here" (Review information about audio file types.)	**1** Capture Music Tracks from a CD **2** Extract Audio Tracks from a DVD **8** Add Tags to Audio Tracks

---

So you have folders full of imported music of every file type, and you want to *convert* some of those files to another format. For instance, if you want to edit a file, using the WAV format is by far the best option, but keeping all your files in this format is unrealistic due to their size (about 10MB per minute of audio). A number of compressed audio formats can help you store your music more efficiently, and Easy Media Creator supports several of them.

There are plenty of opportunities within Easy Media Creator to convert your files from one type to another. When you are importing them, you can choose your capture settings. If you load your Audio CD project with MP3s, Easy Media Creator automatically converts them to WAV files so you can listen to your disc on a conventional CD player. But if your goal is simply to change one file format to another, the following steps help you do so easily.

▶ KEY TERM

Convert—To change a file from one format to another.

■ Select Audio in the Project Pane

Select the **Audio** button in the **project** pane to open the **Audio** menu.

2 Select Advanced Projects

Selecting the **Advanced Projects** option displays the **Music Disc Creator** project wizard. You use this wizard to determine what audio tracks you would like to convert, from what source, and where you will save them.

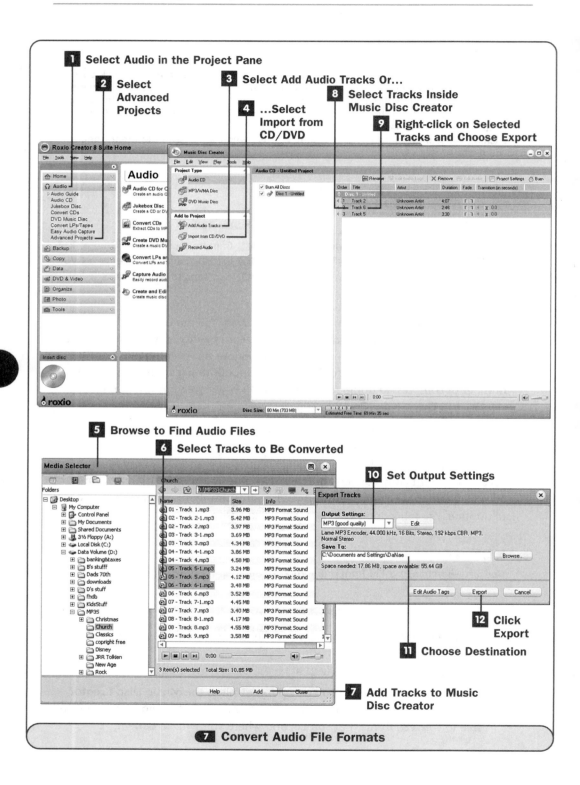

1 Select Audio in the Project Pane

2 Select Advanced Projects

3 Select Add Audio Tracks Or...

4 ...Select Import from CD/DVD

8 Select Tracks Inside Music Disc Creator

9 Right-click on Selected Tracks and Choose Export

5 Browse to Find Audio Files

6 Select Tracks to Be Converted

10 Set Output Settings

12 Click Export

11 Choose Destination

7 Add Tracks to Music Disc Creator

7 Convert Audio File Formats

3 Select Add Audio Tracks Or...

After you have launched **Music Disc Creator**, select the **Add Audio Tracks** option to open the **Media Selector** window. This enables you to browse for audio files already saved on your computer (or network drives).

4 ...Select Import from CD/DVD

After you have launched **Music Disc Creator**, select the **Import from CD/DVD** option to open **Media Manager**. This allows you to import tracks from an audio CD or to take the audio from a DVD track. This is an alternative method of extracting audio from a DVD. The other method is described in **2** Extract Audio Tracks from a DVD.

5 Browse to Find Audio Files

After you have opened **Media Manager**, you need to browse through your drives and files to find the audio you would like to import. If you are searching for a file, it can be found on your hard disks. If you are importing from a CD or DVD, you need to select your CD/DVD drive.

6 Select Tracks to Be Converted

After you have browsed to the location of the tracks that you would like to edit, you can select one or more tracks to be imported into **Music Disc Creator**. Preview your tracks using the playback control buttons on the lower part of the screen. You can select multiple tracks by holding down the **Control** key as you select each one.

7 Add Tracks to Music Disc Creator

When you have selected the tracks you would like to convert, click the **Add** button at the bottom of your window. This does not automatically close **Media Manager**; you can continue to add files until you are finished. When you are finished, select **Close**.

8 Select Tracks Inside Music Disc Creator

When you have imported the tracks you are going to convert into **Music Disc Creator**, select them by clicking on each one while you hold the **Control** key down (or the **Shift** key if they are shown contiguously in **Media Manager**) or drag the mouse over them.

9 Right-click on Selected Tracks and Choose Export

With your mouse positioned over any part of the selected track, right-click to bring up the **Edit** menu. Choose **Export** to bring up the **Export Tracks** window.

10 Set Output Settings

After you have brought up the **Export Tracks** window, you need to choose the type of file to which you would like to convert your tracks. A WAV file is the highest quality file available. It is also the best option if you are planning to edit the audio file in any way. An MP3 or WMA file is the popular choice for use with your computer or digital media player. They take up a significantly smaller amount of space but can still be very good quality. Either one is a good choice; it just depends on your preference. If you are limited on space and don't mind giving up quality, choose the lower-quality settings for the MP3 or WMA formats.

For the advanced user, you can also customize your audio. This option enables you to apply your own combination of settings, including an alternate file format, encoder type, bit rate, and file location. To define custom settings, click the **Edit** button to the right of the **Output settings** menu.

11 Choose Destination

When you have decided on your export settings, choose the location to which you would like the file saved. Make this a folder that is conveniently accessible and easy to remember. When it comes time to add these tracks to a project, you'll want to be able to find them again.

▶ **NOTE**

You can change the tags of your audio files in either **Music Disc Creator** or in the **Export** window by choosing the **Edit Audio Tags** button. If you would like help with this process, see 8 Add Tags to Audio Tracks.

12 Click Export

When you are sure your settings are correct, click **Export** to save your files. You have successfully converted your files to a new format.

> ### 8   Add Tags to Audio Tracks
>
> → **SEE ALSO**
>
> **120** Auto-fill the Label Menu from Your Disc (on the Web)

Editing your audio *tags* can be done in almost any interface involving individual audio tracks, not only in Easy Media Creator, but also in Windows. All you need to do is select the tracks you would like to add tags to and select the **Edit Audio Tags** option. This brings up the **Edit Audio Tags** window where you have quite a few options to make changing the tag on your tracks as easy as possible.

▶ **KEY TERM**

Tags—Embedded data for a particular file. A tag can be added to an audio file, a data file, a photo file, or a video file. A tag can also have several components, such as a date, title, and so forth.

▶ **NOTE**

Changing the audio tags does not change the name of your audio file. The tags are embedded inside your audio track and are recognized by Easy Media Creator as well as other playback software and devices. Windows Media Player displays audio tags, as will most digital audio players and newer CD players.

8

1 Select Audio Track

Select your audio track from anywhere in Easy Media Creator or even any-where on your computer.

2 Select Edit Audio Tags

If you are in Easy Media Creator, chances are you have an **Edit Audio Tags** icon in your taskbar; simply click on it. If you don't see the **Edit Audio Tags** option or you are browsing through Windows, right-click on your selected tracks and select **Edit Audio Tags** from the menu. This brings up the **Edit Audio Tags** window.

3 Add Tags Or...

After you have launched the **Edit Audio Tags** window, you see a list of your selected tracks in the left side of the window. You can select any or all of these tracks and change their name, artist, album, genre, track number, and year by filling in the appropriate field. Preview your tracks by using the playback buttons on the bottom of the window.

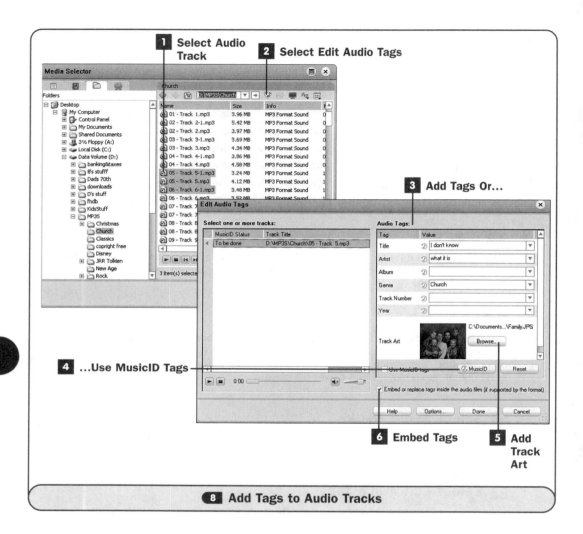

1 Select Audio Track

2 Select Edit Audio Tags

3 Add Tags Or...

4 ...Use MusicID Tags

6 Embed Tags

5 Add Track Art

8 Add Tags to Audio Tracks

8

4 ...Use MusicID Tags

You can also assign tags to your tracks by using MusicID. The **MusicID** button allows you to search the Gracenote online database for your track information. This works if your tracks have been recorded in their entirety and you haven't made any major changes to them.

The MusicID status of each track is listed in the window along with the track name. You will find one of the following status indicators:

- **To be done**—MusicID has not been used to identify the track.

- **Identified**—One matching music database entry has been found by MusicID.

- **Multiple matches**—More than one music database entry matches your audio track. If this is the case, the status listing **Multiple matches** is a highlighted link. Click on this link to open up a window listing the matches found. If the correct name of your track is there, select it and click **OK**.

- **Could not identify**—Your audio track did not match any of the database entries. In this instance, you have to enter your tag manually.

5 Add Track Art

You can also add track art to your audio tag. Browse for the picture that you would like to associate with the track and click **OK**.

6 Embed Tags

Put a check mark next to the **Embed or replace tags inside the audio file** option if you would like your audio tags to be permanently embedded into your audio file. This enables other applications and software to recognize your audio tag.

---

9 Add Tracks to Sound Editor

→ SEE ALSO

1 Capture Music Tracks from a CD
2 Extract Audio Tracks from a DVD
4 Capture Audio Using Easy Audio Capture
5 Capture Audio Using the LP and Tape Assistant
6 Use the LP and Tape Assistant to Edit Newly Captured Audio

Sound Editor is the full-fledged audio-editing application within Easy Media Creator. You can edit, mix, and add fun effects to your audio files using this application.

Sound Editor has all the capabilities of **LP and Tape Assistant** and **Quick Sound Editor**, plus a whole lot more. In **LP and Tape Assistant** you capture your audio file and then edit it. **Quick Sound Editor** is launched after the tracks you would like to edit are in place in a project, but **Sound Editor** is launched separately and requires you to import your audio files.

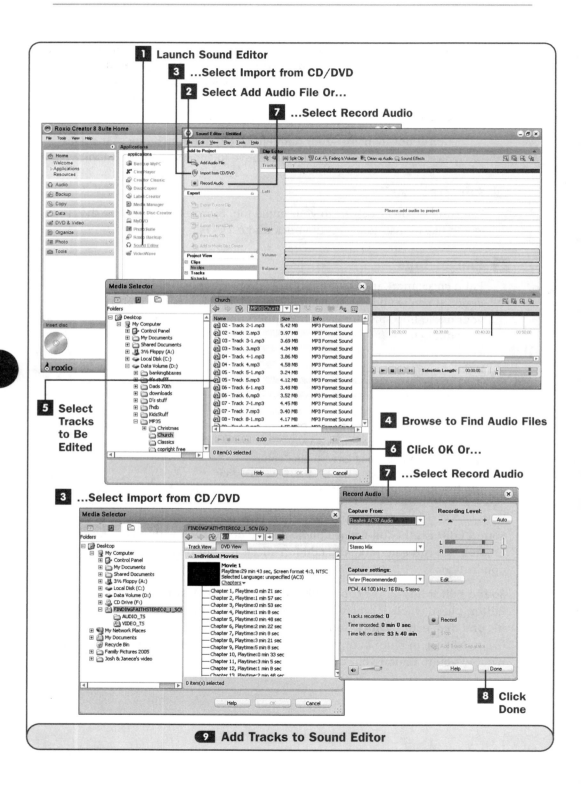

1 Launch Sound Editor

3 ...Select Import from CD/DVD

2 Select Add Audio File Or...

7 ...Select Record Audio

5 Select Tracks to Be Edited

4 Browse to Find Audio Files

6 Click OK Or...

7 ...Select Record Audio

3 ...Select Import from CD/DVD

8 Click Done

9 Add Tracks to Sound Editor

1 Launch Sound Editor

The easiest way to launch **Sound Editor** is in the Easy Media Creator **Home** page. Choose the **Home** menu in the **project** pane, select **Applications**, and then select **Sound Editor** in the **Applications** window.

2 Select Add Audio File Or...

After you have launched **Sound Editor**, select the **Add Audio File** option to open the **Media Selector** window. This allows you to browse for audio files already saved on your computer (or network drives).

3 ...Select Import from CD/DVD

After you have launched **Sound Editor**, select the **Import from CD/DVD** option to open **Media Manager**. This allows you to import tracks from an audio CD or to take the audio from a DVD track. This is an alternative method of extracting audio from a DVD. The other method is described in **2** Extract Audio Tracks from a DVD.

4 Browse to Find Audio Files

After you have opened **Media Manager**, you need to browse through your drives and files to find the audio you would like to import. If you are searching for a file, it is found on your hard discs. If you are importing from a CD or DVD, you need to select your CD/DVD drive.

5 Select Tracks to Be Edited

After you have browsed to the location of the tracks that you would like to edit, you can select one or more tracks to be imported into **Sound Editor**. Preview your tracks using the playback control buttons on the lower part of the screen. You can select multiple tracks by holding down the **Control** key as you select each one.

6 Click OK Or...

When you have selected the tracks you would like to edit, click **OK**.

7 ...Select Record Audio

After you have launched **Sound Editor**, select the **Record Audio** option to open the **Record Audio** window. The **Record Audio** interface is almost exactly the same as the **Easy Audio Capture** interface described in **4** Capture Audio Using Easy Audio Capture. The only additional feature of the **Record Audio** interface is the **Add Track Separator** button. This allows you to split your audio into two or more tracks as it is being recorded.

9

▶ **TIP**

If you are planning to record several tracks, it is much more convenient to use **LP and Tape Assistant**. You can set options within **LP and Tape Assistant** that automatically detect and separate your tracks. By doing this, you won't be required to closely monitor your recording.

8 Click Done

When you are finished recording the audio you would like to edit, click **Done**.

---

10 Split, Crop, and Join Tracks

✔ BEFORE YOU BEGIN	→ SEE ALSO
9 Add Tracks to Sound Editor	**11** Fade Volume of an Audio Track
	15 Mix Multiple Audio Tracks

There are two windows to view your tracks, the **Clip Editor** and the **Mix Editor**. Use the **Clip Editor** to edit the track and the **Mix Editor** to position your clips.

1 Add Markers

Launch **Sound Editor** and add the audio tracks you would like to edit. Click anywhere inside the clips shown in the **Clip Editor** to place a selection line. Right-click on the selection line and select **Add/Remove Marker**. This adds a marker to your audio track. Of course, you can remove a marker in the same way.

▶ **TIPS**

A faster way to add markers to your clip is to place the selection line and then use the **M** key to add each marker.

You can also automatically detect tracks within your audio file to add markers to it. This is helpful if you have recorded audio that contains more than one music track. Select **Track Detection** from the **Tools** drop-down menu.

2 Click on Split Clip

After you have set markers in place, click on **Split Clip**. This opens the **Split Clip** window.

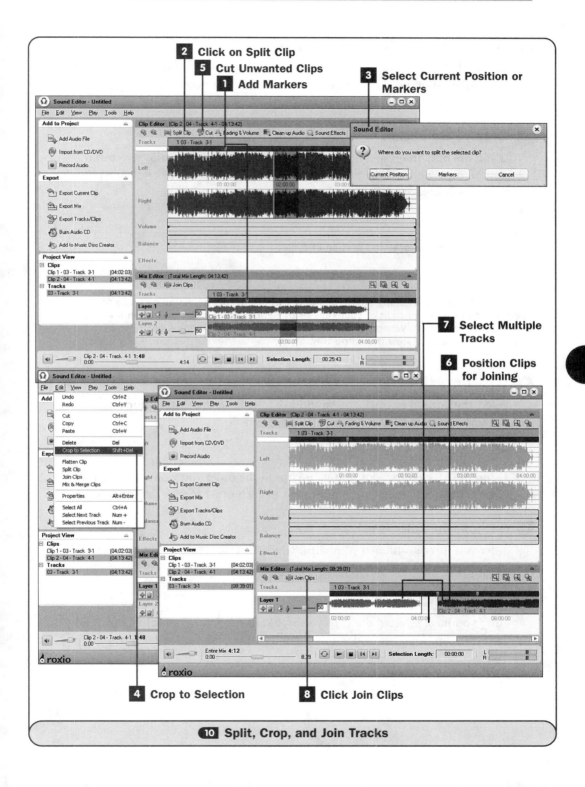

2 Click on Split Clip

5 Cut Unwanted Clips

1 Add Markers

3 Select Current Position or Markers

7 Select Multiple Tracks

6 Position Clips for Joining

4 Crop to Selection

8 Click Join Clips

3 Select Current Position or Markers

The **Split Clip** window gives you the option to split the clip at your current position or at all markers. Choose which option you would like and the operation is completed.

4 Crop to Selection

If you are only interested in editing a small portion of the track, select that portion and choose **Crop to Selection** in the **Edit** menu. This *crops* the picture and deletes anything that is not selected.

▶ KEY TERM

Crop—To delete the unselected portion of a file.

▶ TIP

Any time you have something selected, you can zoom to that selection by using the zoom tools in the upper right of your view or by right-clicking on the selection and choosing **Zoom to selection**. When you are done editing your particular selection, you can zoom back to your full view the same way.

10

5 Cut Unwanted Clips

Select the portion of track you would like to crop in the **Clip Editor** and click the **Cut** option in the taskbar.

6 Position Clips for Joining

Using the **Mix Editor**, position your clips in the order you would like them joined. They don't need to be right next to each other for the joining to work.

7 Select Multiple Tracks

After you have positioned your clips, select the tracks you would like to join by holding down the **Control** key and clicking on each one.

8 Click Join Clips

After you have selected the clips you would like to join, click **Join Clips**. This pulls the clips together and seams them as if there had never been a split.

11   Fade Volume of an Audio Track

✔ BEFORE YOU BEGIN	→ SEE ALSO
9 Add Tracks to Sound Editor	12 Set the Right and Left Audio Track

Setting the volume and fading your audio tracks are two of the most obvious changes you can make. Fading a clip into the next one creates a very nice transition between the two. Of course, that is an obvious use of volume control. You can change the volume—or the balance—of any portion of your track for any number of reasons. You might want to adjust the volume in order to add a sound effect or change the balance to create a sound effect.

▶ NOTE

These steps offer a more precise way to adjust the volume of your track. You can also adjust the volume manually by right-clicking on the **Volume** or **Balance** windows and placing one or more nodes on the line. You can move these nodes at will to adjust the volume or balance settings.

1 Select the Track to Fade

Select the track you would like to fade by clicking on it in the **Mix Editor**; this places it in the **Clip Editor**.

2 Select Area of Track to Fade

Choose a portion of the track to fade by either placing a selector line in the place that you would like to fade or by selecting a portion of the track.

3 Click the Fading & Volume Button

After you have selected the portion of the track you would like to fade, click the **Fading & Volume** button. The **Fading & Volume** menu is displayed.

4 Choose Your Fading Option

The **Fading & Volume** menu has the following options:

- **Fade In**—Used primarily at the beginning of a track (although it can be used anywhere), this option brings the track from silence up to its set volume level. If you have placed a selector line without highlighting a portion of the track, the fade in carries through the rest of the track, coming up to its set volume in the end.

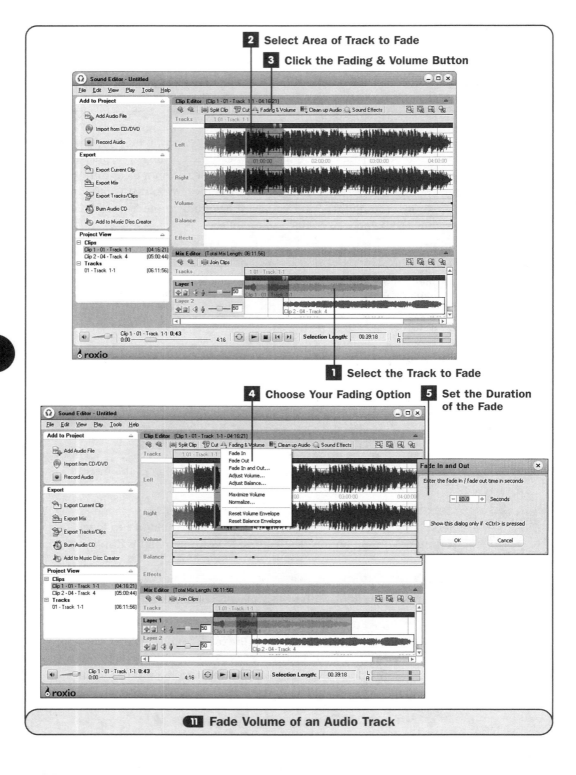

2 Select Area of Track to Fade

3 Click the Fading & Volume Button

1 Select the Track to Fade

4 Choose Your Fading Option

5 Set the Duration of the Fade

11 Fade Volume of an Audio Track

- **Fade Out**—Used primarily at the end of a track (although it can be used anywhere), this option brings the track from its set volume level down to silence. If you have placed a selector line without highlighting a portion of the track, the fade out carries through the rest of the track, finally fading to silence in the end.

- **Fade In and Out**—This option can be used for a variety of reasons. For example, you can soften the transition between merged tracks, or soften a section of music to allow for a voice-over. If you have placed a selector line without highlighting a portion of the track, you are prompted to enter the duration of the fade effect in seconds.

- **Adjust Volume**—This option allows you to adjust the volume of your selected track.

- **Adjust Balance**—This option allows you to adjust the volume *balance* of the right and left channels at different volume settings.

▶ KEY TERM

Balance—The volume of the right channel relative to the volume of the left channel of audio.

After you have selected your option, the fade takes effect.

5 Set the Duration of the Fade

If you selected **Fade In and Out**, you are prompted to set the duration of the fade in seconds. Set the duration and click **OK**.

▶ TIP

If you are dissatisfied with your volume or balance settings, you can quickly reset these values by choosing **Reset Volume Envelope** or **Reset Balance Envelope** in the **Fading & Volume** menu.

12 **Set the Right and Left Audio Track**

✔ BEFORE YOU BEGIN	→ SEE ALSO
9 Add Tracks to Sound Editor	**11** Fade Volume of an Audio Track
	15 Mix Multiple Audio Tracks

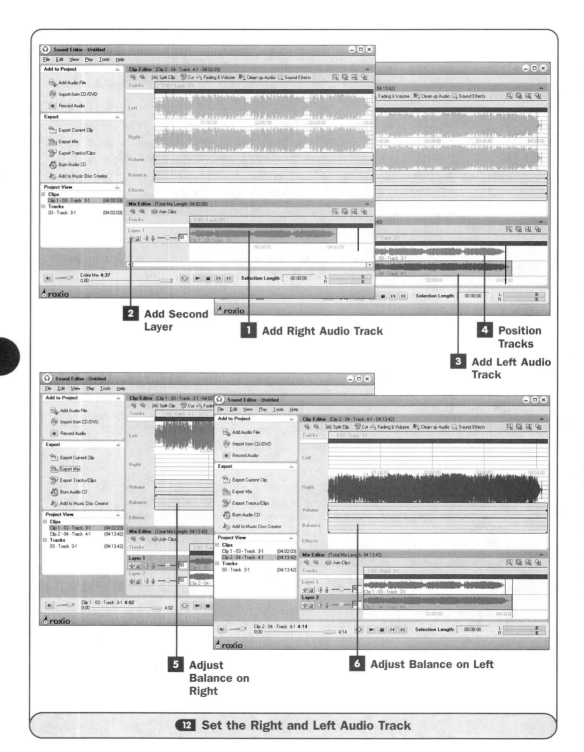

2 Add Second Layer

1 Add Right Audio Track

4 Position Tracks

3 Add Left Audio Track

5 Adjust Balance on Right

6 Adjust Balance on Left

12 Set the Right and Left Audio Track

In order to set a right and left audio track, you need two tracks that coincide with each other. You can do this by adding layers to your project. This is really a very simple task that gives you the capability to add fun effects to your audio.

1 Add Right Audio Track

Add the audio track you would like to play in the right channel to **Sound Editor**.

2 Add Second Layer

Add *layers* to your **Sound Editor** project by clicking on the **Add Layer** button (the plus sign) in the left of the **Mix Editor** under the layer name.

▶ **KEY TERM**

Layer—A separate component within a larger project that can be manipulated independently of the other components of the project.

3 Add Left Audio Track

After you add a second layer, select it. Add the audio track for the left channel.

4 Position Tracks

Position your tracks in the desired location. You can do this simply by dragging them into place inside the **Mix Editor**.

5 Adjust Balance on Right

Select the top track, displaying it in the **Clip Editor**. Set the balance to the right channel by dragging the line in the balance area all the way down.

6 Adjust Balance on Left

Select the bottom track, displaying it in the **Clip Editor**. Set the balance to the left channel by dragging the line in the balance area all the way up.

---

13 Clean, Enhance, and Equalize an Audio Track

✔ BEFORE YOU BEGIN	→ SEE ALSO
9 Add Tracks to Sound Editor	**6** Use LP and Tape Assistant to Edit Newly Captured Audio

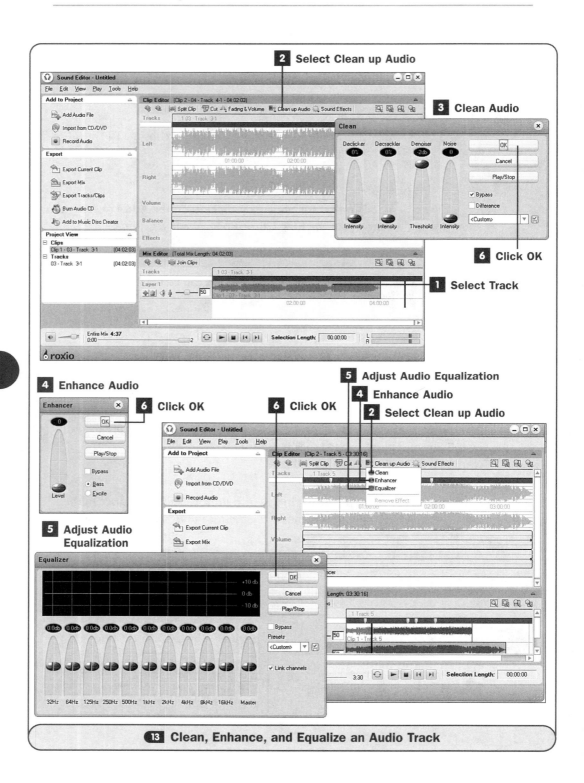

2 Select Clean up Audio

3 Clean Audio

6 Click OK

1 Select Track

4 Enhance Audio

6 Click OK

5 Adjust Audio Equalization

4 Enhance Audio

6 Click OK

2 Select Clean up Audio

5 Adjust Audio Equalization

13 Clean, Enhance, and Equalize an Audio Track

1 Select Track

Select the track (or portion of track) you would like to clean, enhance, or equalize by clicking on it in the **Mix Editor**.

2 Select Clean up Audio

After the track is selected, click on the **Clean up Audio** button in the **Clip Editor** taskbar to bring up the menu. From this menu you can choose **Clean**, **Enhancer**, or **Equalizer**.

3 Clean Audio

After you have opened the **Clean up Audio** menu, click the **Clean** button. In the **Clean** dialog that opens, you can declick, decrackle, denoise, or add noise manually by selecting **Custom** (the default) at the bottom right of the pane and adjusting the sliders for each function until the cleaning effect is properly applied. You can also have the effect applied via **Sound Editor** presets by choosing a low, medium, or high setting from the bottom-right drop-down menu. Play the track that you are cleaning to hear the effect as you adjust it.

▶ TIP

Because the cleaning effects are layered on top of each other as you apply them, you should add the effects one at a time, adjusting each as necessary.

13

4 Enhance Audio

After you have cleaned your audio, you can enhance it by selecting the **Enhancer** option. You can choose to enhance the **Bass**, or make your audio brighter by enhancing the **Excite**. There are no presets for either enhance function, so you need to adjust the effects manually with the slider provided.

5 Adjust Audio Equalization

When you are satisfied with the enhancement settings of your audio, choose the **Equalizer** option to use Easy Media Creator's 10-band equalizer to change the levels of your audio track. You can use the presets, or customize your settings by adjusting the levels manually. Customizing your settings is mostly a trial-and-error process, so change one setting at a time and listen to your track to monitor the differences. There is a left and right channel indicator for each band. You can adjust these separately by deselecting the **Link channels** option.

6 Click OK

After you are done with each of these options, click **OK** to close the windows.

▶ **NOTE**

As you add effects to your audio, you will notice a **Bypass** and (sometimes) a **Difference** selection in the effect adjustment windows. As you preview your audio, you can select **Bypass** to listen to your audio without the effect, or **Difference** to hear the difference the effect is having on the audio without the rest of the audio. Where **Difference** isn't available, simply deselect **Bypass** to preview the audio with the effect applied.

14 Add Effects to an Audio Track	
✔ **BEFORE YOU BEGIN**	→ **SEE ALSO**
9 Add Tracks to Sound Editor	**10** Split, Crop, and Join Tracks
	11 Fade Volume of an Audio Track
	12 Set the Right and Left Audio Track
	13 Clean, Enhance, and Equalize an Audio Track
	15 Mix Multiple Audio Tracks

After you have cleaned up your audio, you might want to add effects. Effects allow you to apply a filter to the audio that adjusts the sound of the track. You can apply effects to set a uniform volume level for tracks, improve the quality of the track, convert a track from mono to stereo, or just add a fun element to the sound of the audio.

Sound Editor allows you to add multiple effects to the same track, a portion of the track, or multiple portions of tracks. This feature allows you to be very creative in making the most of the effects available for audio tracks.

1 Normalize Track

The one effect that you will want to use on virtually every audio track is **Normalize**. The **Normalize** effect enables you to give audio tracks a uniform level of volume by increasing the loudest level in the track to match a specific range in the sound editor. The entire volume level of the track is either increased or decreased to make the loudest part match the maximum level you specify. You can normalize your track by following these steps:

1. Select the Track

If you have multiple tracks loaded in the project, make sure you select the one you want to normalize or apply audio effects to.

2. Select Normalize

Select the **Fading & Volume** button and choose **Normalize**. This brings up the **Normalize** effect window.

3. Set Volume Level

Use the slider to adjust the volume to the level desired for audio in this project.

4. Preview the Audio

You can preview the loudness by pressing the **Play/Stop** button. While listening to the audio, you can select the **Bypass** check box to quickly bypass the normalization effect to hear the original audio.

5. Click OK

After you have the normalize level set to the appropriate value, click **OK**.

▶ **NOTE**

You can also maximize the volume of a clip. Maximizing the clip renders each layer to play at the same volume, and can be a critical function if the volume variance is easily distinguishable. This is not always recommended, however. If the volume of a clip is very low, you might cause the audio to become distorted or clipped if you maximize it. Maximized clips also tend to be a little bit louder than normal audio CDs, forcing you to adjust the volume of the playback device.

14

2 **Add Effects**

With the track selected, select **Sound Effects** and choose one of the following effects to apply to the audio track. You can also apply effects to a specific portion of the track by highlighting only that portion of the track:

- **Alienizer**—Adds a metallic timbre to the sound.

- **DeVoicer**—Attemps to remove voices from the audio.

- **Digital Hall**—Adds the echo effect that you might get in a large building.

- **Maturizer**—Adds static and other effects to make audio sound like an old LP or radio signal.

- **Mono to Stereo**—Changes mono audio to sound like stereo with different tracks in each speaker.

- **Parametric Equalizer**—Allows you to equalize the audio with an easy-to-use interface.

1 Normalize Track

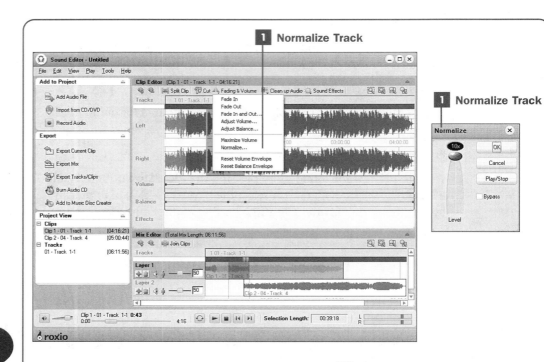

1 Normalize Track

2 Add Effects

3 Preview the Effect

4 Adjust the Effect Settings

5 Click OK

14 Add Effects to an Audio Track

- **Pitch**—Adjusts the pitch of the audio.

- **RoboVoice**—Adds an electronic timbre to the sound.

- **Stereo Enhancer**—Amplifies the stereo effect of the audio to make it more apparent.

3 Preview the Effect

You can preview the loudness by pressing the **Play/Stop** button. While listening to the audio, you can select the **Bypass** check box to quickly bypass the normalization effect to hear the original audio.

4 Adjust the Effect Settings

Each effect has its own controls, allowing you to adjust what the effect does to the audio. Adjust the effects while the audio is playing and tweak the effect until you get the best result.

5 Click OK

After you have the desired effect, click **OK**. You can add additional effects to the track by repeating steps 2 through 5.

15

▶ NOTE

As you add effects to your tracks, you can undo them at any time by selecting **Edit, Undo** in the **File** menu. Keep in mind that although you can continue to undo several actions, your effects are undone in the reverse order that you applied them.

▶ TIP

You should always normalize all audio tracks for a project to the same level. This makes the volume of each track match and removes the risk of having one track sound much softer than the other tracks.

---

15 Mix Multiple Audio Tracks

✔ BEFORE YOU BEGIN	→ SEE ALSO
9 Add Tracks to Sound Editor	**11** Fade Volume of an Audio Track
10 Split, Crop, and Join Tracks	**12** Set the Right and Left Audio Track
	13 Clean, Enhance, and Equalize an Audio Track
	14 Add Effects to an Audio Track

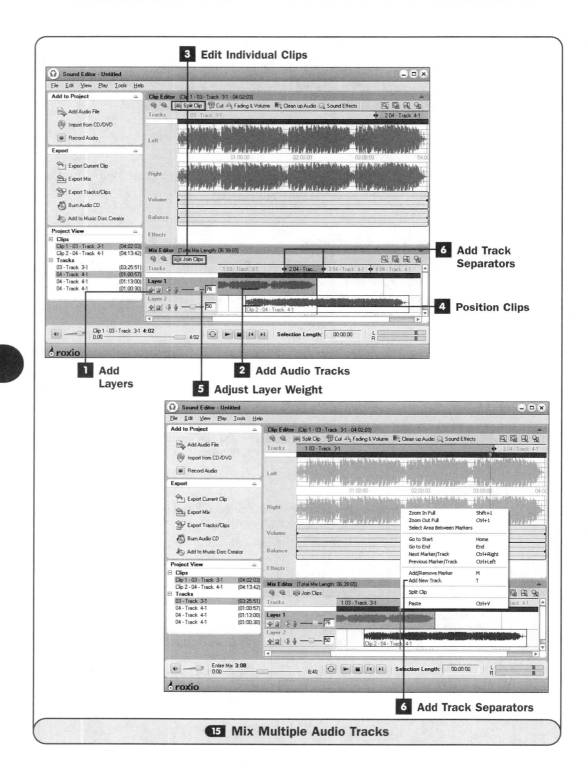

3 Edit Individual Clips

6 Add Track Separators

4 Position Clips

1 Add Layers

2 Add Audio Tracks

5 Adjust Layer Weight

6 Add Track Separators

15 Mix Multiple Audio Tracks

1 Add Layers

Add Layers to your **Sound Editor** project by clicking on the **Add Layer** button (the plus sign) in the left of the **Mix Editor** under the layer name.

2 Add Audio Tracks

After you have added an appropriate number of layers, add the audio tracks you would like to mix. Select the layer you would like the track dropped into before you import it.

3 Edit Individual Clips

After you have imported your clips, edit your clips individually to suit your needs. For example, you probably want to crop or join some of your clips or set the channels on each clip.

4 Position Clips

Position your tracks in the desired location. You can do this simply by dragging them in place inside the **Mix Editor**.

5 Adjust Layer Weight

After you have edited each clip, adjust the weight of each layer by moving the slider in the layer window back and forth. The heavier the layer weight, the louder that layer sounds in comparison to the other layers.

15

6 Add Track Separators

After you are done mixing your clips, you can add track separators to create new tracks within your mix. Position the selection line in the location that you would like to divide the tracks. You can do this in the **Clip Editor** or the **Mix Editor**. Right-click on the selection line and choose **Add New Track**. The clip is split and identified as two separate tracks.

▶ NOTE

After you have edited and mixed your audio to your satisfaction, you want to save your new tracks. Use the **Export** options on the right of the **Sound Editor** window to export your tracks to a file, to a **Music Disc Creator** project, or to burn it onto a CD.

16   Export Audio

✔ BEFORE YOU BEGIN	→ SEE ALSO
Chapter 1, "Start Here" (Review information about audio file types.)	**6** Use LP and Tape Assistant to Edit Newly Captured Audio **20** Create and Burn an Audio CD Project

After you are done editing your audio in **Sound Editor**, there are many options for exporting it. You can export just an edited clip or track, export the whole mix, burn the mix to CD, or add it to **Music Disc Creator**. You can also save an unfinished project so you can open and finish it later.

It is important to review the information on file formats in Chapter 1, "Start Here," so you know what your best option is for saving your mix.

Also, be sure to choose a destination for your files that is organized and easy to find so you can find the files when it comes time to add them to a project.

16

1 Save Sound Editor Project

If you would like to save an unfinished project, choose **Save Project** from the **File** menu. This brings up the standard **Save As** window where you are able to choose a file name and destination. The file will have a **.dmse** extension that enables **Sound Editor** to locate it when you ask the program to open an existing project.

2 Export Current Clip

If you would like to save a single edited clip, select the clip you would like to export and click **Export Current Clip** in the **Export** menu to open the **Export Current Clip** window. You can choose the file format you would like to save your clip to, the destination, and the name. After you are finished selecting these options, click **Export**.

3 Export Mix

If you would like to save the mix you have created, click **Export Mix** in the **Export** menu to open the **Export Mix** window. You can choose the file format you would like to save your clip to, the destination, and the name. After you are finished selecting these options, click **Export**.

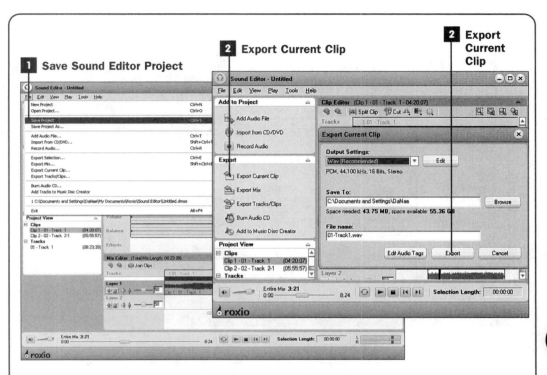

1 Save Sound Editor Project

2 Export Current Clip

2 Export
Current
Clip

3 Export Mix

3 Export Mix

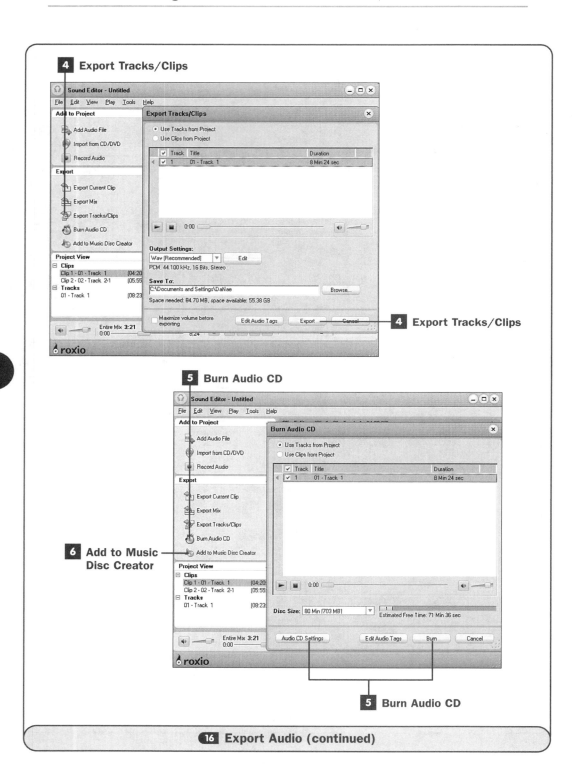

4 Export Tracks/Clips

4 Export Tracks/Clips

5 Burn Audio CD

6 Add to Music Disc Creator

5 Burn Audio CD

16 Export Audio (continued)

4 Export Tracks/Clips

To save one or more tracks or clips from your project, click **Export Tracks/Clips** in the **Export** menu to open the **Export Tracks/Clips** window. In this window you can choose whether to export the tracks or the clips and you can deselect any that you do not want to export. Choose the file format you would like to save your clip to, the destination, and the name. After you are finished selecting these options, click **Export**.

5 Burn Audio CD

To burn your mix to a CD, click **Burn Audio CD** in the **Export** menu to open the **Burn Audio CD Wizard**. You can use the tracks or the clips from the project and deselect any tracks that you do not want burned. By clicking the **Audio CD Settings** button, you can name the disc and the artist and choose to maximize the volume as the CD is being burned to ensure that the audio is burned at the same level. In this settings window you can also choose to have CD-text information stored on the disc. Make sure that you will have enough room on your CD to hold the tracks, and place an empty CD in your burner. When you are finished with the settings, click **OK** to exit the settings window, and then click **Burn**.

16

6 Add to Music Disc Creator

To add your mix to an advanced audio project as a track, click **Add to Music Disc Creator** in the **Export** menu to open **Music Disc Creator**. The mix is automatically added to **Music Disc Creator** as it is opened, and you can continue to add tracks from Sound Editor projects or other sources to your advanced project so you can save it or burn it to CD.

4

Creating Audio Projects

IN THIS CHAPTER:

Creating audio projects is why you captured and edited your audio. Roxio Easy Media Creator 8 has more capabilities than it has ever had before for creating audio projects and burning them to CD or to DVD. Whether you want to create your own music mix on a standard audio CD or you want to create intricate menus for an audio DVD, you can do it easily in Easy Media Creator.

Before creating your audio projects, you should have already captured and edited any audio you would like to place in the projects. You can capture your audio as you are creating these projects, but unless you are simply ripping a few tracks from a CD, it might be much simpler to capture ahead of time. Any editing should be done ahead of time.

17 | Burn Audio Files to an Audio CD

✔ BEFORE YOU BEGIN	→ SEE ALSO
Chapter 1, "Start Here" (Review information on choosing the correct disc format)	**18** Create a Jukebox Disc **19** Create and Burn an MP3/ WMA Disc **20** Create and Burn an Audio CD Project

17

It is a simple task to create a basic audio CD within Easy Media Creator. With just a few steps you can record your own CD mix on a recordable disc and play it in any conventional CD player. Because it is such a widely used feature and can be either a simple process or a more detailed one if you would like more advanced settings, it is handled in two areas of Easy Media Creator.

This task focuses on the quick and easy method of creating an audio CD. You simply drop your files into the project and burn them to a CD. Because you can only create a conventional CD with this interface, your files are automatically converted to WAV files so they will play on any standard CD player.

If you would like to create a more advanced project, please refer to **20** **Create and Burn an Audio CD Project**.

1 Select Audio

Select the **Audio** button in the **project** pane to open the **Audio** menu.

2 Select Audio CD

After the **Audio** menu is displayed, select the **Audio CD** option to open the **Audio CD Wizard**.

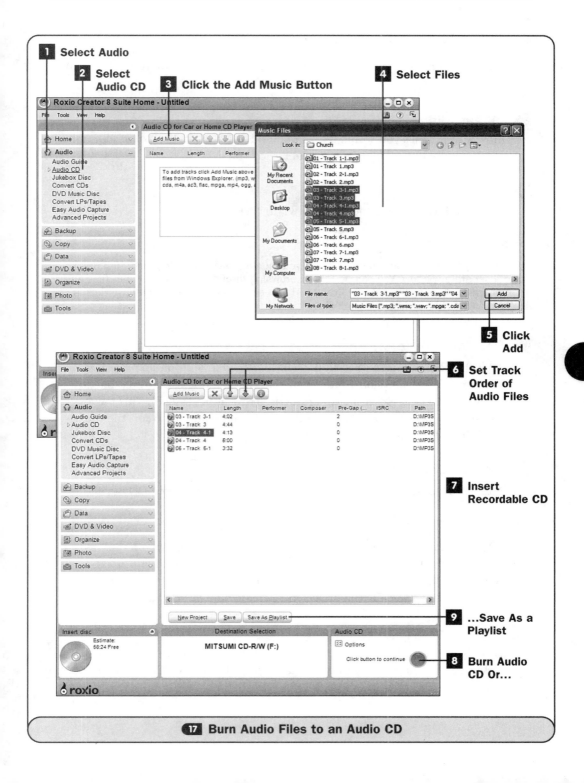

1 **Select Audio**

2 **Select Audio CD**

3 **Click the Add Music Button**

4 **Select Files**

5 **Click Add**

6 **Set Track Order of Audio Files**

7 **Insert Recordable CD**

8 **Burn Audio CD Or...**

9 **...Save As a Playlist**

17 Burn Audio Files to an Audio CD

3 Click the Add Music Button

After the **Audio CD Wizard** is open, click the **Add Music** button to add audio files to your project.

4 Select Files

Browse to the files you would like to add and select them. You can add multiple files by holding down the **Control** key as you click on them.

5 Click Add

After you have selected the files you want, click **Add**.

▶ **TIP**

Another way to import your audio files into your audio project is to drag and drop them from a separate window. You can do this by browsing through Windows for your files and then dragging them to Easy Media Creator. This is an easier method if you have files in several locations to add to your project.

17

6 Set Track Order of Audio Files

After the files you have selected have been placed in your audio project, you can re-order the tracks on your disc by selecting the track you would like to move and clicking either the **up** or **down arrow** in the taskbar. This moves the track up or down one track at a time. You can continue to sort the tracks until they are in the order you would like them to be.

7 Insert Recordable CD

After your tracks are in place, insert a recordable CD into your CD burner.

8 Burn Audio CD Or...

After you have your recordable disc in your CD burner, click the round, red button on the bottom of the **Audio CD** window to start the burn process. When your CD has been burned, it is automatically ejected and you are given the option to close the project or to create a label for your disc.

9 ...Save As a Playlist

When your tracks are in place, you can choose to save your project as a playlist. Select the **Save As Playlist** button and choose the destination of the playlist file. This playlist is recognized by most digital media software.

▶ **TIP**

You can save your project so you can burn the same CD at anytime by clicking **Save** in the **File** menu.

18 Create a Jukebox Disc	
✔ **BEFORE YOU BEGIN**	→ **SEE ALSO**
Chapter 1, "Start Here" (Review information on choosing the correct disc format)	**17** Burn Audio Files to an Audio CD **19** Create and Burn an MP3/WMA Disc **20** Create and Burn an Audio CD Project

Creating a *jukebox disc* is similar to creating an audio CD with the exception that the files are burned in MP3 format so you can play the disc in your MP3/WMA player. The steps are also very similar to the audio CD process with the exception that you can add folders to create playlists to a jukebox disc.

Like creating an audio CD, this is a project that can be simplified enough to warrant two interfaces within Easy Media Creator. In this easier interface you simply drag your files into the **Jukebox Disc** menu and then burn them to a CD or DVD. For more advanced options see **19** **Create and Burn an MP3/WMA Disc**.

▶ **KEY TERM**

Jukebox disc—A music CD that is made up of MP3 files and folders. It can hold a lot more than a conventional CD and the folders become playlists.

1 Select Audio

Select **Audio** in the **project** pane to open the **Audio** menu.

2 Select Jukebox Disc

From the **Audio** menu, select **Jukebox Disc** to bring up the **Jukebox Disc Wizard**.

3 Add Files to Jukebox Disc Project Or...

When the **Jukebox Disc Wizard** has launched, select **Add Files** from the **Add Music** drop-down menu to add files to your project.

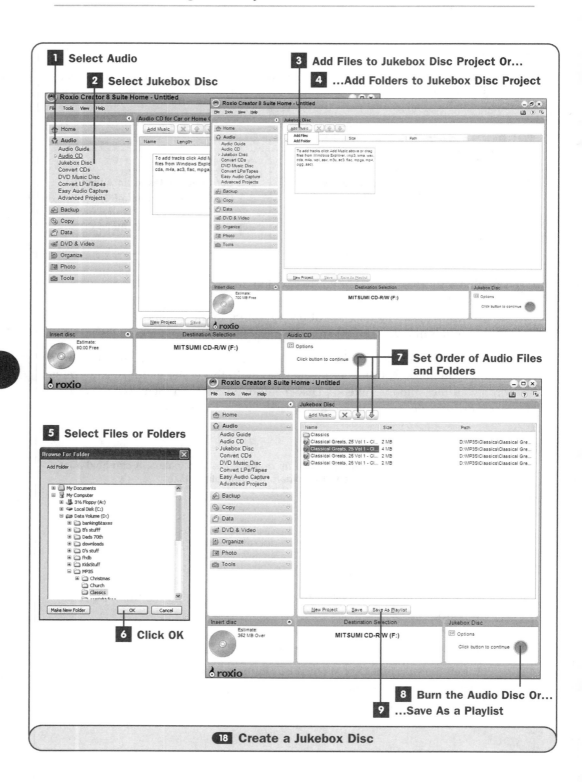

1 Select Audio

2 Select Jukebox Disc

3 Add Files to Jukebox Disc Project Or...

4 ...Add Folders to Jukebox Disc Project

5 Select Files or Folders

6 Click OK

7 Set Order of Audio Files and Folders

8 Burn the Audio Disc Or...

9 ...Save As a Playlist

18 Create a Jukebox Disc

4 ...Add Folders to Jukebox Disc Project

When the **Jukebox Disc Wizard** has launched, select **Add Folders** from the **Add Music** drop-down menu add folders to your project. These folders will become *playlists* on your MP3 disc.

▶ KEY TERM

Playlist—A file that contains a list of music tracks, usually with something in common, that can be played together.

5 Select Files or Folders

Browse to the files you would like to add and select them. You can add multiple files by holding down the **Control** key as you click on them.

6 Click OK

After you have selected the files you want, click **OK**.

7 Set Order of Audio Files and Folders

After the files you have selected have been placed in your audio project, you can re-order them on your disc by selecting the file or folder you would like to move and clicking either the **up** or **down arrow** in the taskbar. This moves the file up or down one location at a time. You can continue to sort your files and folders until they are in the order you would like them to be.

18

8 Burn the Audio Disc Or...

After you have your files and folders in place, click the round, red button on the bottom of the **Jukebox Disc** window to start the burn process. When your CD has been burned, it is automatically ejected and you are given the option to close the project or to create a label for your disc.

9 ...Save As a Playlist

When your tracks are in place, you can choose to save your project as a playlist. Select the **Save As Playlist** button and choose the destination of the playlist file. This playlist is recognized by most digital media software.

19 **Create and Burn an MP3/WMA Disc**

✔ BEFORE YOU BEGIN	→ SEE ALSO
Chapter 1, "Start Here" (Review information on choosing the correct disc format)	**17** Burn Audio Files to an Audio CD **18** Create a Jukebox Disc **20** Create and Burn an Audio CD Project

When you go out shopping for your next CD player, you will probably notice that many of them are capable of playing MP3 discs as well as the discs that contain conventional CD audio tracks. MP3s are so popular because they take up less than a quarter of the disc space that a conventional CD track uses and sacrifice little of the quality if they're properly encoded. This opens the doors to creating discs that not only carry more music, but can be formatted with playlists and menus.

This is the more advanced interface for creating your MP3/WMA disc; **18** **Create a Jukebox Disc** is the more simplified method.

19

▶ **TIP**

You should put the blank disc in your CD/DVD recorder prior to adding files and folders. Easy Media Creator automatically detects what size the audio disc is so the **Estimated Free Space** number is correct. Even though most audio CDs available today are labeled as 80-minute/700MB discs, there are always slight variations in disc capacity that can affect your audio projects if you fill your discs to the maximum.

1 **Select Audio**

Select **Audio** in the **project** pane to open the **Audio** menu.

2 **Select Advanced Projects**

After the **Audio** menu is displayed, select the **Advanced Projects** to bring up **Music Disc Creator**.

3 **Select MP3/WMA Disc**

From within **Music Disc Creator**, select **MP3/WMA Disc** to start a MP3/WMA disc project.

4 **Select Disc Size**

After you have started a new disc project, choose the size of the recordable disc you will be using from the **Disc Size** drop-down menu. The size of the disc is usually printed somewhere on the disc itself.

Selecting the correct size of your disc ensures that the **Estimated Free Space** status bar is correct so you do not add more files to the project than can actually fit on the disc.

5 Add/Name Folders

After setting the disc size, add folders to the project by clicking on the **New Folder** button. You want to give the folders meaningful names. Most MP3 players now allow you to view the folder names when selecting music to play. Using meaningful names makes it easier to navigate and find the music you want to play. You can change the name of a folder at any time before burning by right-clicking on the folder and selecting **Rename** from the context menu.

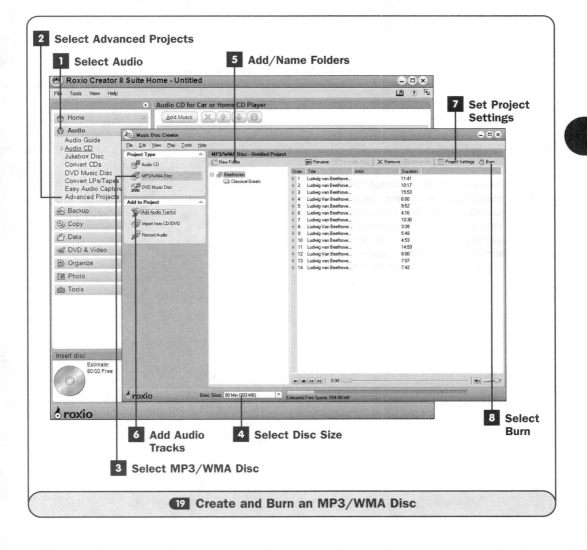

2 Select Advanced Projects

1 Select Audio

5 Add/Name Folders

7 Set Project Settings

19

8 Select Burn

6 Add Audio Tracks

4 Select Disc Size

3 Select MP3/WMA Disc

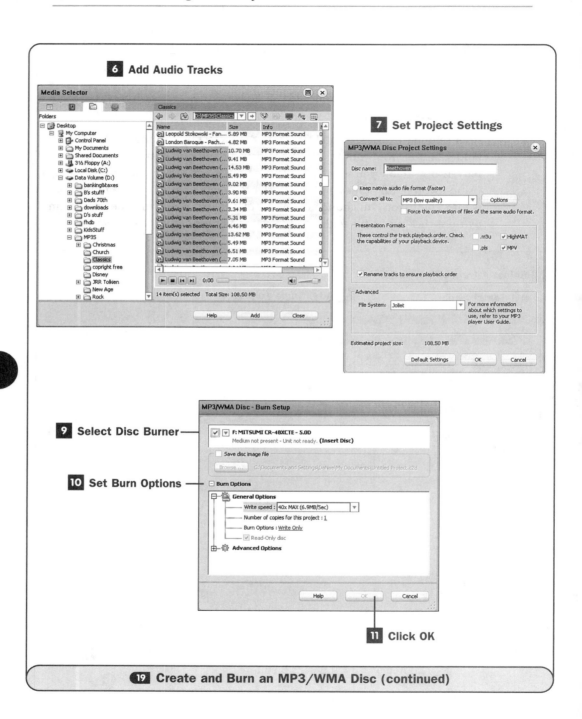

6 **Add Audio Tracks**

7 **Set Project Settings**

9 **Select Disc Burner**

10 **Set Burn Options**

11 **Click OK**

19 **Create and Burn an MP3/WMA Disc (continued)**

6 Add Audio Tracks

After you have your folders created, you can start adding audio tracks to them. There are three ways to add audio tracks. The first is to click on **Add Audio Tracks** and then find the audio files you want to add in **Media Manager**. You can select several by holding down the **Control** key while you click on them. After you have selected the tracks you want, click **OK**.

You can also import audio directly into the project by clicking **Import from CD/DVD** or **Record Audio** and then following the instructions listed in **1 Capture Music Tracks from a CD** and **4 Capture Audio Using Easy Audio Capture**.

7 Set Project Settings

After you have imported your audio, you need to set the project settings prior to burning it to disc. Select the **Project Settings** button in the taskbar to set the following options:

- **Disc name**—You should give your disc a meaningful name because this name will be displayed in the MP3 player.

- **Keep native audio file format**—If your audio is already in a format that is supported by your MP3 player, you can keep the audio format the same. This method is the fastest because no audio conversion is necessary, and it's also preferable because you won't have to worry about losing quality in additional format conversions.

- **Convert all to**—If your audio files are in formats that are not supported by your MP3 player, you want to select the **Convert all to** option and specify the audio format as MP3 or WMA.

- **Options**—If you are converting the audio files, you should take some time to make certain that the conversion options are correct. The **Options** button brings up a window that allows you to specify the format, encoder, and quality of the audio file.

- **Presentation Formats**—You can also specify the presentation formats to add to the MP3 disc. These formats are playlist files that specify the order that the MP3 player uses to play back the audio tracks. The most common formats are **.m3u** or **.pls**.

- **Rename tracks to ensure playback order**—You can force the playback order even on players that do not support presentation formats by checking the **Rename tracks to ensure playback order** check box. Only use this option if necessary because the filenames will be altered.

19

- **File System**—You can also specify which type of file system to use when burning the disc. Typically you want to use the Joliet file system; however, you might want to use the ISO 9660 or UDF 102 if your MP3 player is having problems with the Joliet file system. With ISO 9660, you are limited to eight-character filenames for all your tracks.

8 Select Burn

After you have set the project options, you are ready to burn the disc. Start the burn process by clicking on the **Burn** button in the taskbar to bring up the **Burn Setup** window.

9 Select Disc Burner

If you have multiple CD/DVD recorders, you need to specify which drive you will be using to burn the disc by checking it. If your preferred destination drive does not appear in the recorder drop-down menu, check your connections. Open **My Computer** in the **Start** menu if necessary to make sure it has been assigned a drive letter.

19

▶ **TIP**

You also have the option in the **Burn Setup** window to save an image of the disc you are burning. This enables you to store the disc image as a file to archive, transfer it to another computer, or burn copies later.

10 Set Burn Options

After you have selected the disc burner, you can specify options by expanding the **Options** menu. From the **Options** menu, you can specify the write speed, number of copies, and other settings.

▶ **NOTE**

A buffer under-run is a condition where all the files have not been burned to disc, but the computer is not fast enough to keep sending data to the disc burner. When a buffer under-run occurs, the burn fails and the disc is useless. You can help prevent buffer under-runs by closing any unnecessary programs when burning discs and by using a slower write speed.

11 Click OK

After you have finished setting the burn options, click **OK** to burn the disc. After the burn process is completed, the disc is automatically ejected.

20 | Create and Burn an Audio CD Project

✔ BEFORE YOU BEGIN	→ SEE ALSO
Chapter 1, "Start Here" (Review information on choosing the correct disc format)	**17** Burn Audio Files to an Audio CD **18** Create a Jukebox Disc **19** Create and Burn an MP3/WMA Disc

This is the more advanced method of creating an audio CD to play on your conventional CD player. Unlike the simple wizard in the Easy Media Creator interface, this task uses **Music Disc Creator** to create an audio CD. This gives you many more options in creating your CD.

1 Select Audio

Select **Audio** in the **project** pane to open the **Audio** menu.

2 Select Advanced Projects

Select **Advanced Projects** from the **Audio** menu to bring up **Music Disc Creator**.

3 Select Audio CD

From within **Music Disc Creator** select **Audio CD**. This brings up the **Audio CD** project window.

4 Select Disc Size

After you have started a new disc project, choose the size of the recordable disc you will be using from the **Disc Size** drop-down menu. The size of the disc is usually printed somewhere on the disc itself.

Selecting the correct size of your disc ensures that the **Estimated Free Space** status bar (to the right of the **Disc Size** menu) is correct so you do not add more files to the project than can actually fit on the disc.

5 Add Audio Tracks

After you have selected your disc size, you can start adding audio tracks to your project. There are three ways to add audio tracks. The first is to click on **Add Audio Tracks** to open **Media Manager** and then find the audio files you want to add. You can select several by holding down the **Control** key while you click on them. After you have selected the tracks that you want, click **OK**.

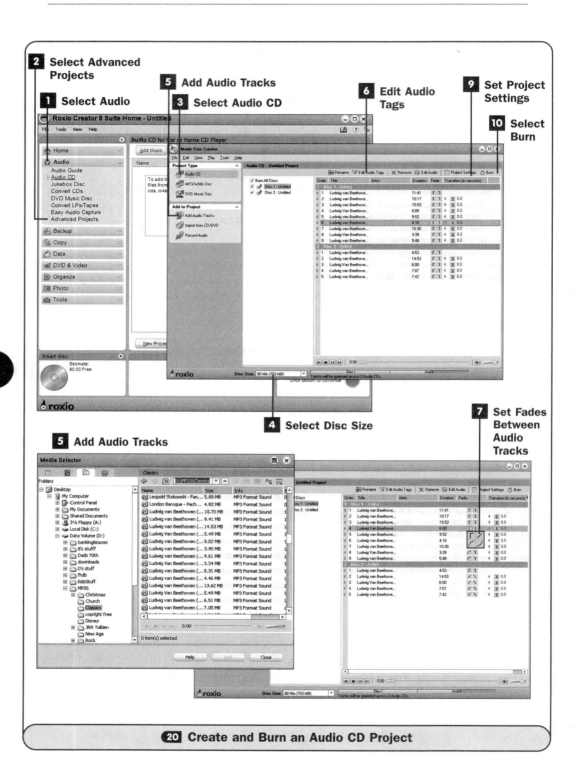

2 Select Advanced Projects

1 Select Audio

5 Add Audio Tracks

3 Select Audio CD

6 Edit Audio Tags

9 Set Project Settings

10 Select Burn

4 Select Disc Size

7 Set Fades Between Audio Tracks

5 Add Audio Tracks

20 Create and Burn an Audio CD Project

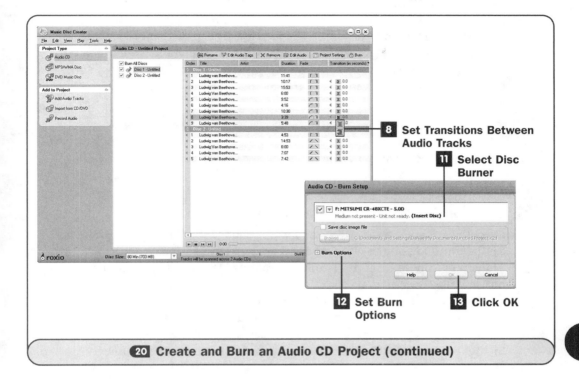

8 Set Transitions Between
Audio Tracks

11 Select Disc
Burner

12 Set Burn
Options

13 Click OK

20 Create and Burn an Audio CD Project (continued)

20

▶ **TIP**

Another way to import your audio files into your audio project is to drag and drop them
from a separate window. You can do this by browsing through Windows for your files and
then dragging them to Easy Media Creator. This is an easier method if you have files in
several locations to add to your project.

You can also import audio directly into the project by clicking the **Import
from CD/DVD** or **Record Audio** and then following the instructions listed in
1 **Capture Music Tracks from a CD** and **4** **Capture Audio Using Easy Audio
Capture**.

6 **Edit Audio Tags**

You can edit the tags of your audio tracks by clicking the **Edit Audio Tags**
button in the taskbar. Follow the steps in **8** **Add Tags to Audio Tracks**.

7 **Set Fades Between Audio Tracks**

You can set the fades between two or more of the audio tracks in your project.
Select the track or tracks on which you would like to set fades. Click on the

left **Fade** button in the **Fade** column to determine how the track fades in and the right **Fade** button to determine the fade out. The preset option (looking like an upside down L) represents no fade. A diagonal line is a standard fade. The diagonal line curved up is a slow fade and curved down is a quick fade. Changing the setting in any one of the selected tracks changes the setting for all.

▶ TIP

You can save your project so you can burn the same CD at any time by clicking **Save** in the **File** menu.

8 Set Transitions Between Audio Tracks

Select the tracks for which you would like to change the transition settings. Set the transition option and time between tracks by clicking on the **Transition** icon inside of the **Transition** column. The preset option is a gap and looks like two brackets backed up to each other. The other option is an overlap. This looks similar to a buckled seat belt. You can choose either option on any of the tracks you have selected and the option is changed in all the tracks. Set the duration of your transition by changing the number to the right of the **Transition** icons. This sets your duration time in number of seconds.

9 Set Project Settings

You can change the name of the disc and artist as well as maximize your volume by clicking the **Project Settings** icon in the taskbar.

10 Select Burn

After you have set the project options, you are ready to burn the disc. Start the burn process by clicking on the **Burn** button in the taskbar to bring up the **Burn Setup** window.

11 Select Disc Burner

If you have multiple CD/DVD recorders, you need to specify which drive you will be using to burn the disc.

▶ TIP

You also have the option in the **Burn Setup** window to save an image of the disc you are burning. This enables you to store the disc image as a file to archive, transfer it to another computer, or burn copies later.

20

12 Set Burn Options

After you have selected the disc burner, you can specify options by expanding the **Options** menu. From the **Options** menu, you can specify the write speed, number of copies, and other settings.

13 Click OK

After you have finished setting the burn options, click **OK** to burn the disc. After the burn process is completed, the disc is automatically ejected.

---

21 Use the DVD Music Assistant to Create a DVD Music Disc

✔ BEFORE YOU BEGIN	→ SEE ALSO
Chapter 1, "Start Here" (Review information on choosing the correct disc format)	**22** Add Tracks to an Advanced DVD Music Disc Project **23** Use Predefined Styles for a DVD Music Disc Menu **24** Add Photos to a DVD Music Disc Menu **25** Organize Titles in a DVD Music Disc Menu **26** Change the DVD Music Disc Project Settings **27** Preview a DVD Music Disc

---

DVD Music Assistant is a three-step wizard that makes audio DVD creation fun and easy to do. It is a good place to start if you have never created an audio DVD. After you are familiar with the basic steps of creating an audio DVD, you can go on to the more advanced steps that are covered in the rest of this chapter.

1 Select Audio

Select **Audio** in the **project** pane to open the **Audio** menu.

2 Select DVD Music Disc

After the **Audio** menu is displayed, select **DVD Music Disc** to bring up the **DVD Music Assistant**.

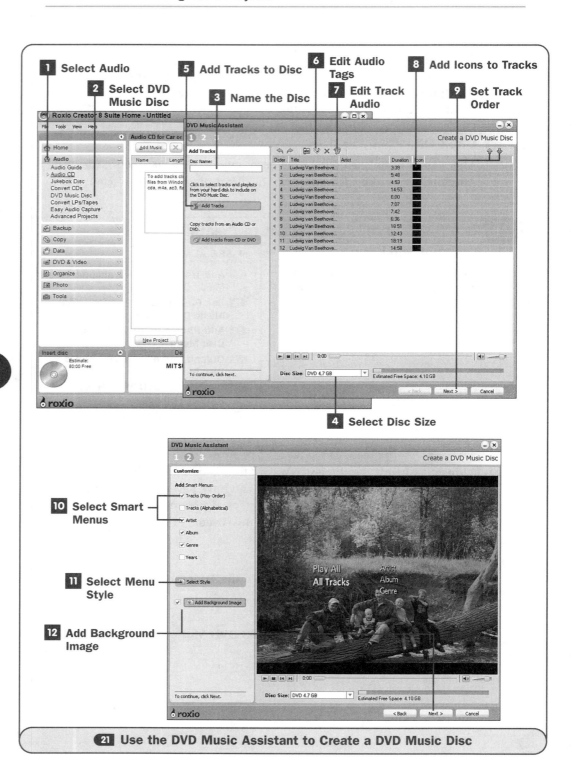

1 Select Audio

2 Select DVD Music Disc

3 Name the Disc

5 Add Tracks to Disc

6 Edit Audio Tags

7 Edit Track Audio

8 Add Icons to Tracks

9 Set Track Order

4 Select Disc Size

10 Select Smart Menus

11 Select Menu Style

12 Add Background Image

21 Use the DVD Music Assistant to Create a DVD Music Disc

21

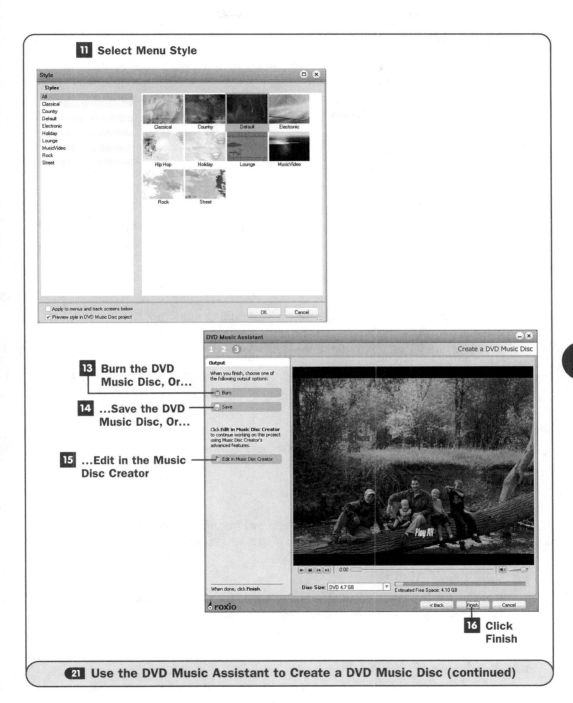

11 Select Menu Style

13 Burn the DVD Music Disc, Or...

14 ...Save the DVD Music Disc, Or...

15 ...Edit in the Music Disc Creator

16 Click Finish

21 Use the DVD Music Assistant to Create a DVD Music Disc (continued)

3 Name the Disc

When the **DVD Music Assistant** comes up, type in the name you want to use for the DVD music disc. This name is displayed in the DVD menu as well as the display of some DVD players, so you want to use a name that enables you to recognize the contents of the disc.

4 Select Disc Size

After you have started a new disc project, choose the size of the recordable disc you will be using from the **Disc Size** drop-down menu. The size of the disc is usually printed somewhere on the disc itself.

Selecting the correct size of your disc ensures that the **Estimated Free Space** status bar is correct so you do not add more files to the project than can actually fit on the disc.

5 Add Tracks to Disc

After you have set the disc size, you can start adding audio tracks. There are two ways to add audio tracks. The first is to click on **Add Tracks** to use the **Media Manager** to find and add the audio files.

You can also import audio directly into the project by clicking the **Add Tracks from CD or DVD** and selecting the tracks directly on the disc.

▶ NOTE

You can only add 97 tracks to a DVD music disc, regardless of the capacity of the media.

6 Edit Audio Tags

You can edit the tags of your audio tracks by clicking the **Edit Audio Tags** button in the taskbar. Follow the steps in **8** **Add Tags to Audio Tracks**.

7 Edit Track Audio

If necessary, you can also edit the track by clicking on the **Edit Audio** icon. This brings up **Quick Sound Editor**. See the tasks in Chapter 3, "Editing Audio," for more information about editing audio.

8 Add Icons to Tracks

You can also add graphic icons to the tracks that will make your DVD menus look cool and make it easier to identify tracks. To add icons to the tracks, click on the blank graphic in the **Icon** column next to the track to which you would like to add an icon. This brings up **Media Manager**, where you can find a graphic file to use for the track icon.

9 Set Track Order

After you have added icons to the tracks, you can re-order the tracks on your disc by dragging and dropping the tracks in the order you would like them to be or by selecting a track and using the **up** and **down arrows** to move it up or down one track at a time.

After you have the tracks in the correct order, click the **Next** button to customize the DVD menu.

10 Select Smart Menus

After you have the tracks in order, you can add different types of *smart menus* that make it easier to navigate the DVD to play audio. Select the smart menus that you want to be displayed on the DVD menu by checking the box next to the appropriate menu.

▶ KEY TERM

Smart menu—A menu that is automatically created based on the content of the DVD.

21

11 Select Menu Style

DVD Music Assistant also includes a number of predefined *menu styles* that include specific background images and fonts in the DVD menu. Click on **Select Style** and use the **Style** window to select a predefined style to use for the DVD menu.

▶ KEY TERM

Menu style—A template for the menu that has predefined elements, such as the background, font, and layout.

12 Add Background Image

After you have selected a menu style, you might want to add a different background to the DVD menu. Click on the **Smart Objects** option in the **DVD Music Disc** menu and then click the **Add Background Image** button. Use the **Media Manager** to select your own image file to use as the background.

After the DVD menu is set, click the **Next** button to bring up the **Output** menu. The **Output** menu gives you several options for continuing with your DVD project.

⒀ Burn the DVD Music Disc, Or...

When you have brought up the **Output** menu, click on the **Burn** button to bring up the **Burn Setup** dialog box. If you have multiple CD/DVD recorders, you need to specify which drive you will be using to burn the disc. After you have selected the disc burner, you can specify options by expanding the **Options** menu. From the **Options** menu, you can specify the write speed, number of copies, and other settings. When you have finished setting the burn options, click **OK** to burn the disc. After the burn process is completed, the disc is automatically ejected.

⒁ ...Save the DVD Music Disc, Or...

You also have the option to save the music disc project to a file by clicking on the **Save** button.

⒂ ...Edit in the Music Disc Creator

If you want to enhance the DVD music disc more, you can open the project in **Music Disc Creator** by clicking on the **Edit in Music Disc Creator** button.

⒃ Click Finish

Click **Finish** to close the project.

---

22   Add Tracks to an Advanced DVD Music Disc Project

✔ BEFORE YOU BEGIN	→ SEE ALSO
Chapter 1, "Start Here" (Review information on choosing the correct disc format)	㉑ Use the DVD Music Assistant to Create a DVD Music Disc ㉓ Use Predefined Styles for a DVD Music Disc Menu ㉔ Add Photos to a DVD Music Disc Menu ㉕ Organize Titles in a DVD Music Disc Menu ㉖ Change the DVD Music Disc Project Settings ㉗ Preview a DVD Music Disc

Creating a DVD music disc with menus and photos is definitely one of the fun aspects of advancing technology. It goes without saying that a DVD can hold numerous music files of any type. You can sort your music into menus of your own creation or use smart menus that sort them by genre, album, artist, and so forth.

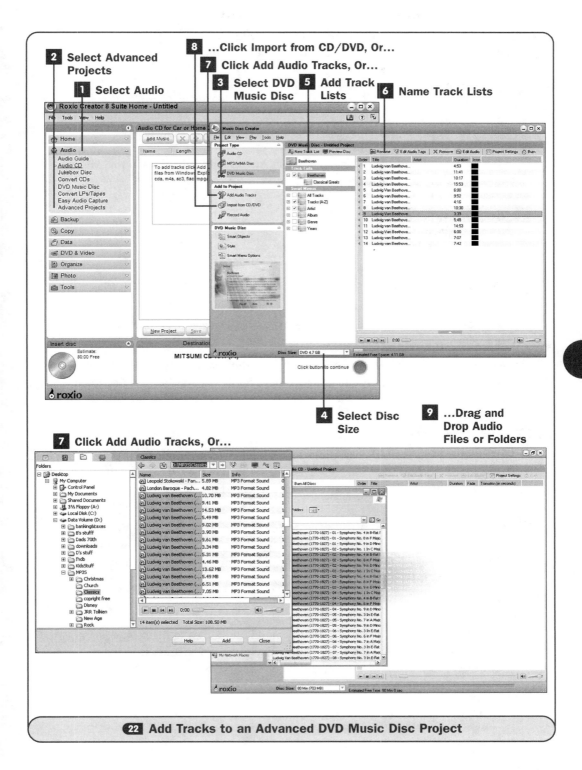

2 Select Advanced Projects

8 ...Click Import from CD/DVD, Or...

7 Click Add Audio Tracks, Or...

1 Select Audio

3 Select DVD Music Disc

5 Add Track Lists

6 Name Track Lists

4 Select Disc Size

9 ...Drag and Drop Audio Files or Folders

7 Click Add Audio Tracks, Or...

22 Add Tracks to an Advanced DVD Music Disc Project

The first step in creating a DVD music disc is to add files to your project. You can add files by themselves or you can drop entire folders into your project.

1 Select Audio

Select **Audio** in the **project** pane to open the **Audio** menu.

2 Select Advanced Projects

After the **Audio** menu is displayed, select **Advanced Projects** from the **Audio** menu to bring up **Music Disc Creator**.

3 Select DVD Music Disc

From within **Music Disc Creator**, select **DVD Music Disc** to start a DVD music disc project.

4 Select Disc Size

After you have started a new disc project, choose the size of the recordable disc you will be using from the drop-down menu labeled **Disc Size**. The size of the disc is usually printed somewhere on the disc itself.

Selecting the correct size of your disc ensures that the **Estimated Free Space** status bar is correct so you do not add more files to the project than can actually fit on the disc.

5 Add Track Lists

When a new DVD music disc project is created, there is only one track list that exists. You can add new track lists by selecting an existing track list and clicking on the **New Track List** button in the taskbar.

6 Name Track Lists

After you have added the number of track lists you think that you will need, give them meaningful names by selecting them and clicking on the **Rename** button in the taskbar.

7 Click Add Audio Tracks, Or...

After the track lists are in place, you can add audio files to them by selecting a track list and clicking the **Add Audio Tracks** button to bring up **Media Manager**. Use **Media Manager** to add files or folders.

22

8 **...Click Import from CD/DVD, Or...**

You can also import tracks directly from a CD or DVD by clicking on **Import from CD/DVD**.

9 **...Drag and Drop Audio Files or Folders**

You can also simply drag and drop audio files from **Windows Explorer** (or any open window) into track lists.

▶ **TIP**

If you add folders instead of files when you are adding audio tracks, those folders and any subfolders are added as track lists and all audio files contained in each folder appear in each matching track list.

---

23 **Use Predefined Styles for a DVD Music Disc Menu**

✔ BEFORE YOU BEGIN	→ SEE ALSO
Chapter 1, "Start Here" (Review information on choosing the correct disc format)	**21** Use the DVD Music Assistant to Create a DVD Music Disc
22 Add Tracks to an Advanced DVD Music Disc Project	**24** Add Photos to a DVD Music Disc Menu
	25 Organize Titles in a DVD Music Disc Menu
	26 Change the DVD Music Disc Project Settings
	27 Preview a DVD Music Disc

23

You can set a predefined style to your menu to make it fun and easy to navigate around your audio DVD. Each menu can be set to a different style depending on what type of music you have in that menu.

1 **Select Smart Menus**

Roxio allows you to add different types of smart menus that make it easier to navigate the DVD to play audio. Select the check boxes of the smart menus that you want to be displayed on the DVD menu.

2 **Set Menu Styles**

After you have selected the smart menus to display in the DVD menu, you can set menu styles for each track list and smart menu. Easy Media Creator includes a number of predefined menu styles that include specific background images and fonts. To set a menu style for a track list or smart menu, select the list or menu and click on **Style** to bring up the **Style** window. Use the **Style** window to select a predefined style to use for the track list or smart menu.

3 Set Preview Options

From the **Style** menu, select the **Preview style in DVD Music Disc project** check box to preview the menu in the **Music Disc Creator** project window prior to accepting the style.

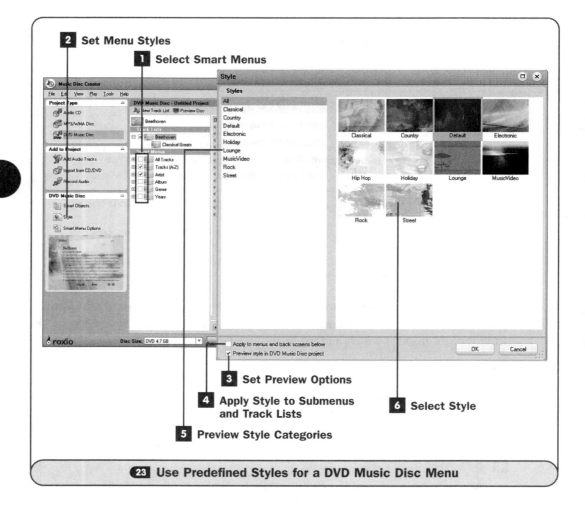

23 Use Predefined Styles for a DVD Music Disc Menu

4 **Apply Style to Submenus and Track Lists**

You can check the **Apply to menus and track screens below** check box if you want the style to be applied to any track lists or menus below the one that is selected.

5 **Preview Style Categories**

Click on each style category to view the available predefined styles.

6 **Select Style**

After you find the style you like, select it and click the **OK** button to apply it to the menu or task list.

---

24 **Add Photos to a DVD Music Disc Menu**

✔ BEFORE YOU BEGIN	→ SEE ALSO
Chapter 1, "Start Here" (Review information on choosing the correct disc format) **22** Add Tracks to an Advanced DVD Music Disc Project	**21** Use the DVD Music Assistant to Create a DVD Music Disc **23** Use Predefined Styles for a DVD Music Disc Menu **25** Organize Titles in a DVD Music Disc Menu **26** Change the DVD Music Disc Project Settings **27** Preview a DVD Music Disc

24

Music Disc Creator allows you to add photos to the disc, smart menus, and track lists. These images make it easier to navigate the DVD menu and give your project a personal touch. You can use your own photos instead of, or in conjunction with, Easy Media Creator's predefined styles.

1 **Select Disc, Smart Menu, Track List, or Track**

Within your DVD music disc project, select **Disc**, **Smart Menu**, **Track List**, or **Track** to add an image.

2 **Select Smart Objects**

When you have selected the item you would like to add an image to, click **Smart Objects** to bring up the **Smart Objects** window.

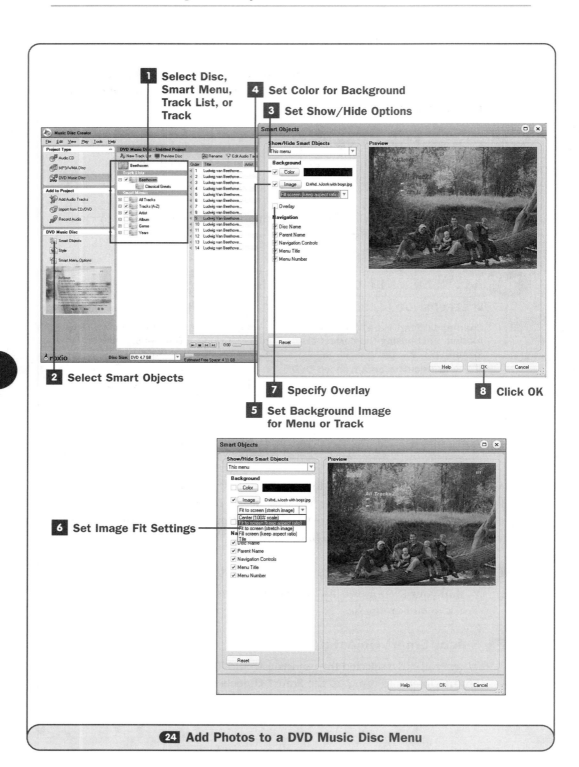

1 Select Disc, Smart Menu, Track List, or Track

4 Set Color for Background

3 Set Show/Hide Options

2 Select Smart Objects

7 Specify Overlay

8 Click OK

5 Set Background Image for Menu or Track

6 Set Image Fit Settings

24 Add Photos to a DVD Music Disc Menu

24

3 Set Show/Hide Options

After the **Smart Objects** window opens, choose where you would like the icon to be displayed by selecting one of the following from the **Show/Hide Smart Objects** drop-down menu:

- This menu
- This menu and below
- All menus
- Selected track screen
- Track screens below
- All track screens
- All menus and track screens

4 Set Color for Background

After you have set the **Show/Hide** options for the image, click the **Color** button to change the background color. This color is displayed behind the image if the image does not fill the entire screen. You can also save the color alone as the icon without choosing an image.

5 Set Background Image for Menu or Track

When you have set the background color, add the image that will be displayed behind the menu by clicking on the **Image** button to bring up **Media Manager**. After you have found your image, close **Media Manager**.

6 Set Image Fit Settings

After you have set the background image, use the drop-down menu to specify whether the image will be centered, tiled, fit to screen, or fill the screen. If the original aspect ratio (or shape) of your image doesn't conform to the 4:3 ratio of a standard TV screen, the image might be distorted if you select the **Fit to screen (stretch image)** option.

7 Specify Overlay

Check the **Overlay** check box to add an interesting effect to the color or image you have chosen. The *overlay* effect depends on the style you have chosen for your menus.

▶ KEY TERM

Overlay—One image that is laid on top of another to create a layered effect.

8 Click OK

After you have set all options in the **Smart Objects** window, click **OK** to return to **Music Disc Creator**.

---

25 | **Organize Titles in a DVD Music Disc Menu**

✔ BEFORE YOU BEGIN	→ SEE ALSO
Chapter 1, "Start Here" (Review information on choosing the correct disc format) **22** Add Tracks to an Advanced DVD Music Disc Project	**21** Use the DVD Music Assistant to Create a DVD Music Disc **23** Use Predefined Styles for a DVD Music Disc Menu **24** Add Photos to a DVD Music Disc Menu **26** Change the DVD Music Disc Project Settings **27** Preview a DVD Music Disc

25

You want to make your DVD music disc menus easy to use by setting navigation settings for each one of your menu objects. This seems complicated but is actually very easy to do, and it will save you time when it comes to enjoying your music DVD.

1 Set Navigation Settings for Disc Object

Select the **Disc** icon and click **Smart Objects** to bring up the **Smart Objects** window. Check the boxes next to the **Navigation** options that you want to be visible on the DVD menu when the DVD is played. Click **OK** when you are finished.

2 Set Navigation Settings for Track Lists

Select the track list and click **Smart Objects** to bring up the **Smart Objects** window. Check the boxes next to the **Navigation** options that you want visible on the **Track List** menu when the DVD is played. Click **OK** when you are finished.

3 Set Navigation Settings for Smart Menus

Select the smart menu and click **Smart Objects** to bring up the **Smart Objects** window. Check the boxes next to the **Navigation** options that you want to be visible on the smart menu when the DVD is played. Click **OK** when you are finished.

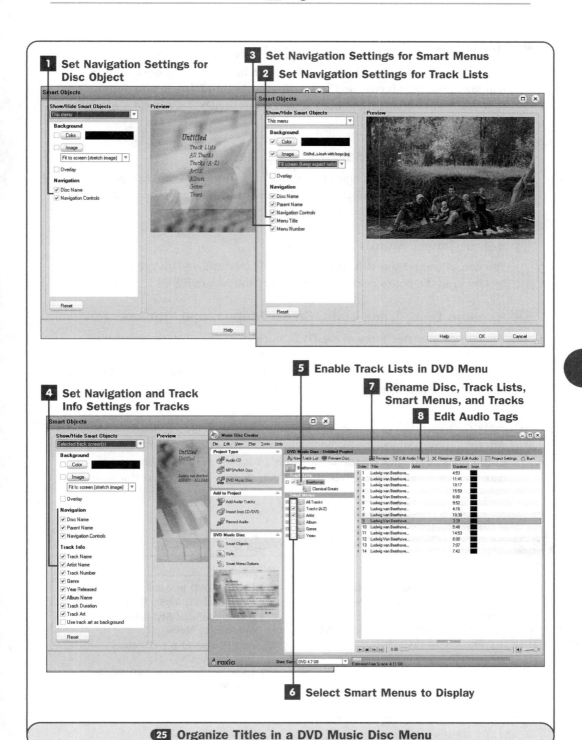

1 Set Navigation Settings for Disc Object

3 Set Navigation Settings for Smart Menus

2 Set Navigation Settings for Track Lists

5 Enable Track Lists in DVD Menu

7 Rename Disc, Track Lists, Smart Menus, and Tracks

8 Edit Audio Tags

4 Set Navigation and Track Info Settings for Tracks

6 Select Smart Menus to Display

25 Organize Titles in a DVD Music Disc Menu

4 Set Navigation and Track Info Settings for Tracks

Select the track(s) and click **Smart Objects** to bring up the **Smart Objects** window. Check the boxes next to the **Navigation and Track Info** options that you want visible on the track screen when the DVD is played. Click **OK** when you are finished.

5 Enable Track Lists in DVD Menu

After you have set the navigation settings for your menus and tracks, check the box next to the root track list if you want the track list to be visible in the DVD menu.

6 Select Smart Menus to Display

You can also specify which smart menus will be displayed on the DVD menu by checking the boxes next to the ones that you want visible.

7 Rename Disc, Track Lists, Smart Menus, and Tracks

You can change the name of the DVD music disc, track lists, smart menus, and audio tracks at any time to make them more meaningful. These names are displayed in the DVD menu, so you want to use a name that enables you to easily navigate through the DVD menu.

8 Edit Audio Tags

After you have named the audio tracks and menus properly, you can select audio tracks and click on the **Edit Audio Tags** button to edit the tags associated with each track. See task **8** **Add Tags to Audio Tracks** for more information.

---

26 Change the DVD Music Disc Project Settings

✔ BEFORE YOU BEGIN	→ SEE ALSO
Chapter 1, "Start Here" (Review information on choosing the correct disc format)	**21** Use the DVD Music Assistant to Create a DVD Music Disc
22 Add Tracks to an Advanced DVD Music Disc Project	**23** Use Predefined Styles for a DVD Music Disc Menu
	24 Add Photos to a DVD Music Disc Menu
	25 Organize Titles in a DVD Music Disc Menu
	27 Preview a DVD Music Disc

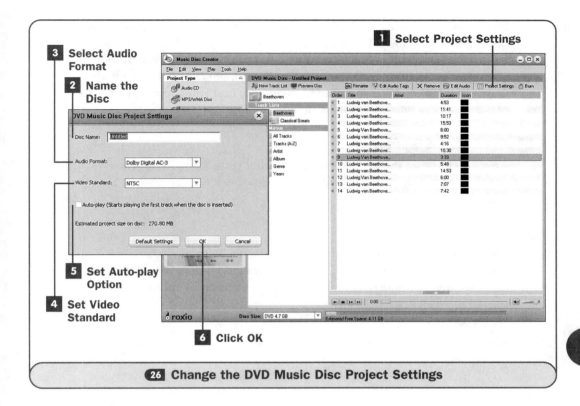

Before you are ready to burn your DVD music disc, you want to make sure the project settings are correct. This ensures that the DVD is the quality that you want and that it will play on your machine.

1 Select Project Settings

Select **Project Settings** from the taskbar to bring up the **DVD Music Disc Project Settings** dialog.

2 Name the Disc

From within the **DVD Music Disc Project Settings** dialog, type in a meaningful name for the DVD music disc.

3 Select Audio Format

After you have named the music disc, select the audio format for the DVD music disc from the **Audio Format** drop-down list. The best option to use is Dolby Digital. Dolby Digital is a compressed format that saves space; however, the quality is virtually indistinguishable from audio CD quality, even on home theater systems. The highest quality setting is PCM, which is the standard format for audio CDs. PCM is not compressed and takes a great deal more space on the disc. MPEG-1, Layer 2 is a compressed file format that gives your project the same size as Dolby Digital, but the quality is inferior. Only use MPEG audio if you need to save space and you know that your DVD playback device does not support Dolby Digital.

4 Set Video Standard

After you have set the audio format, select the video standard for the DVD music disc from the **Video Standard** drop-down list. NTSC is used in North America; PAL is used everywhere else.

5 Set Auto-play Option

When you have set the video standard, check the **Auto-play** check box if you want the DVD to automatically play the first music track when it is inserted into the player instead of defaulting to the disc's main menu.

6 Click OK

After you have finished setting the project options, click the **OK** button to apply them.

► **TIP**

Look at the **Estimated Free Space** status bar to determine if your project will fit on your blank disc.

---

27 Preview a DVD Music Disc

✔ BEFORE YOU BEGIN	→ SEE ALSO
Chapter 1, "Start Here" (Review information on choosing the correct disc format) **22** Add Tracks to an Advanced DVD Music Disc Project	**21** Use the DVD Music Assistant to Create a DVD Music Disc **23** Use Predefined Styles for a DVD Music Disc Menu **24** Add Photos to a DVD Music Disc Menu **25** Organize Titles in a DVD Music Disc Menu **26** Change the DVD Music Disc Project Settings

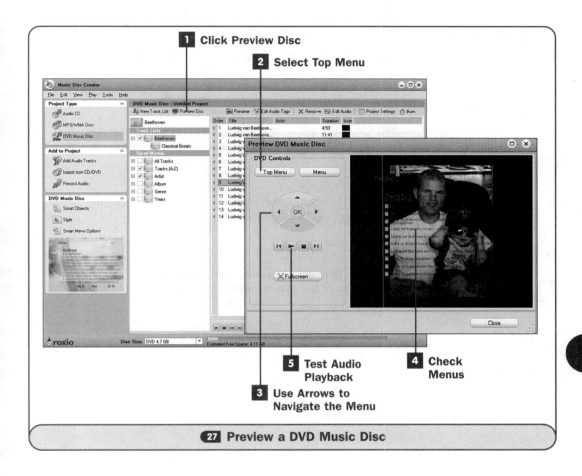

1 Click Preview Disc

2 Select Top Menu

5 Test Audio Playback

3 Use Arrows to Navigate the Menu

4 Check Menus

27 Preview a DVD Music Disc

Be sure to preview the menu of your new DVD disc before you burn it to ensure that it is what you were expecting and to catch any mistakes you might have made.

This is also a fun way to learn more about how the menu setup works and can help you decide how to set your options.

1 Click Preview Disc

Click **Preview Disc** from the taskbar to bring up the **Preview DVD Music Disc Assistant**.

2 Select Top Menu

Select **Top Menu** to begin previewing the disc at the menu that has the highest hierarchy.

3 Use Arrows to Navigate the Menu

Use the arrow keys to navigate through the menu to verify that the menu flows the way you want it to.

4 Check Menus

After you have verified the main menu, navigate through each menu and verify that the options, tracks, and information on each menu are correct.

5 Test Audio Playback

After you have verified that the menus are correct (or as you are verifying menus), select the audio tracks to verify that they play properly.

▶ **TIP**

You can click the **Fullscreen** button to make the preview fill the entire screen to more closely simulate what you will see when the DVD is playing.

27

5

Importing Photos

IN THIS CHAPTER:

Capturing photos into digital format is a great way to organize, preserve, and share them. Whether you use a film-based or digital camera, there is an easy way for you *import* your photos into Roxio Easy Media Creator 8.

▶ KEY TERM

Import—To place a file on the computer. You can import by digitizing an external source such as audio, video, or a photo, or you can import files from another digital source, such as an external hard drive or a network.

---

28 | **Import Photos from a Disc**

→ **SEE ALSO**

29 Import Photos from a Digital Camera or Removable Media

28

A CD-ROM is a great way to store photos, and because of that, it is becoming a very popular media for them. If you use a film-based camera, you have the option to get a photo CD when you have your film developed. Many professional photographers will sell you a photo CD along with your prints. You might have burned your photos to CD to back them up. For whatever reason, you have a photo CD, and here's how to import the photos into your computer.

1 Select Photo in the Project Pane

Select the **Photo** button in the **project** pane to open the **Photo** menu.

2 Select Import Photos

After you have opened the **Photo** menu, select **Import Photos** to launch **Media Import**.

3 Click Photo on the Import Menu

Make sure the **Photo** tab is selected. This brings up the **Photo Import Wizard**.

4 Insert Photo CD into CD/DVD Drive

Place the CD or DVD that you would like to take your photos from in the CD/DVD drive on your computer.

Media Manager

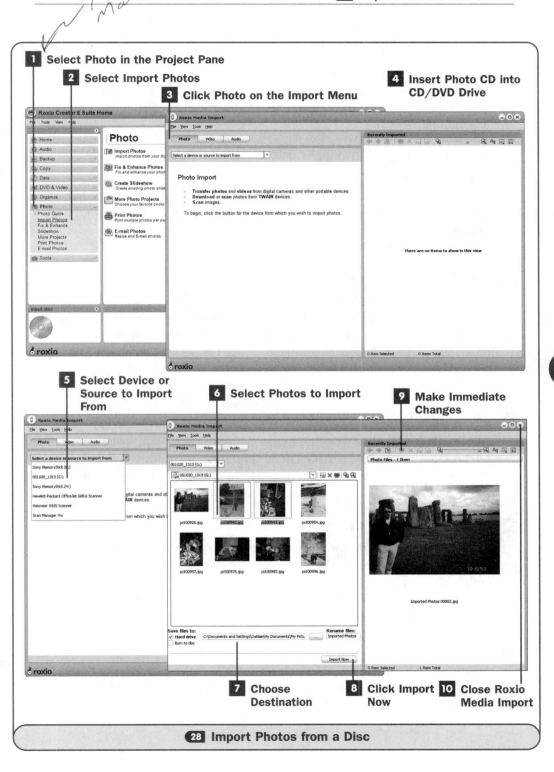

1 Select Photo in the Project Pane

2 Select Import Photos

3 Click Photo on the Import Menu

4 Insert Photo CD into CD/DVD Drive

5 Select Device or Source to Import From

6 Select Photos to Import

9 Make Immediate Changes

7 Choose Destination

8 Click Import Now

10 Close Roxio Media Import

28 Import Photos from a Disc

28

5 Select Device or Source to Import From

After you have inserted your photo CD, choose your CD/DVD drive from the **Select device or source to import from** drop-down menu. This brings up a menu of the disc in the drive. If you need to browse to the pictures you would like to import, do so.

6 Select Photos to Import

After your photo CD menu has opened, select the photos you would like to import. You can select all the files on the disc at once by clicking the **Select all** button in the taskbar at the top of the menu, or you can hold down the **Control** key as you select multiple files, or hold down the **Shift** key to select multiple contiguous files.

7 Choose Destination

When you have selected the photos you want to import, you need to specify a destination path on your computer to which to save the photos. The destination path is a location on a hard disk or any directly writable device, such as an SD card, USB drive, and so forth. Make this a folder that is conveniently accessible and easy to remember. When it comes time to add these photos to a project, you want to be able to find them again.

8 Click Import Now

After you have specified a destination, click **Import Now**. This saves your photos in the destination specified and brings them up in the **Recently Imported** window. You can continue to import photos as long as **Media Import** is open.

9 Make Immediate Changes

In the **Recently Imported** window, you have the opportunity to make a few quick, but sometimes vital, changes to your photos. By selecting the **Preview** option in the taskbar, you can quickly fix red eye, rotate your picture, or do some basic color correction. The steps here are pretty intuitive, but if you would like some help, refer to Chapter 6, "Editing Photos."

10 Close Roxio Media Import

After you are finished importing your photos and making changes to them, close **Media Import**. This takes you back to the Easy Media Creator **Home** page where you have many opportunities to have fun with the photos you have just imported.

29 Import Photos from Digital Camera or Removable Media

→ **SEE ALSO**

28 Import Photos from a Disc

Digital camera manufacturers are continually making it easier to connect your camera to your computer. This is one of the reasons that the digital camera market has exploded over the past few years. A digital camera usually comes with a USB cable or cradle that can be plugged into your USB port, which is usually found on the front of your computer.

There are many types of removable media. Any external drive or USB device falls into this category. The most common is a card or Memory Stick—SD cards, xD cards, and Sony Memory Stick media being the most frequently used. Most digital cameras and even some video cameras use these types of cards to store photos and sometimes small video files. Although you can plug a digital camera directly into your computer, most digital camcorders are usually plugged into a FireWire port and recognized by the computer solely as a video input device and the computer captures only what's on the DV tape. In order to retrieve still shots from a camcorder, you need to remove the memory card from the camera and plug it into a card reader that is either built into your machine (on newer PCs) or an external device plugged into a USB port.

Another device you might want to import pictures from is a USB flash drive. These are small, portable, thumb-sized drives that plug directly into a USB port and can hold a gigabyte or more of data. This makes them a fantastic way to store and share quite a lot of photos, as well as other files.

When anything is plugged into a USB port, your computer recognizes it as a new drive and labels it with the next available drive letter.

29

1 Select Photo in the Project Pane

Select the **Photo** button in the **project** pane to open the **Photo** menu.

2 Select Import Photos

After you have opened the **Photo** menu, select **Import Photos** to launch **Media Import**.

3 Click Photo in the Import Menu

Make sure that the **Photo** tab is selected. This brings up the **Photo Import Wizard**.

Media Manager

29   **Import Photos from a Digital Camera or Removable Media**

4 Select Device or Source to Import From

After you have opened the **Photo Import Wizard,** choose your removable device from the **Select device or source to import from** drop-down menu. This brings up the menu of your removable device. Browse to the pictures you would like to import.

5 Select Photos to Import

After you have browsed to your photo files, select the photos you would like to import. You can select all the photos in the designated folder at once by clicking the **Select all** button in the taskbar at the top of the menu, or you can hold down the **Control** key as you select multiple files.

6 Choose Destination

After you have selected the photos you want to import, you need to specify a destination path on your computer to which to save the photos. Make this a folder that is conveniently accessible and easy to remember. When it comes time to add these photos to a project, you want to be able to find them again.

7 Click Import Now

After you have specified a destination, click **Import Now.** This saves your photos in the destination specified and brings them up in the **Recently Imported** window. You can continue to import photos as long as **Media Import** is open.

29

8 Make Immediate Changes

In the **Recently Imported** window, you have the opportunity to make a few quick, but sometimes vital, changes to your photos. By selecting the **Preview** option in the taskbar, you can quickly fix red eye, rotate your picture, or do some basic color correction. The steps here are pretty intuitive, but if you would like some help, refer to Chapter 6, "Editing Photos."

9 Close Roxio Media Import

After you are finished importing your photos and making changes to them, close **Media Import.** This takes you back to the Easy Media Creator **Home** page where you have many opportunities to have fun with the photos you have just imported.

30 | **Import Photos from a Scanner**

→ **SEE ALSO**

28 Import Photos from a Disc
29 Import Photos from a Digital Camera or Removable Media

A scanner is a device much like a copy machine that allows you to digitize a hard copy of an image or photo. Some scanners are also capable of scanning in slides and negatives as well.

Most scanners plug into a USB port, just like any removable media. After you have installed the driver and software, your scanner is ready to use.

You can use Easy Media Creator to quickly scan your photos.

▶ **TIP**

Clean your scanner before scanning in photos. This ensures that the quality of your photo is not compromised by fingerprints or dust that has accumulated on your scanner. You can buy anti-static cleaner at any office supply store, or just wipe it off well with a microfiber cloth.

30

1 Select Photo in the Project Pane

Select the **Photo** button in the **project** pane to open the **Photo** menu.

2 Select Import Photos

After you have opened the **Photo** menu, select **Import Photos** to launch **Media Import**.

3 Click Photo in the Import Menu

Make sure that the **Photo** tab is selected. This brings up the **Photo Import Wizard**.

4 Select Device or Source to Import From

After you have opened the **Photo Import Wizard**, choose your scanner from the **Select device or source to import from** drop-down menu. This brings up the **Scanning Wizard**.

5 Place Photo on Scanner

After the **Scanning Wizard** has opened, place a photo on the scanner bed.

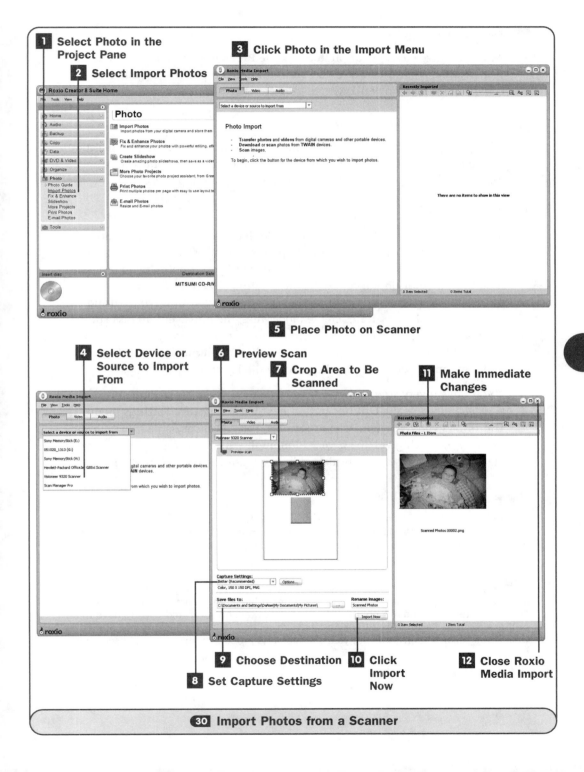

1 Select Photo in the Project Pane

2 Select Import Photos

3 Click Photo in the Import Menu

4 Select Device or Source to Import From

5 Place Photo on Scanner

6 Preview Scan

7 Crop Area to Be Scanned

8 Set Capture Settings

9 Choose Destination

10 Click Import Now

11 Make Immediate Changes

12 Close Roxio Media Import

30 Import Photos from a Scanner

6 Preview Scan

After you have placed your photo, click the **Preview scan** button. You hear your scanner running for a few seconds, and then a preview of your image comes up in the scan window.

7 Crop Area to Be Scanned

After your photo is showing in the preview window, you can use the selection box to crop to the area you would like to scan. Not only is your picture imported pre-cropped, but this saves time in the scanning process.

8 Set Capture Settings

After you have selected the area you would like to scan, set your capture settings from the **Capture Settings** drop-down menu. You set your capture settings based on what you would like to do with your photo. If you are planning to print your photo, choose the best setting (300 dpi). The smaller your picture (or selection inside your picture), the higher you want your setting to be. Although higher settings create bigger files, the massive hard disk space on modern computers can easily accommodate many large picture files. If you need to put a large number of picture files in a limited source of memory and don't mind sacrificing quality, choose the lower quality settings.

If you have a very small picture or would like to make a very large print of your picture, click the **Options** button next to the **Capture Settings** menu. This allows you to customize your settings. You can increase your picture size to 600 *dpi*, which gives you a very high-quality file. You can also choose your file extension and set options determined by that choice.

▶ KEY TERM

DPI (dots per inch)—A term used to quantify the digital dots per actual inch of an image. For instance, 300 dpi means that a printed image has 300×300 (90,000) dots per square inch. The higher the dpi is, the higher the quality of the printed image is.

▶ NOTE

Most scanners can scan up to 1200 or 2400 dpi in black and white, grayscale, or color. The scan interface in Easy Media Creator is very limited, however and doesn't have many of these options. Several file extensions that are related to image files are not offered as well. If you received software with your scanner, it is probably a more capable scan interface.

9 Choose Destination

After you have set the capture settings, you need to specify a destination path on your computer to which to save the scans. The destination path is a location on a hard disk or any directly writable device, such as an SD card, USB drive, and so on. Make this a folder that is conveniently accessible and easy to remember. When it comes time to add these photos to a project, you want to be able to find them again.

10 Click Import Now

After you have specified a destination, click **Import Now**. This saves your photos in the destination specified and brings them up in the **Recently Imported** window. You can continue to scan photos as long as **Media Import** is open.

11 Make Immediate Changes

In the **Recently Imported** window, you have the opportunity to make a few quick, but sometimes vital, changes to your photos. By selecting the **Preview** option in the taskbar, you can quickly fix red eye, rotate your picture, or do some basic color correction. The steps here are pretty intuitive, but if you would like some help, refer to Chapter 6, "Editing Photos."

12 Close Roxio Media Import

After you are finished importing your photos and making changes to them, close **Media Import**. This takes you back to the Easy Media Creator **Home** page where you have many opportunities to have fun with the photos you have just imported.

---

31 Capture Still Shots from a Video

→ SEE ALSO

72 About the VideoWave Interface

76 Extract a Still Shot from a Video Clip

Taking a still shot from a video file is a completely different process from capturing photos from other sources. Because you are working with video, you need to use **VideoWave**, Easy Media Creator's video-editing application.

Capturing still shots from a video is not to be confused with extracting the still shots you have taken with a camcorder using a memory card. In this task you are capturing one frame from a video file and saving it as a photo.

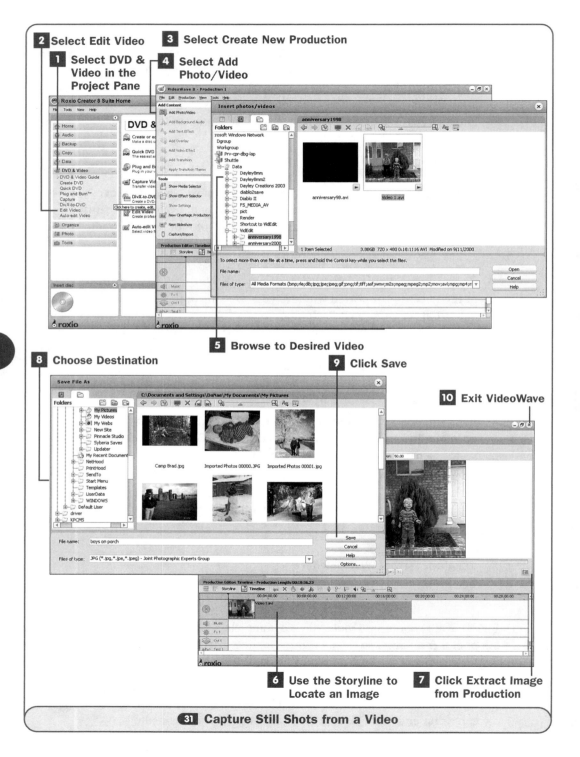

2 Select Edit Video   **3** Select Create New Production

1 Select DVD & Video in the Project Pane   **4** Select Add Photo/Video

5 Browse to Desired Video

8 Choose Destination   **9** Click Save

10 Exit VideoWave

6 Use the Storyline to Locate an Image   **7** Click Extract Image from Production

31 Capture Still Shots from a Video

► **NOTE**

A video file is not nearly as high a quality as most photo files. The pictures you capture from a video file are not very big, and won't look very good printed out. Captured pictures are great to add to a video production or slideshow, however.

1 Select DVD & Video in the Project Pane

Select the **DVD & Video** option in the **project** pane. This brings up the **DVD & Video** menu.

2 Select Edit Video

From the **DVD & Video** menu, select **Edit Video**. This launches **VideoWave**, Easy Media Creator's video-editing application.

3 Select Create New Production

After **VideoWave** has launched, you are given the choice to create a new production or to edit an existing production. Unless you have a **VideoWave** production that you would like to take a photo from, select **Create New Production** and set your format to the original format of the video file from which you would like to capture the photo.

4 Select Add Photo/Video

After you have opened a new production, you need to add the video file from which you want to capture a photo. Select **Add Photo/Video** from the **Add Content** menu. This brings up **Media Manager**.

5 Browse to Desired Video

After you have brought up **Media Manager**, browse to the location of the video file from which you would like to import a photo. Select it and click **Open**.

6 Use the Storyline to Locate an Image

You can locate your image on the storyboard in a number of ways. You can use the **jog dial** to gradually make your way through the video, you can drag the **selection line** through the video until you come to the right spot, or you can play the video back and stop it at the right spot. You can take as many photos out of the video as you want, so your choice might depend on whether you are looking for something specific or just trying to capture photos of an experience.

31

7 **Click Extract Image from Production**

After your image is displayed in the **Preview** window, click on the **Extract Image from Production** button (the camera icon) in the lower right of the video preview window. This brings up the **Save File As** window.

8 **Choose Destination**

After you have brought up the **Save File As** window, browse to the destination path on your computer to which to save the images. The destination path is a location on a hard disk or any directly writable device, such as an SD card, USB drive, and so on. Make this a folder that is conveniently accessible and easy to remember. When it comes time to add these photos to a project, you want to be able to find them again.

9 **Click Save**

After you have chosen a destination for your image, click **Save**. This takes you back to **VideoWave** where you can capture as many still shots as you would like before exiting **VideoWave**.

31

10 **Exit VideoWave**

After you are done capturing your still shots, exit **VideoWave**. This takes you back to the Easy Media Creator **Home** page where you have many opportunities to have fun with the photos you have just imported.

6

Editing Photos

IN THIS CHAPTER:

You can fix photos in Roxio Easy Media Creator 8 at almost any time. When you are importing them, for instance, you have the chance to make a few essential changes. You can also use the pocket editor while you are placing your photos into such projects as calendars and gift cards.

But if you really want to make more than just basic changes to your pictures, you want to use **PhotoSuite**. **PhotoSuite** is Easy Media Creator's full-fledged photo-editing application. Besides the more conventional edits such as color correction, it allows you to add special effects to your photos using advanced tools such as masks.

You can also edit multiple photos at once, not only auto fixing them as a batch, but also renaming them and converting them to different file formats—a particularly useful tool in archiving photos to a convenient location on your computer.

These tasks assume that you have already imported your photo files onto your computer and are ready to edit. If you need to import your photos, see Chapter 5, "Importing Photos."

▶ **NOTE**

32

Many of the tasks within **PhotoSuite** take effect when you close the window for the task. That means you very rarely see an **OK**, **Close**, or **Apply** button in the task windows.

32 Open Photos in PhotoSuite	
✔ **BEFORE YOU BEGIN**	→ **SEE ALSO**
Chapter 5, "Importing Photos"	**122** View a Collection of Photos as a QuickShow (on the Web)

The first vital step in editing your photos is being able to open **PhotoSuite** and import photos to edit. **PhotoSuite** has a handy **Open Files** window at the bottom of the screen that showcases thumbnails of all the photos you have imported into **PhotoSuite**. The **Open Files** window makes it convenient to choose the photo you would like to edit, but keeps them out of the way when you are not editing them.

This makes it very convenient to edit your pictures as you get them back from the developer or as you are importing them from your camera. If you sit down for a few minutes each time in **PhotoSuite**, your pictures are all edited as you archive them into your computer.

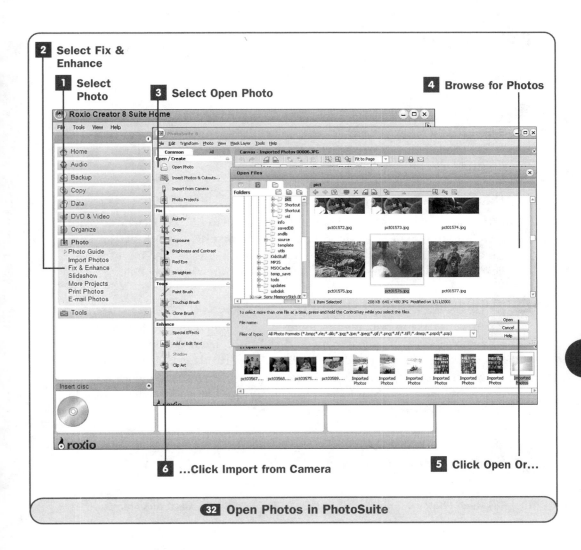

2 **Select Fix & Enhance**

1 **Select Photo**

3 **Select Open Photo**

4 **Browse for Photos**

6 **...Click Import from Camera**

5 **Click Open Or...**

32 Open Photos in PhotoSuite

1 Select Photo

From within the Easy Media Creator **project** pane, select **Photo** to open up the **Photo** menu.

2 Select Fix & Enhance

After you have opened the **Photo** menu, select **Fix & Enhance** to launch the **PhotoSuite** application.

3 Select Open Photo

After **PhotoSuite** has launched, click on the **Open Photo** button in the **tasks** pane to open **Media Manager**.

4 Browse for Photos

When **Media Manager** has opened, browse for the photo or photos you would like to edit. You can select more than one by holding down the **Control** key while you select them.

5 Click Open Or...

After you have selected the photos you would like to edit, click **Open** to place them into the **Open Files** window inside of **PhotoSuite**. From this **Open Files** window, you can choose any photo and bring it up inside the **Canvas** window. Here you can make all the desired changes and save the photo.

6 ...Click Import from Camera

If you would like to import your photos directly from a digital camera, other removable device, or even a scanner, click **Import from Camera** in the **Open/Create** menu to bring up the **Photo Import Wizard**. Refer to Chapter 5, "Importing Photos," for detailed instructions on how to use the **Photo Import Wizard**. After you have completed the import, your photos appear in the **Open Files** window inside of **PhotoSuite**.

33

33	Re-orient, Resize, or Crop a Photo	
✔ **BEFORE YOU BEGIN**	→ **SEE ALSO**	
32 Open Photos in PhotoSuite	**39** Add Edges, Mats, and Frames to a Photo	
	44 Create Cutouts and Masks	
	45 Edit Multiple Photos at Once	

Re-orienting your photos is the most common edit you want to make to them. Many photos are taken in portrait mode, with the camera turned so the photo is taller than it is wide. If you are using a digital camera, those photos are imported lying on their side. You want to turn them upright and then save them again.

The dimension of a photo is the size at which it will be printed. Most digital cameras take photos of high enough quality that they can be printed at a very large size. Notice that the photo in the figures is more than 31×23 inches. If you are planning to print your photo, you can resize it to your desired print dimensions.

2 Quick Rotate 90° or 180° Or...

5 Resize Your Photo

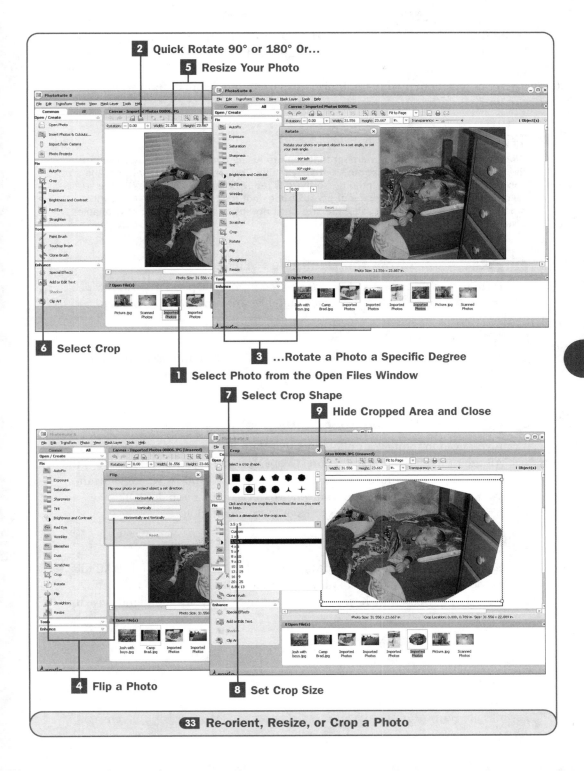

6 Select Crop

3 ...Rotate a Photo a Specific Degree

1 Select Photo from the Open Files Window

7 Select Crop Shape

9 Hide Cropped Area and Close

4 Flip a Photo

8 Set Crop Size

When taking pictures, most people err on the side of getting too much in the pic-ture rather than cutting out something important. This is easy to fix by cropping out the unwanted sections of your photo. Easy Media Creator not only uses a con-ventional rectangular crop, but it also has several other shapes from which to choose.

▶ **TIP**

When resizing your photo, remember that you are losing quality if you reduce the size of the picture. If you print your photo from Easy Media Creator, you can actually set the size you want your photo to be printed at, so there is really no need to resize it. By the same token, if you expand the size of your photo, it does not look as good as it did at the smaller setting because increasing the size does not increase the number of available pixels.

1 **Select Photo from the Open Files Window**

From within **PhotoSuite**, choose the photo from the **Open Files** window at the bottom of the screen that you would like to re-orient, resize, or crop.

2 **Quick Rotate 90° or 180° Or...**

To quickly rotate your photo, click on either the 90° counterclockwise or the 90° clockwise **rotation** button in the taskbar. If your photo needs rotated 180°, click the button again.

3 **...Rotate a Photo a Specific Degree**

If you need to rotate your photo by other than 90° increments, click on the **All** tab at the top of the **tasks** pane to open all your editing options. From the **Fix** menu, select **Rotate**. This brings up the **Rotate** window, where you can set a specific degree to rotate your photo. Click **Reset** if you don't like the results, and your photo returns to its original orientation.

4 **Flip a Photo**

You can flip your photo horizontally, vertically, or both. Click on the **All** tab in the **tasks** pane to open up all your editing options. From the **Fix** menu, select **Flip**. Choose which way you would like to flip your photo and close the window.

5 Resize Your Photo

You can resize your photo by changing the **Height** or **Width** dimension in the taskbar. The proportions of the photo are automatically constrained. That means that if you set the height, the width automatically follows suit to keep the picture proportioned correctly.

▶ **NOTE**

You can choose to delineate the size of your photo by inches, pixels, or centimeters, whichever makes the most sense to you. Use the drop-down menu in the taskbar next to the **Height** and **Width** settings to change this setting.

6 Select Crop

If you would like to crop your photo, click on the **Crop** button in the **Fix** menu to bring up the **Crop** window.

7 Select Crop Shape

After the **Crop** window has come up, you are able to choose from a variety of shapes to crop your picture. Select the one you would prefer by clicking on it.

▶ **NOTE**

When you crop a photo in a shape other than a rectangle, the canvas behind the photo stays rectangular. You can change the color of the canvas to add interest to your photo by choosing the **Edit Canvas** option from the **Tools** drop-down menu in the **File** menu.

8 Set Crop Size

After you have chosen your preferred shape, you can set the crop size. The **Custom** option allows you to drag the selection box in the canvas window to highlight the area to be cropped manually. You can also choose several pre-set sizes from the drop-down menu. You can change an oblong shape to be either portrait (vertical) or landscape (horizontal). If you drag the handles in the corner of the selection box, PhotoSuite maintains the proportions of your photo.

9 Hide Cropped Area and Close

After you have selected the area and size to be cropped, you can preview the final crop by clicking on the **Hide cropped area** box. After you are satisfied with your changes, click the close icon at the top of the **Crop** window. To return the photo to its pre-crop size and shape, click **Reset**.

► **TIP**

You can use the **Straighten** tool to straighten a picture that was scanned crookedly rather than trying to rotate it by small degrees, a guessing game at best. Choose the **Straighten** option from the **Fix** menu and follow the step-by-step instructions to straighten your photo.

---

34   Color Correct a Photo

✔ **BEFORE YOU BEGIN**	→ **SEE ALSO**
32 Open Photos in PhotoSuite	**44** Create Cutouts and Masks
	45 Edit Multiple Photos at Once

---

1 Select Photo from the Open Files Window

From within **PhotoSuite**, choose the photo from the **Open Files** window at the bottom of the screen that you would like to color correct.

2 Change Exposure Settings

Change the *exposure* settings of a photo to adjust the ambient light of the photo. Click on the **Exposure** button in the **Fix** menu to bring up the **Exposure** window. From within the window you can choose to **AutoFix** the exposure (try this out, just to see what it does), or manually fix your photo by using the sliders.

► **KEY TERM**

Exposure—The amount of light a photo is exposed to as it is being taken, usually determined by the aperture of the lens.

As you use the sliders to change the levels of light in your photo, you are able to preview the changes in your photo by checking the **Show Preview** box. Each photo is different, so the settings are a trial-and-error process. Play with them until you feel that you have the best setting for your photo. You can reset the exposure of your photo to the original by clicking on the **Reset** button. When you are satisfied, close the window.

► **TIP**

As you adjust color setting such as exposure, brightness, and contrast, watch the whites in your picture. When they start looking washed out, you've gone too far.

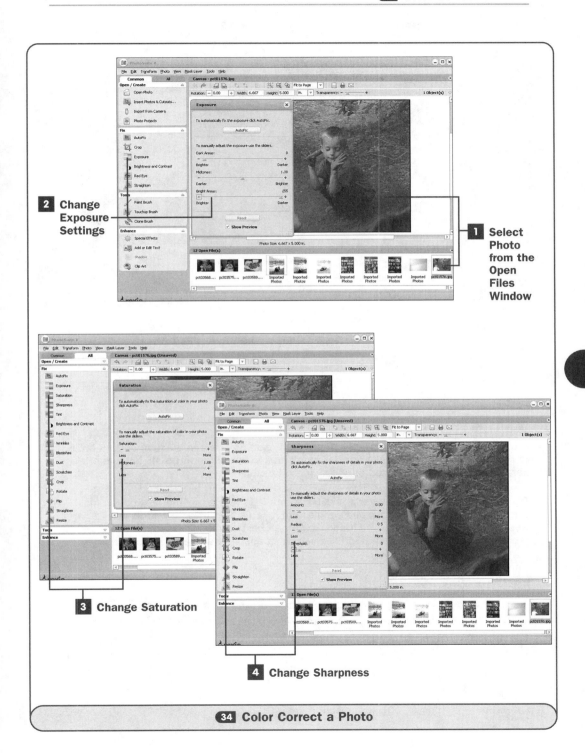

2 Change Exposure Settings

1 Select Photo from the Open Files Window

3 Change Saturation

4 Change Sharpness

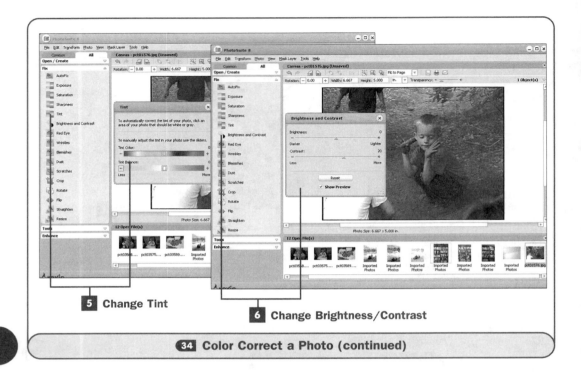

5 Change Tint

6 Change Brightness/Contrast

34 Color Correct a Photo (continued)

▶ **NOTES**

Extremely light or dark photos often do not have enough pixels in the light or dark areas to correct sufficiently. You can correct a small area with the **Clone Brush**, but it is often hard to rescue an overexposed or underexposed picture.

The **AutoFix** option, no matter where you run into it, is very rarely the best option for correcting your photo. It is fast and simple, and it can sometimes be a good way of previewing the changes that *can* be made. To get the best correction for your photo, however, you want to use the hands-on fixes so you can preview and accept each change.

3 Change Saturation

The *saturation* of a photo is simply the amount of color it contains. Think of it as adding food coloring to frosting—the more food coloring you add, the darker, or more saturated, the frosting becomes. When you turn up the saturation of a photo, you make the colors darker and more intense.

▶ **KEY TERM**

Saturation—The density of color present in an image.

Click on the **All** tab at the top of the **tasks** pane to bring up all of your editing options. Select the **Saturation** button from the **Fix** menu to bring up the **Saturation** window. You can **AutoFix** the photo or use the sliders to adjust the saturation of the entire photo or just the midtones. As you decrease the saturation, your picture loses color, looking more like a black-and-white photograph. Play around with these settings until you are satisfied with the result and close the window.

4 Change Sharpness

You can make your photo crisper or more blurred by changing the sharpness setting. Click on the **All** tab at the top of the **tasks** pane to bring up all of your editing options. From the **Fix** menu, select the **Sharpness** button to bring up the **Sharpness** window.

You can **AutoFix** the sharpness by clicking on the **AutoFix** button.

To sharpen your photo, Easy Media Creator detects the pixels within your photo that are different from the surrounding pixels and delineates them as edge *pixels*. These pixels are sharpened, making the edges of objects in the photo clearer.

► **KEY TERM**

Pixel—One single dot within a photo or image. The higher the density of the pixels, the less digitized, or blocky, the photo looks.

As you adjust the **Amount** slider, you are specifying the amount of contrast between the pixels that are being sharpened and those that aren't.

The **Radius** slider determines how many pixels radiating from the edge pixels are also sharpened.

The **Threshold** slider allows you specify how different pixels must be from those around them to be considered edge pixels. The lower the threshold, the more edges you have in your photo.

Each photo is different, so play with the settings until you are happy with the result. Click **Reset** at any time to restore your photo to its presharpened state. After you have made your changes, close the window.

5 Change Tint

The *tint* of your photo is the color cast of your photo. Sometimes when a picture is taken in less-than-ideal lighting (fluorescent, for example), you get an unsightly color cast to your photo. You can correct this by changing the tint of your photo.

34

▶ KEY TERM

Tint—The level of a specific color tone in an image. For instance, a photo taken under fluorescent lighting usually has a yellow tint.

Click on the **All** tab at the top of the **tasks** pane and select the **Tint** button from the **Fix** menu. This brings up the **Tint** window. You can automatically correct the tint of your photo by clicking on a place in your photo that should be white or grey.

To use the sliders to adjust the tint, first use the **Tint Color** slider to adjust the tint color. For example, if you have a picture that has a yellow cast to it after being taken under fluorescent lights, choose the color yellow from the spectrum.

Next, adjust the **Tint Balance** slider to enhance or reduce the color selected in the top slider. To reduce the yellow in your picture, move the slider to the left.

When you are satisfied with your result, close the **Tint** window.

34

6 Change Brightness/Contrast

You can adjust the brightness and contrast of your photo by clicking on the **Brightness and Contrast** button in the **Fix** menu. This brings up the **Brightness and Contrast** window.

Unlike exposure corrections that change the light, midtone, or dark pixels in a photo, changing the brightness of a photo changes the pixels unilaterally. This works well on a universally light or dark picture. Use the **Brightness** slider to make your photo brighter or darker.

As you adjust the **Contrast** slider toward more contrast, the dark tones of your photo become darker and the light tones of your photo become lighter. Most pictures look a little better with a little contrast added. Make sure you don't wash out those whites!

When you are satisfied with your changes, close the **Brightness and Contrast** window.

35 Fix Facial Flaws—Including Red Eye

✔ BEFORE YOU BEGIN	→ SEE ALSO
32 Open Photos in PhotoSuite	**34** Color Correct a Photo
	36 Clean and Fix a Damaged Photo
	37 Use the Clone Brush
	45 Edit Multiple Photos at Once

Ah, the magic touch-ups! We all wish that reducing wrinkles and getting rid of blemishes was as easy as most advertisers would like us to believe. In Easy Media Creator, it really is! The downside is that, unfortunately, you can only touch up your photo.

1 Select Photo from the Open Files Window

From within **PhotoSuite**, choose the photo from the **Open Files** window at the bottom of the screen on which to fix facial flaws.

2 Select Red Eye

After your photo is brought up in the *Canvas* window, select the **Red Eye** icon from the **Fix** menu in the **tasks** pane. This brings up the **Red Eye** window.

▶ KEY TERM

Canvas—The total working area that an image file is capable of using.

3 Click AutoFix Button Or...

After the **Red Eye** window has been brought up, click the **AutoFix** button to quickly fix the red eye.

4 ...Zoom in to Eyes

If the **AutoFix** does not work as well as you would like it to, or if you would like to fix the red eye manually, use the **Zoom** icon in the taskbar to zoom in to the eyes you are trying to fix.

5 Set Brush Size

After you have zoomed close enough to the eyes to have a good view of them, use the slider in the **Red Eye** window to set the brush size just larger than the eye.

35

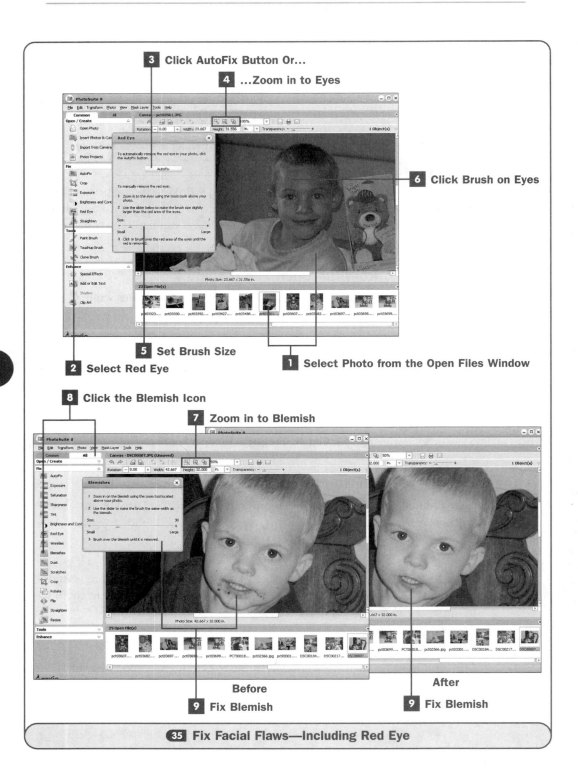

3 Click AutoFix Button Or...

4 ...Zoom in to Eyes

6 Click Brush on Eyes

5 Set Brush Size

2 Select Red Eye

1 Select Photo from the Open Files Window

8 Click the Blemish Icon

7 Zoom in to Blemish

Before

9 Fix Blemish

After

9 Fix Blemish

35 Fix Facial Flaws—Including Red Eye

35

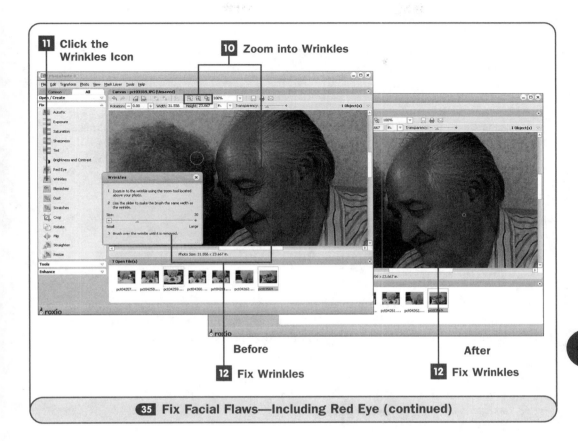

11 Click the Wrinkles Icon

10 Zoom into Wrinkles

Before

12 Fix Wrinkles

After

12 Fix Wrinkles

35

35 Fix Facial Flaws—Including Red Eye (continued)

6 Click Brush on Eyes

When you have the brush size set, cover the red eye with it and click until the red is gone. When you are done, close the **Red Eye** window.

7 Zoom in to Blemish

To fix those embarrassing blemishes and spots, zoom to the flaw by using the **Zoom** icons in the taskbar.

8 Click the Blemish Icon

When you have zoomed into the appropriate spot on the face, click on the **All** tab in the **tasks** pane to open all your editing options. From the **Fix** menu, choose the **Blemish** icon to open the **Blemish** window.

9   Fix Blemish

From the **Blemish** window, set the appropriate brush size and brush over the blemish until it disappears.

▶ **TIP**

Using the **Clone Brush** is sometimes easier than using the **Blemish** tool and it's almost always more effective. Learn how to use the **Clone Brush** in task **37** **Use the Clone Brush**.

10   Zoom into Wrinkles

You can also smooth away wrinkles using Easy Media Creator. Choose the photo you would like to edit and zoom into the wrinkles you would like to fix.

11   Click the Wrinkles Icon

When you have zoomed into the appropriate spot on the face, click on the **All** tab in the **tasks** pane to open all your editing options. From the **Fix** menu, choose the **Wrinkles** icon to open the **Wrinkles** window.

12   Fix Wrinkles

From the **Wrinkles** window, set the appropriate brush size and brush over the wrinkles until they disappear.

---

36   Clean and Fix a Damaged Photo

✔ BEFORE YOU BEGIN	→ SEE ALSO
32 Open Photos in PhotoSuite	**34** Color Correct a Photo
	35 Fix Facial Flaws—Including Red Eye
	37 Use the Clone Brush
	44 Create Cutouts and Masks
	45 Edit Multiple Photos at Once

It's sad to see an older or abused photo that is scratched or dusty. Although editing these photos won't make them look as good as new, removing the dust or taking out scratches can go a long way towards making them look much better.

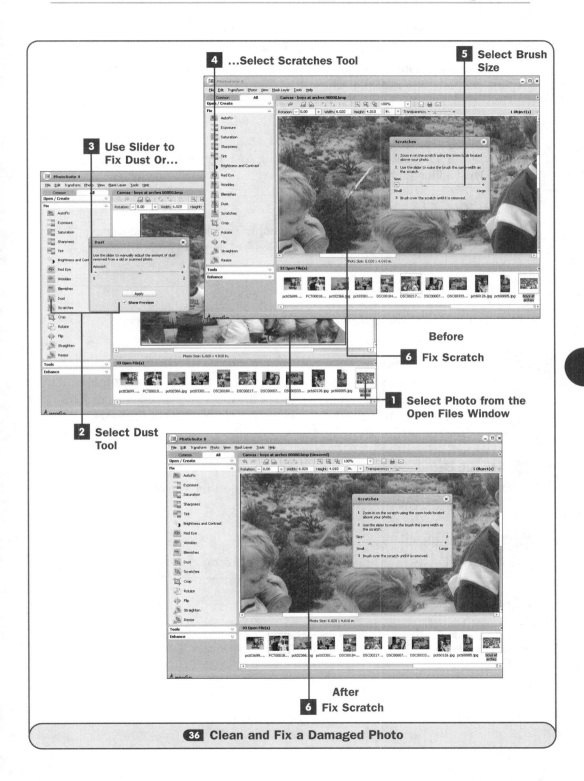

4 ...Select Scratches Tool

5 Select Brush Size

3 Use Slider to Fix Dust Or...

Before

6 Fix Scratch

1 Select Photo from the Open Files Window

2 Select Dust Tool

36

After

6 Fix Scratch

1 Select Photo from Open Files Window

From within **PhotoSuite**, choose the photo from the **Open Files** window at the bottom of the screen on which to remove dust or scratches.

2 Select Dust Tool

To remove dust from a photo, click on the **All** tab in the **tasks** pane to open all of your edit options. Select the **Dust** icon from the **Fix** menu to bring up the **Dust** window.

3 Use Slider to Fix Dust Or...

From the **Dust** window, use the slider to adjust the amount of dust that is removed from the photo. When you are done, click **Apply** and close the window.

▶ NOTE

The more dust you remove from your picture, the blurrier the picture will be.

36

4 ...Select Scratches Tool

To fix a scratch on a photo, zoom into the damaged area using the **Zoom** icons in the taskbar. Click on the **All** tab in the **tasks** pane to open all of your edit options. Select the **Scratches** icon from the **Fix** menu to bring up the **Scratches** window.

5 Select Brush Size

From the **Scratches** window, use the slider to adjust the size of the brush to match the scratch.

6 Fix Scratch

After you have set the brush size, brush over the scratch until it disappears. When you are finished fixing the scratch, close the window.

▶ TIP

Using the **Clone Brush** is sometimes easier than using the **Scratch** tool and it's almost always more effective. Learn how to use the **Clone Brush** in task **37** Use the Clone Brush.

37 Use the Clone Brush

✔ BEFORE YOU BEGIN	→ SEE ALSO
32 Open Photos in PhotoSuite	**35** Fix Facial Flaws—Including Red Eye
	36 Clean and Fix a Damaged Photo
	45 Edit Multiple Photos at Once

The **Clone Brush** is a lot of fun. You can use it to fix small blemishes or scratches or to remove unwanted objects from a photo. Sometimes an unwanted object is a person—remember that horrible prom date? No problem.

The **Clone Brush** works by copying an area in the photo and pasting it in the area that you want to fix. The first time you click on your photo, you are setting the start point, or the area from which to copy. The next click copies the start point onto the area that you select. For example, in this photo I clicked on the lake and then began clicking over the head of the third boy to copy the lake into that space. As you continue to click, the clone tool follows so the area you are cloning over looks natural.

It takes a bit of practice, but the **Clone Brush** tool can accomplish some amazing things.

1 Select Photo from Open Files Window

From within **PhotoSuite**, choose the photo from the **Open Files** window at the bottom of the screen on which to remove dust or scratches.

2 Select Clone Brush

From the **Tools** menu in the **tasks** pane, select the **Clone Brush** to bring up the **Clone Brush** window.

3 Select Brush Size

Your brush size is determined by the area of the photo you would like to clone over. The larger the area, the larger the brush can be.

4 Select Transparency

The **Transparency** slider determines how opaque the **Clone Brush** is. If you want full coverage, choose a less transparent setting; if you want your edit to look more like a blending in, choose a more transparent setting.

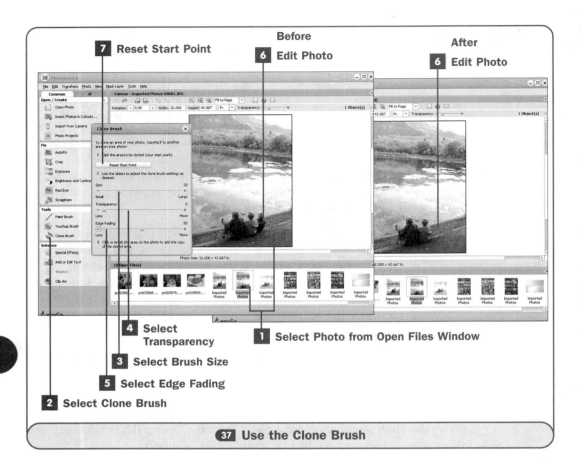

7 Reset Start Point

Before
6 Edit Photo

After
6 Edit Photo

4 Select Transparency

3 Select Brush Size

5 Select Edge Fading

2 Select Clone Brush

1 Select Photo from Open Files Window

37 Use the Clone Brush

5 Select Edge Fading

The **Edge Fading** slider determines how soft the edges of the **Clone Brush** are. The softer the brush, the more the new area blends, but if you make it too soft, you might not get the coverage that you want.

6 Edit Photo

Here's the fun part. If you need to zoom up on the area to be cloned, do that. Now click on the area of your photo to set the start point. Then start clicking over the area to cover. The blemish, scratch, or bad prom date disappears as if by magic.

7 Reset Start Point

The more complicated the photo, the more you will want to reset the start point. For instance, in this photo, I set a start point for the lake, for the log, and for the ground cover. I actually set it more often than that just to get a better clone. The more you practice, the better you'll get.

When you are done with the **Clone Brush**, close the window.

---

38 | **Create a Shadow for a Photo**

✔ BEFORE YOU BEGIN	→ SEE ALSO
32 Open Photos in PhotoSuite	**33** Re-orient, Resize, or Crop a Photo
	39 Add Edges, Mats, and Frames to a Photo
	40 Add Special Effects to a Photo
	41 Add Text to a Photo
	42 Add Clip Art to a Photo
	43 Paint and Draw on a Photo
	44 Create Cutouts and Masks

38

You can add many fun things within Easy Media Creator to your photos to give them a creative, finished look. Creating a shadow for your photo can make it pop and look three dimensional.

You can also add a shadow to any object inside of your canvas. If you have added clip art, for example, you can add a shadow to the clip art to make it seem to jump out of the picture. Have fun!

1 Select Photo from Open Files Window

From within **PhotoSuite**, choose the photo from the **Open Files** window at the bottom of the screen to which you would like to add a shadow. If you want to add a shadow to another object in the canvas, select that object.

2 Select Edit Canvas

After your photo is brought up in the canvas window; select **Edit Canvas** from the **Tools** drop-down menu.

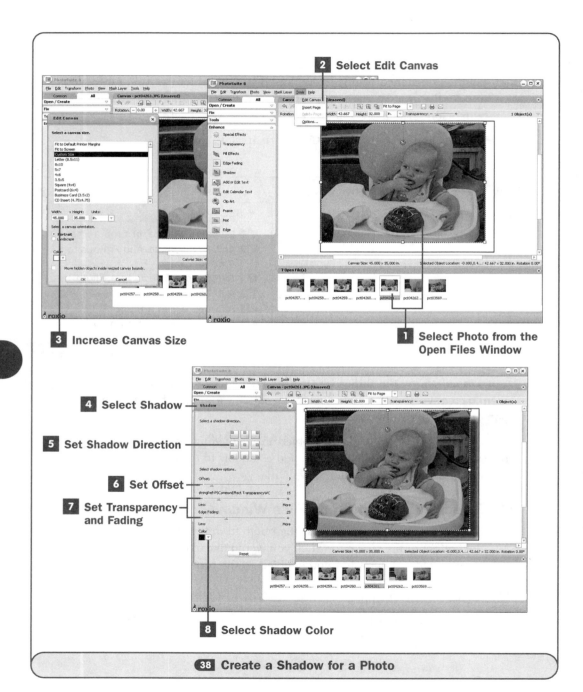

2 Select Edit Canvas

3 Increase Canvas Size

1 Select Photo from the Open Files Window

4 Select Shadow

5 Set Shadow Direction

6 Set Offset

7 Set Transparency and Fading

8 Select Shadow Color

38 Create a Shadow for a Photo

3 Increase Canvas Size

In order to create a shadow for the photo, the canvas must be larger than the photo. Select **Custom Size** and set the canvas slightly larger than the picture. Change the color of the background if you like. When you are done, select **OK**.

4 Select Shadow

When the canvas size is bigger than your photo, select the **Shadow** icon from the **Enhance** menu on the **tasks** pane. This brings up the **Shadow** window.

5 Set Shadow Direction

From the **Shadow** window, you can choose the orientation of the shadow by choosing the appropriate box. If there are shadows within the photo, having the shadows fall in the same direction makes the most sense.

6 Set Offset

When you have set the direction of the shadow, move the **Offset** slider to adjust the length of the shadow. The greater the offset rating, the larger the shadow is.

38

7 Set Transparency and Fading

After you have adjusted the offset, set the **Transparency** and **Edge Fading** sliders. The higher the ratings are on these two options, the softer the edge of the picture is. If you want a crisp look, set these options low.

8 Select Shadow Color

You can change the color of your shadow by clicking on the arrow next to the **Color setting**. Choose from the short list, expand to the full-color spectrum, or use the dropper tool to choose a color from the photo.

▶ **TIP**

The dropper in the **Color** menu can choose any color showing on your monitor. If you would like to choose a color from the taskbar or another photo in your **Open Files** window, just point the dropper and click.

39 Add Edges, Mats, and Frames to a Photo

✔ BEFORE YOU BEGIN	→ SEE ALSO
32 Open Photos in PhotoSuite	**38** Create a Shadow for a Photo
	40 Add Special Effects to a Photo
	41 Add Text to a Photo
	42 Add Clip Art to a Photo
	43 Paint and Draw on a Photo
	44 Create Cutouts and Masks
	45 Edit Multiple Photos at Once

You can add a unique edge, mat, or frame to your photo to jazz it up. This adds a scrapbook look to your photos and makes them even more personal. As you add edges, mats, and frames to your picture, you can add them individually or layer them for a unique look.

▶ TIP

39

Be sure to install the Content disc that came with Roxio Easy Media Creator to get all of the templates for the following tasks and projects. If you have not installed the content CD, your choices are meager.

1 Select Photo from the Open Files Window

From within **PhotoSuite**, choose the photo from the **Open Files** window at the bottom of the screen to which you would like to add an edge, mat, or frame.

2 Select the All Tab

Select the **All** tab at the top of the **tasks** pane to open all of your editing options.

3 Select Edge

Select the **Edge** button from the **Enhance** menu to bring up the **Edge** window.

4 Choose an Edge Style

From the **Edge** window you can click on an album to open up the type of style you want, or you can choose from the drop-down menu. When the style samples are shown in the window, double-click on the one you want to apply to the photo.

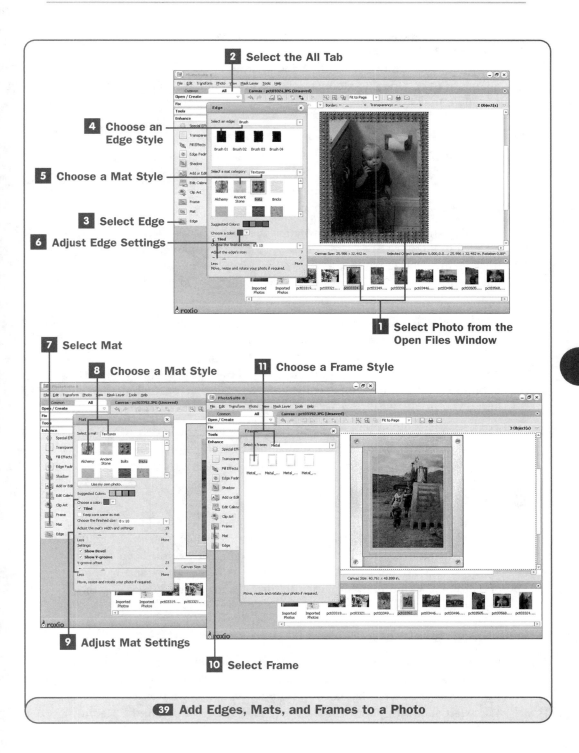

2 Select the All Tab

4 Choose an Edge Style

5 Choose a Mat Style

3 Select Edge

6 Adjust Edge Settings

1 Select Photo from the Open Files Window

7 Select Mat

8 Choose a Mat Style

11 Choose a Frame Style

9 Adjust Mat Settings

10 Select Frame

39

39 Add Edges, Mats, and Frames to a Photo

5 Choose a Mat Style

You can choose a mat style in the **Edge** window. This gives the edge a specific texture or color. Open an album or choose from the drop-down menu and click on a mat style.

6 Adjust Edge Settings

You can choose the color of the edge by clicking on a suggested color or by using the **Choose a color** menu. Use the dropper tool to sample a color on the screen to create a color. If you have chosen a textured mat, the color combines with the style to create a unique look.

The **Tiled** check box determines whether the texture is tiled together tightly to create a uniform look or used on a large scale. For example, if you choose the brick texture, checking the **Tiled** check box gives the mat hundreds of bricks, but unchecking the **Tiled** check box means only a few large bricks are in the edge.

Change the finished size of the edge by choosing from the **Choose the finished size** drop-down menu. The finished size setting does not actually change the size of the edge, but it does adjust the proportion. In other words, if your picture is larger than 8×10, changing the size of the edge to 8×10 does not make it smaller than the picture; it only sets it to an 8×10 proportion so that if you print your picture as an 8×10, it fits into an 8×10 frame.

Change the size of the edge itself by using the **Adjust the edge's size** slider at the bottom of the window. This adjusts the proportion of the edge to your photo. After you are satisfied with the look of your edge, close the window.

7 Select Mat

You can add mats to your photo to give it a three-dimensional look. Whereas the mat style in the **Edge** window only allowed you choose a color or texture for the edge, the Mat enhancement creates a differently colored core to add the three-dimensional look and allows you to adjust the bevel and V-groove of the core. Click on the **Mat** button in the **Enhance** menu to bring up the **Mat** window.

8 Choose a Mat Style

When the **Mat** window is open, you can choose a color or a texture for your mat by opening the appropriate album or using the **Select a mat** drop-down menu. Double-click on the mat you want to apply it to your picture. You can also select your own photo to use as your mat by choosing it in the **Media Manager**.

9 Adjust Mat Settings

You can choose the color of the mat by clicking on a suggested color or by using the **Choose a color** menu. Use the dropper tool to sample a color on the screen. If you have chosen a textured mat, the color combines with the style to create a unique look.

The **Tiled** check box determines whether the texture is tiled together tightly to create a uniform look or used on a large scale. For example, if you choose the brick texture, the mat has hundreds of bricks if it is tiled, but if you uncheck the **Tiled** check box, only a few large bricks are in the mat.

Change the finished size of the mat by choosing from the **Choose the finished size** drop-down menu. The finished size setting does not actually change the size of the edge, but it does adjust the proportion. In other words, if your picture is larger than 8×10, changing the size of the mat to 8×10 does not make it smaller than the picture; it only sets it to an 8×10 proportion so that if you print your picture as an 8×10, it fits into an 8×10 frame.

Change the size of the mat itself by using the appropriate slider. This adjusts the proportion of the mat to your photo.

Check the **Show Bevel** and **Show V-groove** check boxes if you would like a bevel and V-groove and set the offset setting for the V-groove using the **V-groove offset** slider. After you are satisfied with the look of your edge, close the window.

10 Select Frame

Click on the **Frame** button in the **Enhance** menu to bring up the **Frame** window.

11 Choose a Frame Style

Choose the style of frame you want by clicking on an album or use the **Select a frame** drop-down menu. The frames in the style are all the same except for their size. When you choose the frame size, it does not actually change the size of the frame, but it does adjust the proportion. In other words, if your picture is larger than 8×10, changing the size of the frame to 8×10 does not make it smaller than the picture; it only sets it to an 8×10 proportion.

When you are happy with the look of your picture, close the window.

► **TIP**

Remember that you can use the selection box around each of your objects (picture, edge, mat, or frame) to change the size or rotate it to change the look of your finished product.

39

40   Add Special Effects to a Photo

✔ BEFORE YOU BEGIN	→ SEE ALSO
32 Open Photos in PhotoSuite	34 Color Correct a Photo
	42 Add Clip Art to a Photo
	43 Paint and Draw on a Photo
	44 Create Cutouts and Masks

PhotoSuite has a myriad of special effects that you can add to your picture to make it fun. From color effects to textures, you just have to try them out to see everything that can be done.

Easy Media Creator makes it fun and easy. From the **Effect** window you can see a thumbnail example of each effect. By clicking on the thumbnail, you can see the effect previewed on your photo. Go ahead and play around with them!

40

1 Select Photo from the Open Files Window

From within **PhotoSuite**, choose the photo from the **Open Files** window at the bottom of the screen that you would like to add a special effect to and bring it up in the **Canvas** window.

2 Select Special Effects

After your photo is in the **Canvas** window, select the **Special Effects** button from the **Enhance** window in the **tasks** pane to bring up the **Special Effects** window.

3 Select Effect

After the **Special Effects** window opens, choose what type of effect you would like to apply from the drop-down menu at the top of the window, or scroll through all the effects shown to decide which one you would like.

4 Show Effect Preview

Click on the effect you would like to use and make sure that the **Show Preview** box is checked. This allows you to preview what the picture will look like after the effect is applied.

5 Adjust Effect Settings

Depending on the effect you choose, there are different settings. You can adjust these settings to your specifications while previewing the photo to make sure you have just the look you want.

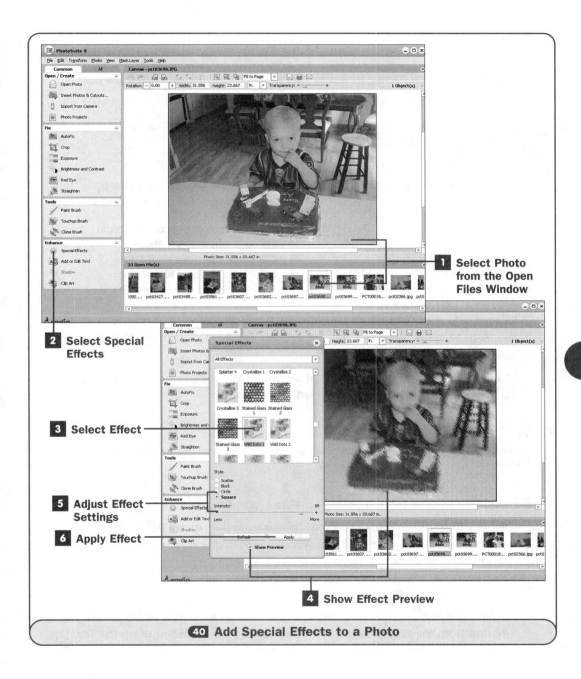

1 Select Photo from the Open Files Window

2 Select Special Effects

3 Select Effect

5 Adjust Effect Settings

6 Apply Effect

4 Show Effect Preview

40 Add Special Effects to a Photo

40

6 Apply Effect

When you are finished, click **Apply Effect** to finalize the effect.

▶ **TIP**

You can revert to the last saved version of your photo at any time by clicking on the **File** drop-down menu and selecting **Revert to Last Saved**. This removes any changes you have not saved, and you can start over.

| **41** | **Add Text to a Photo** |

✔ BEFORE YOU BEGIN	→ SEE ALSO
32 Open Photos in PhotoSuite	**38** Create a Shadow for a Photo
	39 Add Edges, Mats, and Frames to a Photo
	40 Add Special Effects to a Photo
	42 Add Clip Art to a Photo
	43 Paint and Draw on a Photo
	44 Create Cutouts and Masks

41

Adding text to your photo is an easy way to give it a caption or otherwise label it. If you want to really have some fun, add a text bubble to your photo and then add the text.

Your text object is always easy to adjust by using the *nodes*, or handles, around the text to resize, re-orient, or move it within your photo.

▶ **KEY TERM**

Nodes—The handles on the borders of an object that allow you to move it or re-adjust its size.

1 Select Photo from the Open Files window

From within **PhotoSuite**, choose the photo from the **Open Files** window at the bottom of the screen that you would like to add text to and bring it up in the **Canvas** window.

2 Select Add or Edit Text

After your photo is up in the **Canvas** window, select the **Add or Edit Text** button from the **Enhance** window in the **tasks** pane. This brings up the **Text** window and places a text box in the center of your photo.

3 Type in Text

Type the text you would like to place on your photo in the box labeled **Type your text here!**

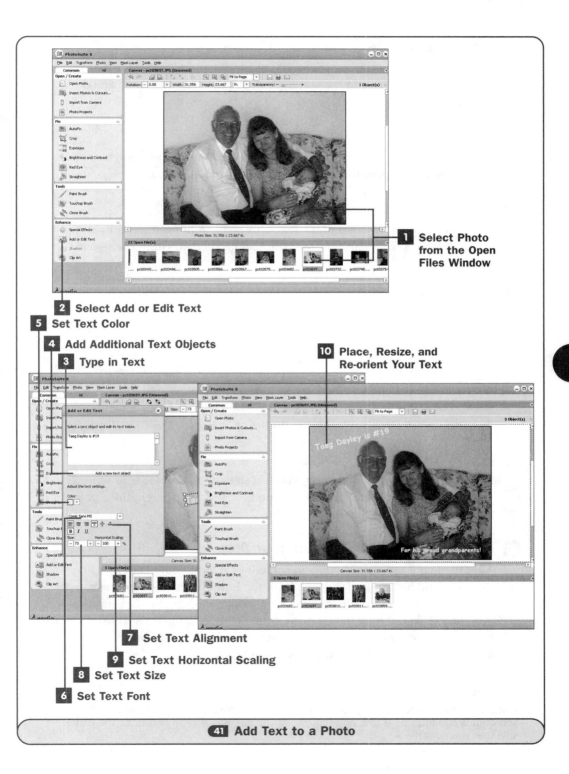

1 Select Photo from the Open Files Window

2 Select Add or Edit Text

5 Set Text Color

4 Add Additional Text Objects

3 Type in Text

10 Place, Resize, and Re-orient Your Text

41

7 Set Text Alignment

9 Set Text Horizontal Scaling

8 Set Text Size

6 Set Text Font

4 Add Additional Text Objects

Add as many text objects as you would like to the photo and enter the text for each one. You can edit the text by selecting the text object you would like to edit.

5 Set Text Color

Set the text color by clicking on the **Color** menu. You can use any color you like, or use the dropper tool to sample a color from the photo.

6 Set Text Font

After you have set the color of the text, choose the font for the text by using the **font** drop-down menu. The font changes for all text within the selected text object.

7 Set Text Alignment

By choosing the appropriate icon, you can align the text right, left, or center, and place it in the top, middle, or bottom of the text box.

41

8 Set Text Size

After you have aligned the text, make it smaller or larger so it fits well with your picture. Within the **Size** box, use the + or – buttons to increase or decrease the size, or just type in the size value.

9 Set Text Horizontal Scaling

Besides setting the size of the text, you can stretch the text wider or scrunch it together by using the **Horizontal Scaling** box. Use the + or – buttons or just type in the percent of the width.

10 Place, Resize, and Re-orient Your Text

After the text is on your photo, you can adjust it to fit your needs by using the bounding box around the text. With the **hand** icon, drag it to the correct location in your photo. Use the individual nodes to resize it to fit your location, and click and hold the orange rotation icon to rotate the text using your mouse. You can also resize and rotate your text by entering values in the **Rotation**, **Width**, and **Height** boxes in the taskbar.

▶ NOTE

Using the nodes to resize text changes the size of the font and the horizontal scaling. It's sometimes easier to do it this way, though, so you can easily change it to be the exact size that you need.

42 Add Clip Art to a Photo

✔ BEFORE YOU BEGIN	→ SEE ALSO
32 Open Photos in PhotoSuite	38 Create a Shadow for a Photo
	39 Add Edges, Mats, and Frames to a Photo
	40 Add Special Effects to a Photo
	41 Add Text to a Photo
	43 Paint and Draw on a Photo

Like using stickers in a scrapbook, adding clip art to your photo can give it a fun look. Easy Media Creator has clip art objects in quite a few categories. For example, you can choose a speech bubble and add text to it, as in the example.

One thing to keep in mind as you add the clip art is that you cannot add it beyond the boundaries of your canvas. Therefore, if you would like the clip art to protrude off your picture, you need to make the canvas larger than the picture. Choose the **Edit Canvas** option in the **Tools** drop-down menu at the top of your screen and enlarge it to a size that will accommodate your needs.

1 Select Photo from the Open Files Window

From within **PhotoSuite**, choose the photo from the **Open Files** window at the bottom of the screen that you would like to add clip art to and bring it up in the **Canvas** window.

2 Select Clip Art

After your photo is in the **Canvas** window, click on the **Clip Art** button in the **Enhance** menu. This brings up the **Clip Art** window.

3 Choose Clip Art Category

After the **Clip Art** window is open, choose the clip art category you want from the drop-down menu or the selection window. This brings up a preview of the clip art in that category.

4 Select the Clip Art

When the clip art in your category is displayed in the selection window, select the clip art you would like to place on your photo and either double-click on it or drag and drop it onto your photo.

42

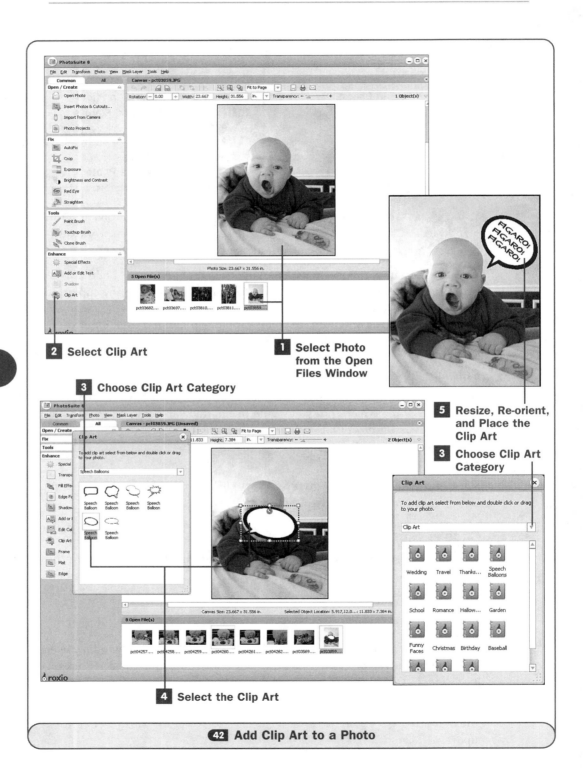

5 Resize, Re-orient, and Place the Clip Art

After the clip art is on your photo, you can adjust it to fit your needs by using the bounding box around the clip art. With the **hand** icon, drag it to the correct location in your photo. Use the individual nodes or handles to resize it to fit your location, and click and hold the orange rotation icon to rotate the clip art using your mouse. You can also resize and rotate your clip art by entering values in the **Rotation**, **Width**, and **Height** boxes in the taskbar. You can also edit it in much the same way as you would edit your photo—for instance, you can add text to it, as is shown in the example.

▶ NOTES

When you drag the center nodes or handles of an object, you stretch it. If you drag the corner nodes, the proportions are constrained.

Adding a shadow to your clip art gives it a three-dimensional look. Add a shadow to any object in your canvas the same way you would add a shadow to a photo. See **38** **Create a Shadow for a Photo.**

▶ TIP

As you add objects to your photo, the file size increases. To reduce your file size, you can flatten the project, combining all the objects into one. Choose the **Flatten Canvas** option in the **Transform** drop-down menu. After you have flattened your canvas, you are no longer able to select the individual objects inside of it.

---

43 **Paint and Draw on a Photo**

✔ BEFORE YOU BEGIN	→ SEE ALSO
32 Open Photos in PhotoSuite	**39** Add Edges, Mats, and Frames to a Photo
	41 Add Text to a Photo
	42 Add Clip Art to a Photo
	44 Create Cutouts and Masks

43

You can use several tools to paint or draw freely on your photo. As you paint, you do not see the results right away. **PhotoSuite** creates a new object out of your paint strokes, which means that you can resize, re-orient, or place it anywhere in the photo, just like any other object in the project.

1 Select Photo from the Open Files Window

From within **PhotoSuite**, choose the photo from the **Open Files** window at the bottom of the screen that you would like to paint and draw on to bring it up in the **Canvas** window.

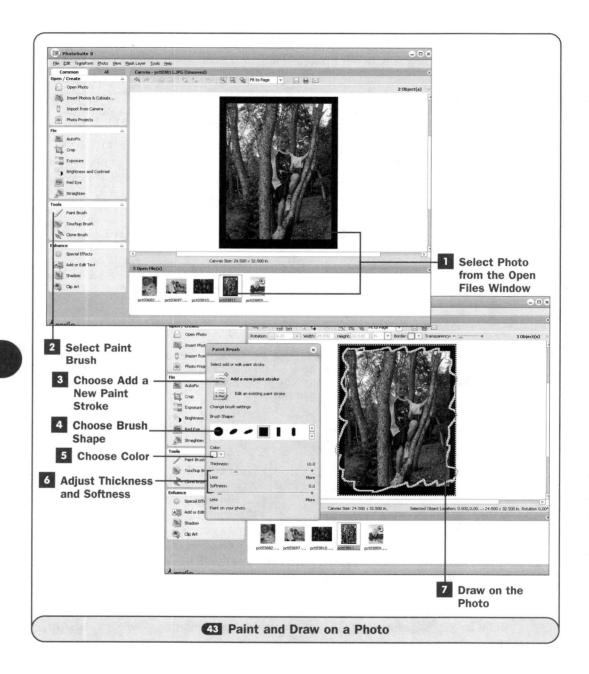

1 Select Photo from the Open Files Window

2 Select Paint Brush

3 Choose Add a New Paint Stroke

4 Choose Brush Shape

5 Choose Color

6 Adjust Thickness and Softness

7 Draw on the Photo

43 Paint and Draw on a Photo

43

2 Select Paint Brush

Select the **Paint Brush** option from the **Tools** menu in the **tasks** pane. This brings up the **Paint Brush** window.

3 Choose Add a New Paint Stroke

From the **Paint Brush** window, select **Add a new paint stroke**. After you have painted on your photo, you can use the **Edit an existing paint stroke** option to edit it. You can add as many paint strokes to a photo as you want, but each stroke has only one set of properties. In other words, you have to create a second paint stroke to draw in a different color.

4 Choose Brush Shape

After you have selected **Add a new paint stroke**, choose the brush shape from the option shown in the **Brush Shape** menu.

5 Choose Color

After you have chosen a brush shape, select the color from the **Color** menu. You can choose any color or use the dropper tool to pick up a color from the photo.

6 Adjust Thickness and Softness

When you have chosen a paint color, move the **Thickness** and **Softness** slider bars to adjust the thickness and softness of the paint brush. The thickness increases or decreases the brush size. The softness determines the amount of transparency at the edges of the stroke.

7 Draw on the Photo

When you have chosen your options for the brush, draw on the photo by dragging the mouse over it while you hold down the left mouse key. The lines do not appear right away, but a dotted line indicates where you have drawn. When you are done drawing, the line appears. To create a new stroke, follow steps 3–7 again.

When you are finished drawing on your photo, close the **Photo** window.

▶ NOTES

When adding anything to a photo, you need to increase the canvas size if you would like it to go out of the bounds of the photo. Choose **Edit Canvas** in the **Tools** drop-down menu at the top of the screen.

You can use the **Flood Fill** option to fill any selected area with color or with several effects. Click on the **All** tab at the top of the **tasks** pane. The **Flood Fill** option is in the **Tools** menu.

43

44 Create Cutouts and Masks

✔ BEFORE YOU BEGIN	→ SEE ALSO
32 Open Photos in PhotoSuite	**34** Color Correct a Photo
	36 Clean and Fix a Damaged Photo
	37 Use the Clone Brush
	40 Add Special Effects to a Photo

What exactly is a *mask*? Think of it as a stencil. A mask is simply a way of selecting part of a photo or photo project in order to edit it separately from the rest of the photo. The portion of the project that is not masked can be changed, while the mask blocks the rest of the photo from the edits. You can add flood fills, color corrections, or special effects to only certain areas in your photo this way.

▶ KEY TERM

Mask—An area that overlays part of an image like a stencil so the effects applied to the rest of the image do not apply to the masked portion of the image.

You can also create *cutouts* to use individually or to place in other pictures. A cutout is just what it sounds like—it has the same effect as taking a pair of scissors to a picture and cutting an object or shape out of it.

▶ KEY TERM

Cutout—An area of an image that has been cut from a larger area.

Several options in creating the shape of the mask give you quite a bit of versatility in what you would like to select, whether you want to ripple every red in your photo, or simply cut a person out of one photo and place her into another photo.

1 Select Photo from Open Files Window

From within **PhotoSuite**, choose the photo to create a mask on from the **Open Files** window at the bottom of the screen and bring it up in the **Canvas** window.

2 Select the All Tab

Select the **All** tab at the top of the **tasks** pane to open all of your editing options.

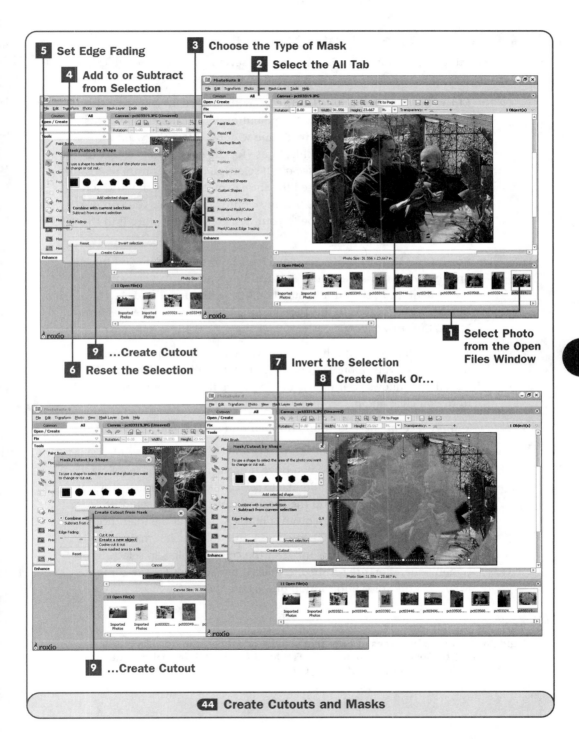

5 Set Edge Fading

4 Add to or Subtract from Selection

3 Choose the Type of Mask

2 Select the All Tab

1 Select Photo from the Open Files Window

9 ...Create Cutout

6 Reset the Selection

7 Invert the Selection

8 Create Mask Or...

9 ...Create Cutout

44 Create Cutouts and Masks

3 Choose the Type of Mask

In creating a mask for your photo, you have several types of mask to choose from:

- **Mask/Cutout by Shape**—In order to create a mask in a specific shape, click on the **Mask/Cutout by Shape** button in the **Tools** menu. This brings up the **Mask/Cutout by Shape** window. From the window, choose the shape you would like to use for the mask. Don't forget to use the up and down arrows to see a full selection of shapes from which to choose. After you have selected the shape you like, click the **Add selected shape** button. This places the mask onto your photo. You can use the handles to drag the shape to your desired size and place it in the right spot on the photo.

- **Freehand Mask/Cutout**—You can choose any shape you want by drawing your mask freehand. This can be as precise as you want if you are patient and your hand is steady. Click on the **Freehand Mask/Cutout** button in the **Tools** menu. This brings up the **Freehand Mask/Cutout** window.

  To create the mask, simply click anywhere inside your picture and begin to draw with your mouse. To pause or to set a point, click again. The dotted line follows your mouse until you are finished, but it won't stick until you click again.

  You must completely surround an area and click directly on your start point before the mask is completed.

- **Mask/Cutout by Color**—If you have a particular color or set of colors in your photo that you would like to select, click on the **Mask/Cutout by Color** button to bring up the **Mask/Cutout by Color** window. From within this window you are given a magic wand. Set the tolerance level for the colors you would like to choose and hold the left mouse key down while you drag the wand over the color or colors to select. Be patient when you are finished; it takes a few seconds for the computer to process the color information and create the mask.

▶ TIP

A great way to clean up areas of color that you did or did not want to select using the **Mask/Cutout by Color** tool is to open the **Freehand Mask/Cutout** tool and manually select the areas to add or subtract from your selection.

44

- **Mask/Cutout Edge Tracing**—This tool differs from the **Freehand** tool because it only selects in straight lines. Click on the **Mask/Cutout Edge Tracing** tool in the **Tools** menu to bring up the window. Click on the place in your photo where you would like to begin the tracing. Each time you click, you can change the direction of the line. Click several times in a row to go around corners.

  You must completely surround an area and click directly on your start point before the mask is completed. After you have clicked back onto your start point, each point that you clicked on becomes a handle that you can edit individually. When you are satisfied with your selection, click on the **Done tracing** box to create the mask.

4 Add to or Subtract from Selection

In each category of mask you have to choose from, you are given the option to **Combine with current selection** or **Subtract from current selection**. You can do this in the window that you are using, or you can choose another type of mask to add to or subtract from your selection. In this example, I have inverted the first shape and added another shape to the selection.

5 Set Edge Fading

Set the edge fading to increase the transparency of the edges by using the **Edge Fading** slide bar. This allows a limited amount of any changes you make to bleed out of the edges of the selection.

6 Reset the Selection

To remove any masks you have created, click the **Reset** button at any time. This allows you to start over if you are unsatisfied with the selections you have made.

7 Invert the Selection

At any time during the masking process, you can invert the selection by clicking on the **Invert Selection** button. Remember that it is the portion of the picture that you can see that is selected, and that the selected areas are the areas that will be changed. So if I applied a special effect to this photo, the star and the area outside of the circle would be affected by the change. To change the opposite area, click on the **Invert Selection** button.

8 Create Mask Or...

When you are finished creating your mask, close the window. *Do not* click on the **Create Cutout** button unless that is what you want to do. Closing the

44

window is sufficient to create the mask. The mask no longer appears as grey shading, but as a dotted line.

9 ...Create Cutout

If you would like to create a cutout of the selected areas, click **Create Cutout**. You are given several options:

- **Cut it out**—This option cuts the selected area out completely, deleting the other areas within the photo.

- **Create a new object**—This option copies the selected area and creates a new object within the canvas that contains the selected areas. The photo behind the new object is still a complete picture.

- **Cookie-cut it out**—This option cuts out the selected area, but does not delete the unselected areas, creating two objects. The photo behind the new object will have a hole in it where the cutout was created.

- **Save masked area to a file**—You can save your cutouts to a file so you can use them later. This way you have the option of bringing them into other photos or photo projects to create a collage.

45

▶ **TIP**

You can revert to the last saved version of your photo at any time by clicking on the **File** drop-down menu and selecting **Revert to Last Saved**. This removes any changes you have not saved, and you can start over.

45 Edit Multiple Photos at Once	
✔ **BEFORE YOU BEGIN**	→ **SEE ALSO**
Chapter 1, "Start Here" (Review information about photo file types.)	33 Re-orient, Resize, or Crop a Photo
	34 Color Correct a Photo
	35 Fix Facial Flaws—Including Red Eye
	36 Clean and Fix a Damaged Photo
	40 Add Special Effects to a Photo

Easy Media Creator gives you the option of editing several photos at once. This saves you time by resizing, renaming, or even adding a few select special effects to several photos at once, rather than individually.

Most of these edits have been covered extensively in the tasks about editing individual photos, so they are lightly covered in this task. If you would like a more detailed description of the process, refer to the individual task.

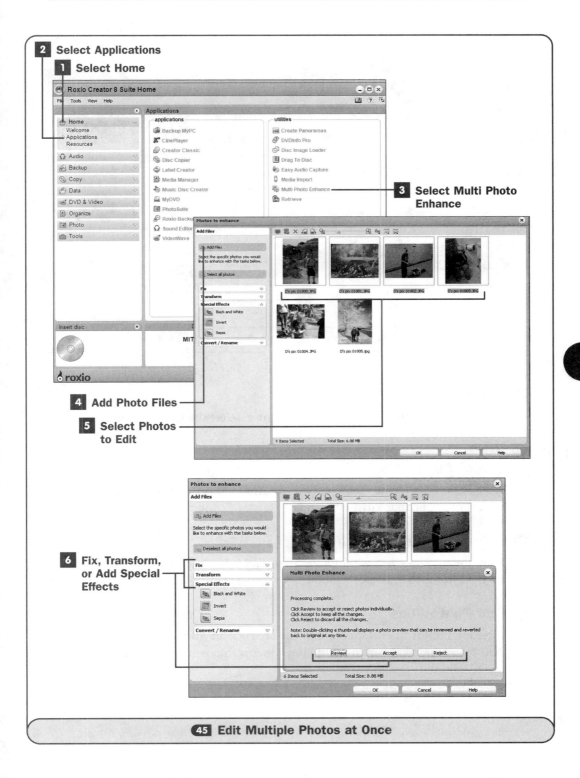

2 Select Applications

1 Select Home

3 Select Multi Photo Enhance

4 Add Photo Files

5 Select Photos to Edit

6 Fix, Transform, or Add Special Effects

45

45 Edit Multiple Photos at Once

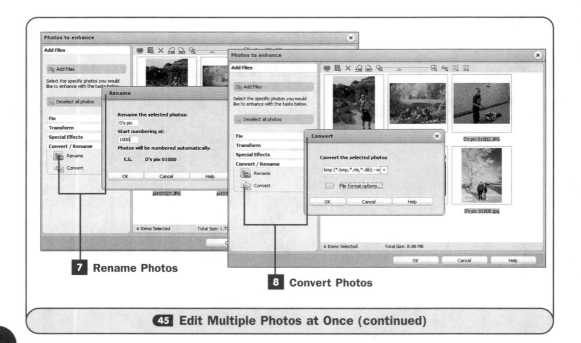

7 Rename Photos

8 Convert Photos

45 Edit Multiple Photos at Once (continued)

45

1 Select Home

From the **project** pane in Easy Media Creator, select the **Home** menu to bring up the **Home** options.

2 Select Applications

From within the **Home** menu, choose the **Applications** option to bring up the list of applications available in Easy Media Creator.

3 Select Multi Photo Enhance

From the utilities window on the right, select **Multi Photo Enhance** to bring up the **Photos to enhance** window.

4 Add Photo Files

After the **Photos to enhance** window is up, click on **Add Files** to bring up the **Add Files** window. From the **Add Files** window, choose the photos you would like to edit and close the window.

5 Select Photos to Edit

Depending on the number of edits you are planning to perform, you might want to select just a few of the pictures you have imported. Make sure that the pictures you want to edit are selected. Use the **Control** key to select more than one photo.

6 Fix, Transform, or Add Special Effects

From the **Photos to enhance** window, choose the **Fix**, **Transform**, or **Special Effects** options that you would like to use on your selected photos. When your edit is complete, you are given the option to review your photos individually, accept the changes, or reject them.

▶ **TIP**

It is highly suggested that you review each photo individually before you accept the changes made, especially if you are fixing your photo. The automatic fixes use a set formula that works for most, but definitely not all, photos. You will find that there are photos you want to fix individually.

45

7 Rename Photos

You can rename your photos as a batch by giving each one of them a different number. This is a great way to store a great quantity of photos so they are easy to find and use. Click on the **Convert/Rename** menu and select **Rename** to bring up the **Rename** window. From within the **Rename** window, type in a prefix for your photos and set the starting number. Click **OK** and accept or reject the changes.

▶ **TIP**

Organize your photos as you number them so the older photos have smaller numbers to make it easy to sort through them later.

8 Convert Photos

You can convert the photos you have selected from one type of file to another. Click the **Convert** button in the **Convert/Rename** menu to bring up the **Convert** window. Choose the type of file to convert your photo files to from the drop-down menu. You can choose the options for the file format by clicking on the **File format options** button. Click **OK** and accept or reject the file format change.

7

PhotoSuite Projects

IN THIS CHAPTER:

The ability to import photos and edit them is invaluable in being able to preserve and share them in the future. Roxio Easy Media Creator 8 includes project assistants to help you use your photos in creative ways. These assistants help you create and output photo albums, calendars, greeting cards, collages, gift tags, posters, and panoramic images.

In this chapter you learn how to use your photos in creative and fun projects. The assistants make it easy for you to add photos to projects and get very professional-looking results quickly. It is also a very good example of the things you can accomplish using **PhotoSuite**. Any one of these projects can be created from scratch using **PhotoSuite**, so after you are familiar with the process, you can create your own projects.

46 Create a Photo Album

✔ BEFORE YOU BEGIN	→ SEE ALSO
Chapter 5, "Importing Photos"	Chapter 6, "Editing Photos"

46

Just like traditional photo albums, the **Photo Album Assistant** is designed to create a place where photos can be put together in a way that is meaningful and looks nice. You can create a photo album to remember a vacation, birthday, or other family event. The following steps describe how to open the **Photo Album Assistant**, add photos to it, customize the album, and output your results.

1 Open Photo Projects Assistant

You can open **Photo Projects Assistant** in three ways, depending on which is easiest for you. If you have the Roxio **Home** page up, simply click on **Photo** and then select **More Projects** from the **Photo** submenu. If you have **PhotoSuite** open, you can select **Photo Projects** from the **Open/Create** options of the **Common** tool menu. You can also open **Photo Projects Assistant** by selecting **Programs**, **Roxio Easy Media Creator 8**, **Photo** from the **Start** menu in Windows.

2 Select Albums

After you have the **Photo Projects Assistant** up, select **Albums** from the **Select project type** menu and click the **Next** button to begin creating a new photo album.

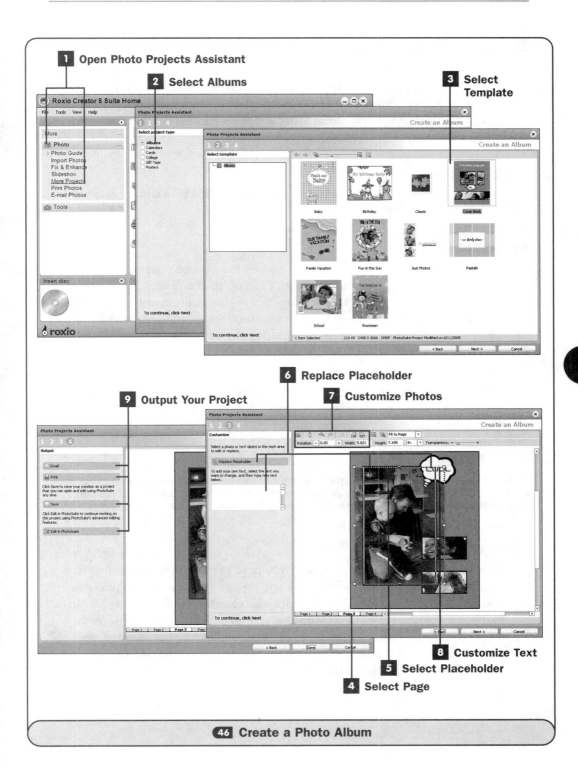

1 Open Photo Projects Assistant

2 Select Albums

3 Select Template

9 Output Your Project

6 Replace Placeholder

7 Customize Photos

8 Customize Text

5 Select Placeholder

4 Select Page

46

3 Select Template

After you have started a new photo album project, you need to select a *template*. The template is a document that predefines the look of the photo album. It includes preset text, photo locations, and some kind of clip art or other graphics in the background. After you have selected the template, click the **Next** button.

▶ KEY TERM

Template—Predefined settings that are applied to a project that save time by automatically setting up basic features.

4 Select Page

The template that you selected in step 3 likely has several pages to add photos to when creating your photo album. Click on the **Page** tabs on the bottom of the view to see the various pages in the photo album until you find a page to which you want to add photos and text. You want to make the changes listed in the steps below to each page in the project.

5 Select Placeholder

46

There are two types of *placeholders* on each template page: text and photos. You need to select and replace these placeholders one at a time. Select a placeholder you want to change.

▶ KEY TERM

Placeholder—Placeholders are photos or text that have been preformatted with specific settings to fit in the template. They are an example to allow you to see where you can add photos and text to the template. You replace these with your own photos and text.

6 Replace Placeholder

After you have selected a placeholder, you need to replace the content with content that is meaningful to you. You can replace the content of a photo by selecting it and then clicking on **Replace Placeholder** to bring up the **Media Manager**. Then use the **Media Manager** to find a photo you want to use in the project. Your photo then becomes the placeholder. You can also replace the text. First select it and then replace the text in the text box on the left. You can also replace the content by double-clicking on it, which also opens the **Media Manager**.

▶ **TIP**

Replace all of the placeholders on a page before customizing the look and feel. Things look different when you add a new photo or new text, and you might spend more time redoing things if you customize each item as it is added to the page.

7 **Customize Photos**

After you have replaced the photo placeholders on the page, you can edit them in several ways to make the project more your own.

To customize a photo, first select it. After the photo is selected, you are able to see the areas of the photo that are inside and outside of the mask. The portions of the photo that will be cropped out by the mask are grayed out in the display.

Resize the photo by dragging the handles on the corners of the photo. After the photo is the size you want it, you can drag it to a position where the proper space is visible inside the template. If you need to, you can also rotate the picture by clicking on the rotate left and right buttons.

If you need to adjust the colors of the photo or fix red eye, click on the *Pocket Editor* button. The **Pocket Editor** provides buttons to autofix, crop, fix red eye, change brightness and contrast, and adjust saturation. You can also open the **Pocket Editor** by double-clicking on the photo after it's in place.

46

▶ **KEY TERM**

Pocket Editor—An application within Easy Media Creator that allows you to quickly edit an image that has already been added to a project.

8 **Customize Text**

After you have replaced the text placeholders on the page, you can edit the text in several ways to make it look the way you want.

To customize text, first select it. After the text is selected, drag it to the location on the page where you want it to be. You can also rotate the text by clicking on the rotate control attached to the top center handle of the text box and dragging the mouse with the left mouse button pressed down.

After the text is in the position you want it to be in, you can use the menu at the top of the display to set the following attributes: color, font, bold/italic/ underline, size, *horizontal scaling*, and *alignment*.

▶ KEY TERMS

Horizontal scaling—Adjusts the width of text in a project based on a scale of 1% to 100%.

Alignment—How an object is lined up in relation to other objects, or how text is lined up in relation to its text box.

9 Output Your Project

After you have completely customized the project, click the **Next** button to bring up the **Output** menu. From the **Output** menu, you can email, print, save, or open the project in **PhotoSuite**.

▶ NOTE

When clicking the **Next** button to move to the final step of the project, you get a warning dialog if you have not replaced all of the placeholders in the project. If you did not deliberately leave a placeholder in the project, click the **Yes** button and go back and replace any placeholders that were missed.

To email your project, click on **Email** to bring up the **Email Assistant**. The **Email Assistant** allows you to specify your email client. It also allows you to specify whether to convert the project into compressed JPEG files, turn it into a WMV slideshow movie, or just send it as is with no conversion. For more information, see **124** **Use Email Assistant to Email a Project** (on the Web).

▶ TIP

When emailing photos to friends, you should convert them to JPEG to conserve space. This speeds up how fast the email is sent and reduces the risk of the email being too big to send.

To print your project, click on **Print** to bring up the **Photo Print Assistant**. The **Photo Print Assistant** gives you the standard options of selecting the printer, setting the paper size and orientation, and specifying how many copies to print.

In addition to those options, the **Photo Print Assistant** provides a powerful layout manager that allows you to specify whether to print one photo per page or multiple photos per page. The **Multiple photos per page** option allows you to select one of many templates that automatically configure where the photos fit on the printed page. For example, you can print a sheet

46

that has two 5"×7" photos or you can print a sheet that has one 5"×7" and two 3"×5" photos. You want to select the **Crop photo to fill the placeholder** and **Auto-rotate to fit the placeholders** buttons to make the pages of your project fit properly. For more information, see **123 Use Print Assistant to Print a Project** (on the Web).

To save the project, click on **Save** to bring up the **Media Manager**. Use the **Media Manager** to find the folder or album where you want to place the project. You can create folders and albums by clicking on the **Create a New Folder** and **Create a New Album** buttons respectively. After you have selected the folder or album, select the file type for your project. The default file type is **.DMSP**, which is a **PhotoSuite** format. Then type in the name of the file and click the **Save** button. If you would like to save your project as an image, choose a different file format to save it in. You can then bring it up in other photo editors and print or make changes to it. However, it will no longer be dynamic, and you will not be able to change the placeholders.

To edit the project further in **PhotoSuite**, click on the **Edit in PhotoSuite** button. This brings up your project in **PhotoSuite**. For more information about editing the project in **PhotoSuite**, see the tasks in Chapter 6, "Editing Photos."

47

47 Create a Calendar

✔ BEFORE YOU BEGIN	→ SEE ALSO
Chapter 5, "Importing Photos"	Chapter 6, "Editing Photos"

The **Calendar Assistant** is designed to help you create nice calendars using your own photos. For example, you can create a personalized calendar for each member of your family or an organization to which you belong. The following steps describe how to open the **Calendar Assistant**, add photos to it, customize the calendar, and output your results.

1 Open Photo Projects Assistant

You can open **Photo Projects Assistant** in three ways, depending on which is easiest for you. If you have the Roxio **Home** page up, simply click on **Photo** and then select **More Projects** from the **Photo** submenu. If you have **PhotoSuite** open, you can select **Photo Projects** from the **Open/Create** options of the **Common** tool menu. You can also open **Photo Projects Assistant** by selecting it from the **Programs, Roxio Easy Media Creator 8, Photo** submenu of the **Start** menu in Windows.

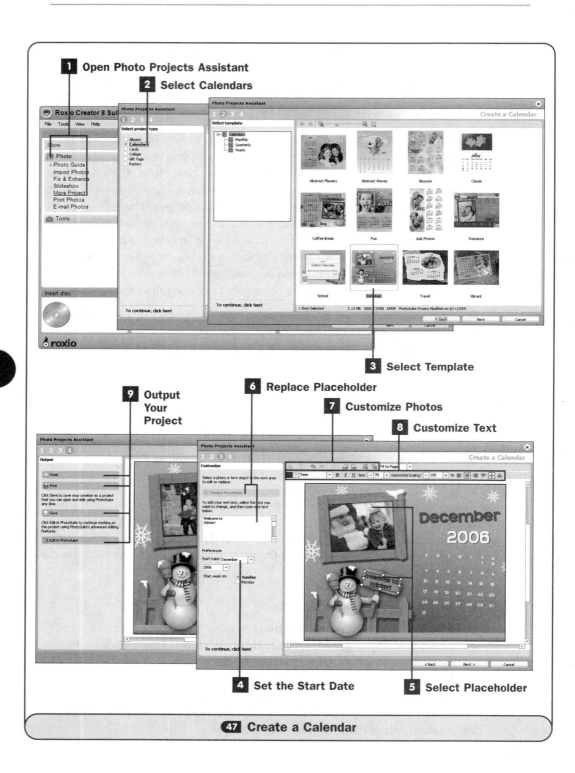

1 Open Photo Projects Assistant

2 Select Calendars

3 Select Template

9 Output Your Project

6 Replace Placeholder

7 Customize Photos

8 Customize Text

4 Set the Start Date

5 Select Placeholder

47 Create a Calendar

2 Select Calendars

After you have the **Photo Projects Assistant** up, select **Calendars** from the **Select project type** menu, and click the **Next** button to begin creating a new calendar.

3 Select Template

After you have started a new calendar project, you need to select a template. The template is a document that predefines the look of the calendar. It includes preset text, photo locations, and some kind of clip art or other graphics in the background. After you have selected the template, click the **Next** button.

4 Set the Start Date

After you have selected the template for the calendar, you need to set the starting month and year in the **Start Date** drop-down boxes. You can also specify if you want the week to start on Sunday or Monday by selecting the radio button next to the day.

5 Select Placeholder

After you have set the date and time for the calendar, you need to select and replace these placeholders one at a time. There are two types of placeholders on each template page: text and photos. Select a placeholder you want to change.

6 Replace Placeholder

After you have selected a placeholder, you need to replace the content with content that is meaningful to you. You can replace the content of a photo by selecting it and then clicking on **Replace Placeholder** to bring up the **Media Manager**. You can also open the **Media Manager** by double-clicking on a placeholder you want to replace. Then use the **Media Manager** to find a photo you want to use in the project. Your photo then becomes the placeholder. You can also replace the text. First select it and then replace the text in the text box on the left.

▶ **TIP**

Replace all the placeholders on a page before customizing the look and feel. Things look different when you add a new photo or new text, and you might spend more time recustomizing if you customize each item as it is added to the page.

47

7 Customize Photos

After you have replaced the photo placeholders on the page, you can edit them in several ways to make the project more your own.

To customize a photo, first select it. After the photo is selected, you are able to see the areas of the photo that are inside and outside of the mask. The portions of the photo that will be cropped out by the mask are grayed out in the display.

Resize the photo by dragging the handles on the corners of the photo. After the photo is the size you want it, you can drag it to a position where the proper space is visible inside the mask. If you need to, you can also rotate the picture by clicking on the rotate left and right buttons.

If you need to adjust the colors of the photo or fix red eye, click on the **Pocket Editor** button. The **Pocket Editor** providesbuttons to autofix, crop, fix red eye, change brightness and contrast, and adjust saturation. You can also open the **Pocket Editor** by double-clicking on your photo.

8 Customize Text

47

After you have replaced the text placeholders on the page, you can edit the text in several ways to make it look the way you want.

To customize text, first select it. After the text is selected, drag it to the location on the page you want it to be. You can also rotate the text by clicking on the rotate control attached to the top center handle of the text box and dragging the mouse with the left mouse button pressed down.

After the text is in the position you want it to be in, you can use the menu at the top of the display to set the following attributes: color, font, bold/italic/underline, size, horizontal scaling, and alignment.

9 Output Your Project

After you have completely customized the project, click the **Next** button to bring up the **Output** menu. From the **Output** menu, you can email, print, save, or open the project in **PhotoSuite**.

▶ NOTE

When clicking the **Next** button to move to the final step of the project, you get a warning dialog if you have not replaced all of the placeholders in the project. If you did not deliberately leave a placeholder in the project, click the **Yes** button and go back and replace any placeholders that were missed.

To email your project, click on **Email** to bring up the **Email Assistant**. The **Email Assistant** allows you to specify your email client. It also allows you to specify whether to convert the project into compressed JPEG files, turn it into a WMV slideshow movie, or just send it as is with no conversion. For more information, see **124 Use Email Assistant to Email a Project** (on the Web).

▶ **TIP**

When emailing photos to friends, you should convert them to JPEG to conserve space. This speeds up how fast the email is sent and reduces the risk of the email being too big to send.

To print your project, click on **Print** to bring up the **Photo Print Assistant**. The **Photo Print Assistant** gives you the standard options of selecting the printer, setting the paper size and orientation, and specifying how many copies to print.

In addition to those options, the **Photo Print Assistant** provides a powerful layout manager that allows you to specify whether to print one photo per page or multiple photos per page. The **Multiple photos per page** option allows you to select one of many templates that automatically configure where the photos fit on the printed page. For example, you can print a sheet that has two 5"×7" photos or you can print a sheet that has one 5"×7" and two 3"×5" photos. You want to select the **Crop photo to fill the placeholder** and **Auto-rotate to fit the placeholders** buttons to make the pages of your project fit properly. For more information, see **123 Use Print Assistant to Print a Project** (on the Web).

To save the project, click on **Save** to bring up the **Media Manager**. Use the **Media Manager** to find the folder or album where you want to place the project. You can create folders and albums by clicking on the **Create a New Folder** and **Create a New Album** buttons respectively. After you have selected the folder or album, select the file type for your project. The default file type is **.DMSP**, which is a **PhotoSuite** format. Then type in the name of the file and click the **Save** button. If you would like to save your project as an image, choose a different file format to save it in. You can then bring it up in other photo editors and print or make changes to it. However, it will no longer be dynamic, and you will not be able to change the placeholders.

To edit the project further in **PhotoSuite**, click on the **Edit in PhotoSuite** button. This brings up your project in **PhotoSuite**. For more information about editing the project in **PhotoSuite**, see the tasks in Chapter 6.

47

48 Create a Card

✔ BEFORE YOU BEGIN	→ SEE ALSO
Chapter 5, "Importing Photos"	Chapter 6, "Editing Photos"

The **Greeting Card Assistant** is designed to help you create personalized greeting cards using your own photos and text. You no longer need to buy expensive greeting cards from a photo company to get your pictures on them, and each card can be personalized to the person to whom you are sending it. The following steps describe how to open the **Greeting Card Assistant**, add photos to it, customize greeting cards, and output your results.

48

1 Open Photo Projects Assistant

You can open **Photo Projects Assistant** in three ways, depending on which is easiest for you. If you have the Roxio **Home** page up, simply click on **Photo** and then select **More Projects** from the **Photo** submenu. If you have **PhotoSuite** open, you can select **Photo Projects** from the **Open/Create** options of the **Common** tool menu. You can also open **Photo Projects Assistant** by selecting it from the **Programs, Roxio Easy Media Creator 8, Photo** submenu of the **Start** menu in Windows.

2 Select Cards

After you have the **Photo Projects Assistant** up, select **Cards** from the **Select project type** menu and click the **Next** button to begin creating a new greeting card.

3 Select Template

After you have started a new greeting card project, you need to select a template. The template is a document that predefines the look of the greeting card. It includes preset text, photo locations, and some kind of clip art or other graphics in the background. After you have selected the template, click the **Next** button.

4 Select Page

After you have selected the template, you see the **Front; Inside Left** or **Top; Inside Right** or **Bottom;** and **Back** page tabs. Click on the page tabs on the bottom of the view to see the various pages in the greeting card until you find a page to which you want to add photos and text. You want to make the changes listed in the following steps to each page in the project.

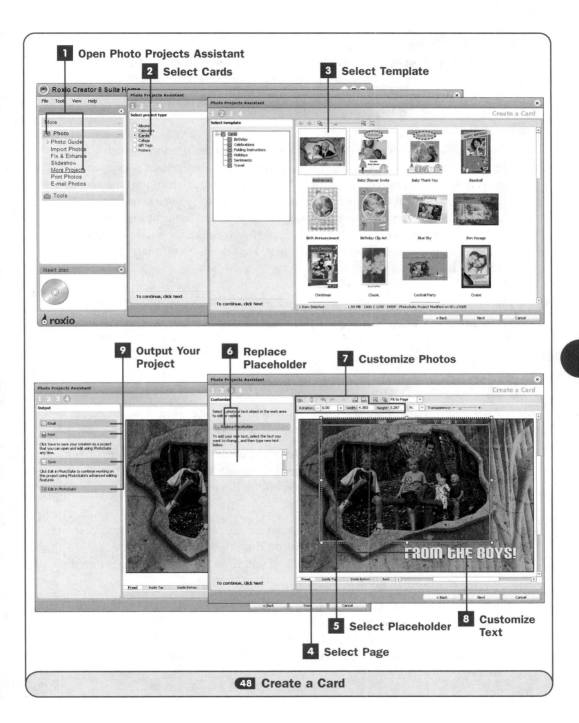

1 Open Photo Projects Assistant

2 Select Cards

3 Select Template

9 Output Your Project

6 Replace Placeholder

7 Customize Photos

48

5 Select Placeholder

8 Customize Text

4 Select Page

48 Create a Card

5 Select Placeholder

There are two types of placeholders on each template page: text and photos. You need to select and replace these placeholders one at a time. Select a placeholder you want to change.

6 Replace Placeholder

After you have selected a placeholder, you need to replace the content with content that is meaningful to you. You can replace the content of a photo by selecting it and then clicking on **Replace Placeholder** to bring up the **Media Manager**. You can also open the **Media Manager** to replace content by double-clicking the placeholder image. Then use the **Media Manager** to find a photo that you want to use in the project. Your photo then becomes the placeholder. You can also replace the text. First select it and then replace the text in the text box on the left.

▶ TIP

Replace all the placeholders on a page before customizing the look and feel. Things look different when you add a new photo or new text, and you might spend more time recustomizing if you customize each item as it is added to the page.

48

7 Customize Photos

After you have replaced the photo placeholders on the page, you can edit them in several ways to make the project more your own.

To customize a photo, first select it. After the photo is selected, you are able to see the areas of the photo that are inside and outside of the mask. The portions of the photo that will be cropped out by the mask are grayed out in the display.

Resize the photo by dragging the handles on the corners of the photo. After the photo is the size you want it, you can drag it to a position where the proper space is visible inside the mask. If you need to, you can also rotate the picture by clicking on the rotate left and right buttons.

If you need to adjust the colors of the photo or fix red eye, click on the **Pocket Editor** button. You can also open the **Pocket Editor** by double-clicking on the image you want to edit. The **Pocket Editor** provides buttons to autofix, crop, fix red eye, change brightness and contrast, and adjust saturation.

8   Customize Text

After you have replaced the text placeholders on the page, you can edit the text in several ways to make it look the way you want.

To customize text, first select it. After the text is selected, drag it to the location on the page where you want it to be. You can also rotate the text by clicking on the rotate control attached to the top center handle of the text box and dragging the mouse with the left mouse button pressed down.

After the text is in the position you want it to be in, you can use the menu at the top of the display to set the following attributes: color, font, bold/italic/underline, size, horizontal scaling, and alignment.

9   Output Your Project

After you have completely customized the project, click the **Next** button to bring up the **Output** menu. From the **Output** menu, you can email, print, save, or open the project in **PhotoSuite**.

▶ **NOTE**

When clicking the **Next** button to move to the final step of the project, you get a warning dialog if you have not replaced all of the placeholders in the project. If you did not deliberately leave a placeholder in the project, click the **Yes** button and go back and replace any placeholders that were missed.

48

To email your project, click on **Email** to bring up the **Email Assistant**. The **Email Assistant** allows you to specify your email client. It also allows you to specify whether to convert the project into compressed JPEG files, turn it into a WMV slideshow movie, or just send it as is with no conversion. For more information, see **124** **Use Email Assistant to Email a Project** (on the Web).

▶ **TIP**

When emailing photos to friends, you should convert them to JPEG to conserve space. This speeds up how fast the email is sent and reduces the risk of the email being too big to send.

To print your project, click on **Print** to bring up the **Photo Print Assistant**. The **Photo Print Assistant** gives you the standard options of selecting the printer, setting the paper size and orientation, and specifying how many copies to print.

In addition to those options, the **Photo Print Assistant** provides a powerful layout manager that allows you to specify whether to print one photo per page or multiple photos per page. The **Multiple photos per page** option allows you to select one of many templates that automatically configure where the photos fit on the printed page. For example, you can print a sheet that has two 5"×7" photos or you can print a sheet that has one 5"×7" and two 3"×5" photos. You want to select the **Crop photo to fill the placeholder** and **Auto-rotate to fit the placeholders** buttons to make the pages of your project fit properly. For more information, see 123 **Use Print Assistant to Print a Project** (on the Web).

To save the project, click on **Save** to bring up the **Media Manager**. Use the **Media Manager** to find the folder or album where you want to place the project. You can create folders and albums by clicking on the **Create a New Folder** and **Create a New Album** buttons respectively. After you have select-ed the folder or album, select the file type for your project. The default file type is **.DMSP**, which is a **PhotoSuite** format. Then type in the name of the file and click the **Save** button. If you would like to save your project as an image, choose a different file format to save it in. You can then bring it up in other photo editors and print or make changes to it. However, it will no longer be dynamic, and you will not be able to change the placeholders.

To edit the project further in **PhotoSuite**, click on the **Edit in PhotoSuite** but-ton. This brings up your project in **PhotoSuite**. For more information about editing the project in **PhotoSuite**, see the tasks in Chapter 6.

49   Create a Collage

✔ BEFORE YOU BEGIN	→ SEE ALSO
Chapter 5, "Importing Photos"	Chapter 6, "Editing Photos"

The **Collage Assistant** is designed to help you create creative collages of your photos. You can use these collages to make creative groups of photos to print or send to family and friends. These collages are also useful for school projects. The **Collage Assistant** even includes a cool utility that automatically arranges the photos in the collage if you need ideas. The following steps describe how to open the **Collage Assistant**, add photos to it, customize the collage, and output your results.

1 Open Photo Projects Assistant

You can open **Photo Projects Assistant** in three ways, depending on which is easiest for you. If you have the Roxio **Home** page up, simply click on **Photo** and then select **More Projects** from the **Photo** submenu. If you have **PhotoSuite** open, you can select **Photo Projects** from the **Open/Create** options of the **Common** tool menu. You can also open **Photo Projects**

Assistant by selecting it from the **Programs, Roxio Easy Media Creator 8, Photo** submenu of the **Start** menu in Windows.

2 Select Collage

After you have the **Photo Projects Assistant** up, select **Collage** from the **Select project type** menu and click the **Next** button to begin creating a new collage.

3 Select Predesigned Template Or...

After you have started a new collage project, you can use a predefined template. The template is a document that predefines the look of the collage. It includes preset text, an area to place photos in, and clip art or other graphics in the background. Select **Pre-designed template** and click the **Next** button to see a selection of available templates. After you have selected the template, click the **Next** button.

4 ...Select from a Blank Page

To create a collage from your own blank page, select **From a blank template** and click the **Next** button to bring up the canvas selector. Then specify the canvas size for the collage and the print orientation, and click the **Next** button.

5 Select Placeholder

The only type of placeholder in a collage is for text. You need to select and replace these placeholders. Select a placeholder you want to change.

6 Replace Placeholder

To replace text in a placeholder, first select it and then replace the text in the text box on the left.

7 Add Photos

You can add photos to the collage by clicking on **Add Photos** to bring up the **Media Manager**. Use the **Media Manager** to add photos to the collage.

8 Shuffle Photos

After you have added all the photos to the collage, you can automatically shuffle them into creative arrangements. To shuffle the photos, first select which of the following operations to perform on the photo when shuffling: **Offset, Rotation, Size,** and **Layer.** Then click **Shuffle Photos** to shuffle the photos around.

49

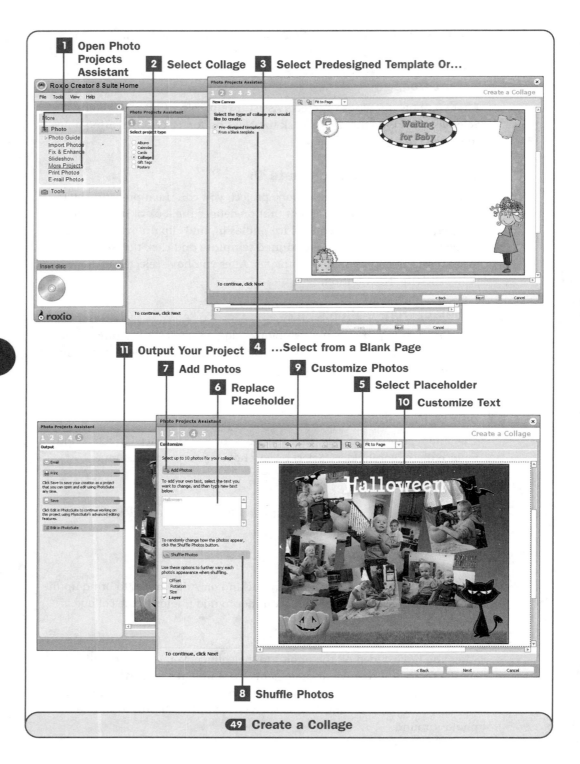

1 Open Photo Projects Assistant

2 Select Collage

3 Select Predesigned Template Or...

4 ...Select from a Blank Page

11 Output Your Project

7 Add Photos

9 Customize Photos

6 Replace Placeholder

5 Select Placeholder

10 Customize Text

8 Shuffle Photos

49 Create a Collage

9 Customize Photos

After the shuffled photos look good, you can edit them further in several ways to make the project more your own.

To customize a photo, first select it and then resize the photo by dragging the handles on the corners of the photo. After the photo is the size you want it, you can adjust the rotation by clicking on the rotate control attached to the top center handle of the photo box and dragging the mouse with the left mouse button pressed down.

If you need to adjust the colors of the photo or fix red eye, click on the **Pocket Editor** button. The **Pocket Editor** provides buttons to autofix, crop, fix red eye, change brightness and contrast, and adjust saturation. You can also open the **Pocket Editor** by double-clicking the photo you want to edit.

10 Customize Text

After you have replaced the text placeholders on the page, you can edit the text in several ways to make it look the way you want.

To customize text, first select it. After the text is selected, drag it to the location on the page where you want it to be. You can also rotate the text by clicking on the rotate control attached to the top center handle of the text box and dragging the mouse with the left mouse button pressed down.

After the text is in the position you want it to be in, you can use the menu at the top of the display to set the following attributes: color, font, bold/italic/underline, size, horizontal scaling, and alignment.

11 Output Your Project

After you have completely customized the project, click the **Next** button to bring out the **Output** menu. From the **Output** menu, you can email, print, save, or open the project in **PhotoSuite**.

▶ **NOTE**

When clicking the **Next** button to move to the final step of the project, you get a warning dialog if you have not replaced all of the placeholders in the project. If you did not deliberately leave a placeholder in the project, click the **Yes** button and go back and replace any placeholders that were missed.

To email your project, click on **Email** to bring up the **Email Assistant**. The **Email Assistant** allows you to specify your email client. It also allows you to specify whether to convert the project into compressed JPEG files, turn it into a WMV slideshow movie, or just send it as is with no conversion. For more information, see **124 Use Email Assistant to Email a Project** (on the Web).

▶ **TIP**

When emailing photos to friends, you should convert them to JPEG to conserve space. This speeds up how fast the email is sent and reduces the risk of the email being too big to send.

To print your project, click on **Print** to bring up the **Photo Print Assistant**. The **Photo Print Assistant** gives you the standard options of selecting the printer, setting the paper size and orientation, and specifying how many copies to print.

In addition to those options, the **Photo Print Assistant** provides a powerful layout manager that allows you to specify whether to print one photo per page or multiple photos per page. The **Multiple photos per page** option allows you to select one of many templates that automatically configure where the photos fit on the printed page. For example, you can print a sheet that has two 5"×7" photos or you can print a sheet that has one 5"×7" and two 3"×5" photos. You want to select the **Crop photo to fill the placeholder** and **Auto-rotate to fit the placeholders** buttons to make the pages of your project fit properly. For more information, see 🔢 **Use Print Assistant to Print a Project** (on the Web).

50

To save the project, click on **Save** to bring up the **Media Manager**. Use the **Media Manager** to find the folder or album where you want to place the project. You can create folders and albums by clicking on the **Create a New Folder** and **Create a New Album** buttons respectively. After you have selected the folder or album, select the file type for your project. The default file type is **.DMSP**, which is a **PhotoSuite** format. Then type in the name of the file and click the **Save** button. If you would like to save your project as an image, choose a different file format to save it in. You can then bring it up in other photo editors and print or make changes to it. However, it will no longer be dynamic, and you will not be able to change the placeholders.

To edit the project further in **PhotoSuite**, click on the **Edit in PhotoSuite** button. This brings up your project in **PhotoSuite**. For more information about editing the project in **PhotoSuite**, see the tasks in Chapter 6.

50	**Create a Gift Tag**	
✔ **BEFORE YOU BEGIN**		→ **SEE ALSO**
Chapter 5, "Importing Photos"		Chapter 6, "Editing Photos"

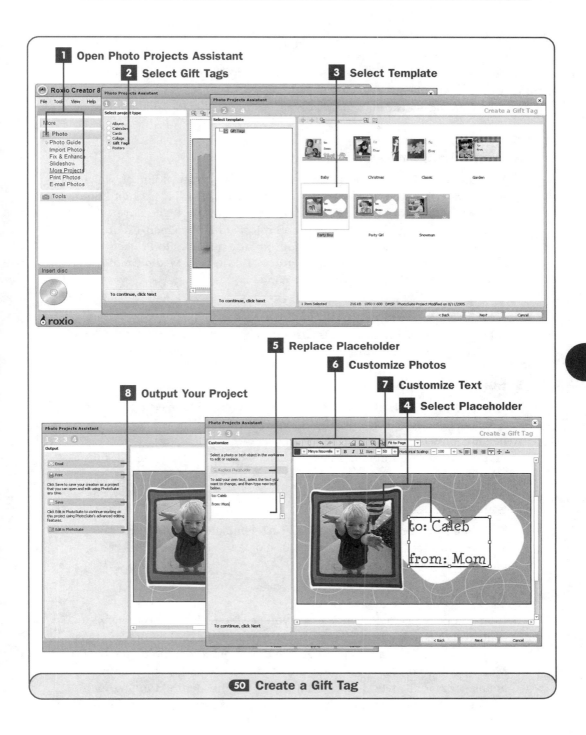

1 Open Photo Projects Assistant

2 Select Gift Tags

3 Select Template

5 Replace Placeholder

6 Customize Photos

7 Customize Text

8 Output Your Project

4 Select Placeholder

50

The **Gift Tag Assistant** is designed to help you create personalized gift tags using your own photos and text. These replace the expensive gift tags you have to order from a photo studio. An additional plus is that each tag can be personalized to the person to whom you are giving the gift. The following steps describe how to open the **Gift Tag Assistant**, add photos to it, customize the tag, and output your results.

1 Open Photo Projects Assistant

You can open **Photo Projects Assistant** in three ways, depending on which is easiest for you. If you have the Roxio **Home** page up, simply click on **Photo** and then select **More Projects** from the **Photo** submenu. If you have **PhotoSuite** open, you can select **Photo Projects** from the **Open/Create** options of the **Common** tool menu. You can also open **Photo Projects Assistant** by selecting it from the **Programs, Roxio Easy Media Creator 8, Photo** submenu of the **Start** menu in Windows.

2 Select Gift Tags

After you have the **Photo Projects Assistant** up, select **Gift Tags** from the **Select project type** menu and click the **Next** button to begin creating a new gift tag.

50

3 Select Template

After you have started a new gift tag project, you need to select a template. The template is a document that predefines the look of the gift tag. It includes preset text, photo locations, and some kind of clip art or other graphics in the background. After you have selected the template, click the **Next** button.

4 Select Placeholder

There are two types of placeholders on each template page: text and photos. You need to select and replace these placeholders one at a time. Select a placeholder you want to change.

5 Replace Placeholder

After you have selected a placeholder, you need to replace the content with content that is meaningful to you. You can replace the content of a photo by selecting it and then clicking on **Replace Placeholder** to bring up the **Media Manager**. You can also open the **Media Manager** to replace content by double-clicking the placeholder image. Then use the **Media Manager** to find a photo you want to use in the project. Your photo then becomes the place-holder. You can also replace the text. First select it and then replace the text in the text box on the left.

▶ **TIP**

Replace all the placeholders on a page before customizing the look and feel. Things look different when you add a new photo or new text, and you might spend more time recustomizing if you customize each item as it is added to the page.

6 Customize Photos

After you have replaced the photo placeholders on the page, you can edit them in several ways to make the project more your own.

To customize a photo, first select it. After the photo is selected, you are able to see the areas of the photo that are inside and outside of the mask. The portions of the photo that will be cropped out by the mask are grayed out in the display.

Resize the photo by dragging the handles on the corners of the photo. After the photo is the size you want it, you can drag it to a position where the proper space is visible inside the mask. If you need to, you can also rotate the picture by clicking on the rotate left and right buttons.

If you need to adjust the colors of the photo or fix red eye, click on the **Pocket Editor** button. You can also open the **Pocket Editor** by double-clicking the photo you want to edit. The **Pocket Editor** provides buttons to autofix, crop, fix red eye, change brightness and contrast, and adjust saturation.

50

7 Customize Text

After you have replaced the text placeholders on the page, you can edit the text in several ways to make it look the way you want.

To customize text, first select it. After the text is selected drag it to the location on the page where you want it to be. You can also rotate the text by clicking on the rotate control attached to the top center handle of the text box and dragging the mouse with the left mouse button pressed down.

After the text is in the position you want it to be in, you can use the menu at the top of the display to set the following attributes: color, font, bold/italic/underline, size, horizontal scaling, and alignment.

8 Output Your Project

After you have completely customized the project, click the **Next** button to bring up the **Output** menu. From the **Output** menu, you can email, print, save, or open the project in **PhotoSuite**.

► **NOTE**

When clicking the **Next** button to move to the final step of the project, you get a warning dialog if you have not replaced all of the placeholders in the project. If you did not deliberately leave a placeholder in the project, click the **Yes** button and go back and replace any placeholders that were missed.

To email your project, click on **Email** to bring up the **Email Assistant**. The **Email Assistant** allows you to specify your email client. It also allows you to specify whether to convert the project into compressed JPEG files, turn it into a WMV slideshow movie, or just send it as is with no conversion. For more information, see 🔢 **Use Email Assistant to Email a Project** (on the Web).

► **TIP**

When emailing photos to friends, you should convert them to JPEG to conserve space. This speeds up how fast the email is sent and reduces the risk of the email being too big to send.

To print your project, click on **Print** to bring up the **Photo Print Assistant**. The **Photo Print Assistant** gives you the standard options of selecting the printer, setting the paper size and orientation, and specifying how many copies to print.

In addition to those options, the **Photo Print Assistant** provides a powerful layout manager that allows you to specify whether to print one photo per page or multiple photos per page. The **Multiple photos per page** option allows you to select one of many templates that automatically configure where the photos fit on the printed page. For example, you can print a sheet that has two 5"×7" photos or you can print a sheet that has one 5"×7" and two 3"×5" photos. You want to select the **Crop photo to fill the placeholder** and **Auto-rotate to fit the placeholders** buttons to make the pages of your project fit properly. For more information, see 🔢 **Use Print Assistant to Print a Project** (on the Web).

To save the project, click on **Save** to bring up the **Media Manager**. Use the **Media Manager** to find the folder or album where you want to place the project. You can create folders and albums by clicking on the **Create a New Folder** and **Create a New Album** buttons respectively. After you have selected the folder or album, select the file type for your project. The default file type is **.DMSP**, which is a **PhotoSuite** format. Then type in the name of the file and click the **Save** button. If you would like to save your project as an image, choose a different file format to save it in. You can then bring it up in other photo editors and print or make changes to it. However, it will no longer be dynamic, and you will not be able to change the placeholders.

To edit the project further in **PhotoSuite**, click on the **Edit in PhotoSuite** button. This brings up your project in **PhotoSuite**. For more information about editing the project in **PhotoSuite**, see the tasks in Chapter 6.

---

51 **Create a Poster**

✔ BEFORE YOU BEGIN	→ SEE ALSO
Chapter 5, "Importing Photos"	Chapter 6, "Editing Photos"

The **Poster Assistant** is designed to help you put together creative posters using your photos. You might want to create individualized posters for a family member or friends. The **Poster Assistant** is also extremely useful for school projects. The following steps describe how to open the **Poster Assistant**, add photos to it, customize the poster, and output your results.

1 Open Photo Projects Assistant

You can open **Photo Projects Assistant** in three ways, depending on which is easiest for you. If you have the Roxio **Home** page up, simply click on **Photo** and then select **More Projects** from the **Photo** submenu. If you have **PhotoSuite** open, you can select **Photo Projects** from the **Open/Create** options of the **Common** tool menu. You can also open **Photo Projects Assistant** by selecting it from the **Programs, Roxio Easy Media Creator 8**, **Photo** submenu of the **Start** menu in Windows.

2 Select Posters

After you have the **Photo Projects Assistant** up, select **Posters** from the **Select project type** menu and click the **Next** button to begin creating a new poster.

3 Select Template

After you have started a new poster project, you need to select a template. The template is a document that predefines the look of the poster. It includes preset text, photo locations, and some kind of clip art or other graphics in the background. After you have selected the template, click the **Next** button.

4 Select Placeholder

There are two types of placeholders on each template page: text and photos. You need to select and replace these placeholders one at a time. Select a placeholder you want to change.

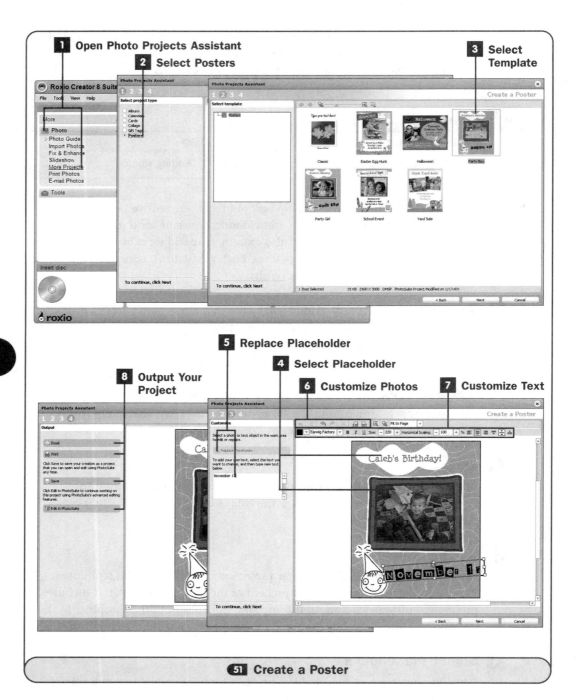

1 Open Photo Projects Assistant

2 Select Posters

3 Select Template

5 Replace Placeholder

4 Select Placeholder

8 Output Your Project

6 Customize Photos

7 Customize Text

51 Create a Poster

5 Replace Placeholder

After you have selected a placeholder, you need to replace the content with content that is meaningful to you. You can replace the content of a photo by selecting it and then clicking on **Replace Placeholder** to bring up the **Media Manager**. You can also open the **Media Manager** to replace content by double-clicking the placeholder image. Then use the **Media Manager** to find a photo you want to use in the project. Your photo then becomes the placeholder. You can also replace the text. First select it and then replace the text in the text box on the left.

▶ **TIP**

Replace all the placeholders on a page before customizing the look and feel. Things look different when you add a new photo or new text, and you might spend more time recustomizing if you customize each item as it is added to the page.

6 Customize Photos

After you have replaced the photo placeholders on the page, you can edit them in several ways to make the project more your own.

To customize a photo, first select it. After the photo is selected, you are able to see the areas of the photo that are inside and outside of the mask. The portions of the photo that will be cropped out by the mask are grayed out in the display.

Resize the photo by dragging the handles on the corners of the photo. After the photo is the size you want it, you can drag it to a position where the proper space is visible inside the mask. If you need to, you can also rotate the picture by clicking on the rotate left and right buttons.

If you need to adjust the colors of the photo or fix red eye, click on the **Pocket Editor** button. You can also open the **Pocket Editor** by double-clicking the photo you want to edit. The **Pocket Editor** provides buttons to autofix, crop, fix red eye, change brightness and contrast, and adjust saturation.

7 Customize Text

After you have replaced the text placeholders on the page, you can edit the text in several ways to make it look the way you want.

To customize text, first select it. After the text is selected, drag it to the location on the page where you want it to be. You can also rotate the text by clicking on the rotate control attached to the top center handle of the text box and dragging the mouse with the left mouse button pressed down.

51

After the text is in the position you want it to be in, you can use the menu at the top of the display to set the following attributes: color, font, bold/italic/underline, size, horizontal scaling, and alignment.

8 Output Your Project

After you have completely customized the project, click the **Next** button to bring up the **Output** menu. From the **Output** menu, you can email, print, save, or open the project in **PhotoSuite**.

▶ **NOTE**

When clicking the **Next** button to move to the final step of the project, you get a warning dialog if you have not replaced all of the placeholders in the project. If you did not deliberately leave a placeholder in the project, click the **Yes** button and go back and replace any placeholders that were missed.

To email your project, click on **Email** to bring up the **Email Assistant**. The **Email Assistant** allows you to specify your email client. It also allows you to specify whether to convert the project into compressed JPEG files, turn it into a WMV slideshow movie, or just send it as is with no conversion. For more information, see **124** **Use Email Assistant to Email a Project** (on the Web).

51

▶ **TIP**

When emailing photos to friends, you should convert them to JPEG to conserve space. This speeds up how fast the email is sent and reduces the risk of the email being too big to send.

To print your project, click on **Print** to bring up the **Photo Print Assistant**. The **Photo Print Assistant** gives you the standard options of selecting the printer, setting the paper size and orientation, and specifying how many copies to print.

In addition to those options, the **Photo Print Assistant** provides a powerful layout manager that allows you to specify whether to print one photo per page or multiple photos per page. The **Multiple photos per page** option allows you to select one of many templates that automatically configure where the photos fit on the printed page. For example, you can print a sheet that has two 5"×7" photos or you can print a sheet that has one 5"×7" and two 3"×5" photos. You want to select the **Crop photo to fill the placeholder** and **Auto-rotate to fit the placeholders** buttons to make the pages of your project fit properly. For more information, see **123** **Use Print Assistant to Print a Project** (on the Web).

To save the project, click on **Save** to bring up the **Media Manager**. Use the **Media Manager** to find the folder or album where you want to place the project. You can create folders and albums by clicking on the **Create a New Folder** and **Create a New Album** buttons respectively. After you have selected the folder or album, select the file type for your project. The default file type is **.DMSP**, which is a **PhotoSuite** format. Then type in the name of the file and click the **Save** button. If you would like to save your project as an image, choose a different file format to save it in. You can then bring it up in other photo editors and print or make changes to it. However, it will no longer be dynamic, and you will not be able to change the placeholders.

To edit the project further in **PhotoSuite**, click on the **Edit in PhotoSuite** button. This brings up your project in **PhotoSuite**. For more information about editing the project in **PhotoSuite**, see the tasks in Chapter 6.

---

52 Create a Panorama

✔ **BEFORE YOU BEGIN**

Chapter 5, "Importing Photos"

The **Panorama Assistant** is designed to help you put together several photos taken at different angles from the same position. For example, you might want to create panoramic images of natural landscapes to remember the entire view. To do this, first take a series of photos from one spot turning slightly left or right between each photo, and then use the following steps to open the **Poster Assistant**, add your photos to it, join the photos into a single panoramic image, and output your results.

1 Open Panorama Assistant

You can open **Panorama Assistant** in two ways, depending on which is easiest for you. If you have the Roxio **Home** page up, simply click on **Home**, select **Applications**, and then select **Create Panoramas** from the submenu. You can also open **Panorama Assistant** by selecting **Create Panoramas** from the **Programs, Roxio Easy Media Creator 8, Photo** submenu of the **Start** menu in Windows.

2 Add Photos

You can add photos to the **Panorama Assistant** project by clicking on **Add Photos** to bring up the **Media Manager**. Use the **Media Manager** to add photos. After all the photos have been added, click the **Next** button to adjust the panoramic image.

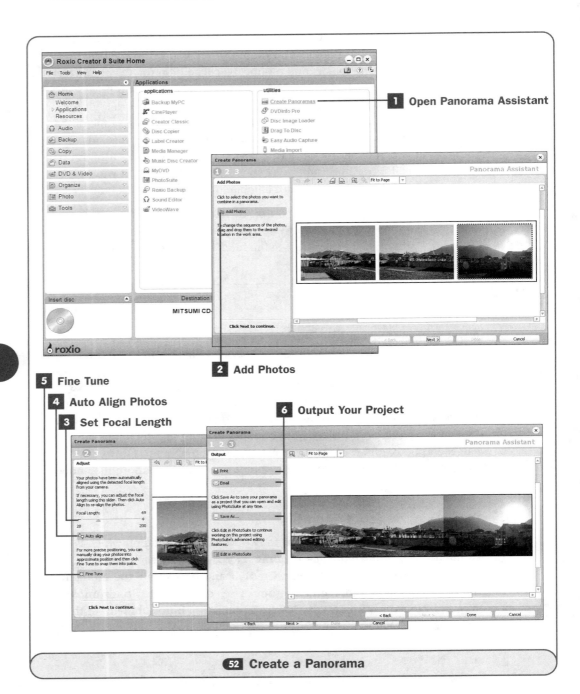

1 Open Panorama Assistant

2 Add Photos

5 Fine Tune

4 Auto Align Photos

6 Output Your Project

3 Set Focal Length

52 Create a Panorama

3 Set Focal Length

After you have added the photos to the panorama, they are initially joined into a panoramic image. This image might need to be adjusted. First set the focal length to change how the edges of the picture are adjusted for the distance from which the photo was taken. For instance, one of these photos might have a different distance from the grass line to the top of the fence. By adjusting the focal length, the picture is warped slightly so these two lines match up.

4 Auto Align Photos

After you have set the focal length, click the **Auto align** button to re-align the photos into a panoramic image.

5 Fine Tune

If the panoramic image is still not exactly the way you want it, use the mouse to drag the images as close to the correct position as you can. Then click the **Fine Tune** button to snap the photos into place.

6 Output Your Project

52

After you have the image the way you want it, click the **Next** button to bring up the **Output** menu. From the **Output** menu, you can email, print, save, or open the project in **PhotoSuite**.

To email your project, click on **Email** to bring up the **Email Assistant**. The **Email Assistant** allows you to specify your email client. It also allows you to specify whether to convert the project into compressed JPEG files, turn it into a WMV slideshow movie, or just send it as is with no conversion. For more information, see **124 Use Email Assistant to Email a Project** (on the Web).

► **TIP**

When emailing photos to friends, you should convert them to JPEG to conserve space. This speeds up how fast the email is sent and reduces the risk of the email being too big to send.

To print your project, click on **Print** to bring up the **Photo Print Assistant**. The **Photo Print Assistant** gives you the standard options of selecting the printer, setting the paper size and orientation, and specifying how many copies to print.

In addition to those options, the **Photo Print Assistant** provides a powerful layout manager that allows you to specify whether to print one photo per page or multiple photos per page. The **Multiple photos per page** option allows you to select one of many templates that automatically configure where the photos fit on the printed page. For example, you can print a sheet that has two 5"×7" photos or you can print a sheet that has one 5"×7" and two 3"×5" photos. You want to select the **Crop photo to fill the placeholder** and **Auto-rotate to fit the placeholders** buttons to make the pages of your project fit properly. For more information, see 🔢 **Use Print Assistant to Print a Project** (on the Web).

To save the project, click on **Save** to bring up the **Media Manager**. Use the **Media Manager** to find the folder or album where you want to place the project. You can create folders and albums by clicking on the **Create a New Folder** and **Create a New Album** buttons respectively. After you have select-ed the folder or album, select the file type for your project. You can choose from several image file types. Then type in the name of the file and click the **Save** button.

To edit the project further in **PhotoSuite**, click on the **Edit in PhotoSuite** but-ton. This brings up your project in **PhotoSuite**. For more information about editing the project in **PhotoSuite**, see the tasks in Chapter 6.

52

8

Creating Slideshows

IN THIS CHAPTER:

So what to do with all those photos you have painstakingly edited and filed neatly away? It's not often that the family gathers around the computer to see the latest photos.

Roxio Easy Media Creator 8 has not one but two applications that enable you to create spectacular *slideshows* out of your photos and save them as a video file for later use or burn them immediately to a DVD (complete with a menu) so you can enjoy your photos on your own TV or share them with your family and friends.

Guess you won't just be sending out a Christmas newsletter this year, will you?

▶ KEY TERM

Slideshow—A sequence of pictures that are added together to create a video.

53	Use Slideshow Assistant to Create a Slideshow

✔ BEFORE YOU BEGIN	→ SEE ALSO
Chapter 5, "Importing Photos"	64 Export a Slideshow to a Video File
	65 Burn a Slideshow to a Disc

53

Like many of the applications within Easy Media Creator, **Slideshow Assistant** is a step-by-step wizard that allows you to create a slideshow quickly and easily even if you have never done it before. In just a few easy steps you can take a group of photos of your choosing, put them in order, add colorful titles, create transitions between them, put them to music, and burn them to a disc to watch at any time.

Of course, **Slideshow Assistant** is easy because it is very simplified. It simply doesn't have the editing capabilities of **VideoWave**, Easy Media Creator's video production software. The application you use really depends on your abilities and needs. If you have never tried creating a slideshow or producing a video, please start here. **Slideshow Assistant** can give you a very good sampling of the slideshow capabilities of **VideoWave**.

You might just decide that **Slideshow Assistant** is more than adequate for your needs. After all, special effects can be fun, but if you just want to showcase your photos, there is little reason to use special effects in a slideshow.

Whatever your reason, there is no disputing that **Slideshow Assistant** is fun and easy to use, so enjoy!

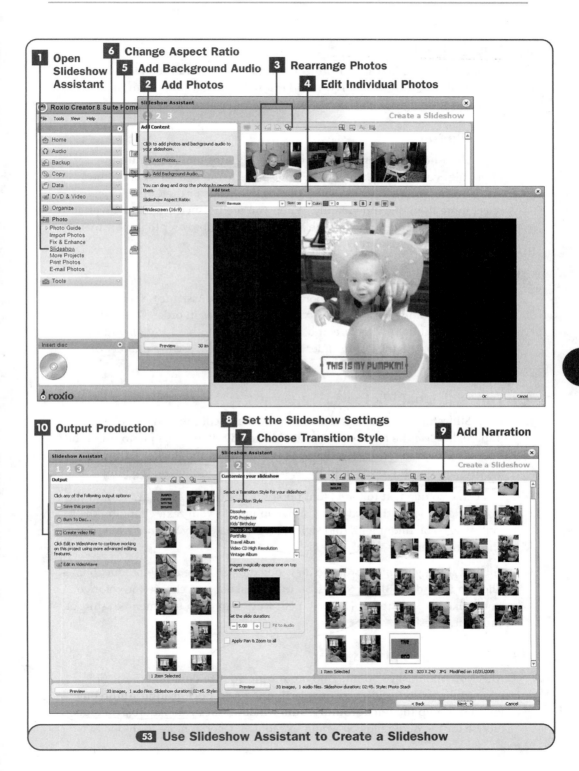

1 Open Slideshow Assistant

From the Easy Media Creator project pane, choose the **Photo** menu and select **Slideshow**, or select **Create Slideshow** from the **Photo** menu that appears to the right. Either choice brings up **Slideshow Assistant**.

2 Add Photos

After **Slideshow Assistant** is open, click **Add Photos** and browse for the photo files you would like to add to your project. You can select more than one by using the **Shift** key to select photos in a series or the **Control** key to select more than one individually. When you are finished selecting the photos you want, click **Add Photos** in the **Media Manager** browser to import them into **Slideshow Assistant**.

3 Rearrange Photos

After your photos have been imported in **Slideshow Assistant**, something you most certainly want to do is to place your photos in order. This is done easily by selecting any picture and dragging it to another location within the photo line-up. Use the **Zoom** slider to increase or decrease the number of photos in your view.

4 Edit Individual Photos

From **Slideshow Assistant** you can do some basic editing of the photos you imported. Select the picture you would like to edit. Rotate the photo using the **Rotate** icons in the taskbar or bring the photo up in the **Pocket Editor** by clicking on the **Preview** icon in the taskbar or double-clicking the photo.

You can also add text to individual photos. Click on the **Add Text** icon in the taskbar to bring up the text editor. You can type in your text, changing the font, size, color, alignment, and style. Place it wherever you want inside the photo and stretch or shrink it to fit.

The last thing you might want to do is add a blank slide to the production. Click on the **Add a Blank Slide** icon in the taskbar and choose the color you would like the slide to be. This is a great way to create a title menu to start or end your slideshow.

5 Add Background Audio

After you are finished editing and organizing your photos, add music or other audio to your slideshow by selecting the **Add Background Audio** button to bring up the **Background Audio** window. Click **Add Audio Track** and browse for the audio file you would like to add. Choose more than one by

53

holding down the **Control** key as you select the files. After you have selected your tracks, click **Add Audio** to go back to the **Background Audio** window.

From the **Background Audio** window, you have the option to loop the tracks if they are too short or to crossfade more than one track. When you are finished setting your options, click **OK.**

6 Change Aspect Ratio

Change the *aspect ratio* of your slideshow to fit your TV. Standard TVs are 4:3; widescreen TVs are 16:9.

▶ **KEY TERM**

Aspect ratio—The width to height ratio to which a video is formatted.

When you have finished making changes to your project, click **Next** to move on to the **Customize your slideshow** screen.

▶ **TIP**

You can preview your slideshow at any time by clicking on the **Preview** button in the **Slideshow Assistant**.

7 Choose Transition Style

From the **Customize your slideshow** screen in **Slideshow Assistant**, you can choose one of several *transition* styles. Click on each to see a short description and to preview an example. Select the transition style you like for your slideshow.

▶ **KEY TERM**

Transition—An effect that defines the change from one video scene to the next.

8 Set the Slideshow Settings

After you have chosen your transition style, you can set the length to play each photo in the slide show, fit the slideshow to audio, and apply the *Pan & Zoom* feature.

▶ **KEY TERM**

Pan & Zoom—An effect that sets a new center point in an image, zooms into the image, or both.

The **Pan & Zoom** feature creates movement within each frame of the slideshow by zooming in or out of the photo and moving the photo back and forth or up and down. If you check the box labeled **Apply Pan & Zoom to all**, **Slideshow Assistant** automatically randomizes a different pan and zoom setting for each photo.

You can manually set what kind of pan and zoom you would like for each picture by selecting that picture and clicking on the **Pan & Zoom settings** icon in the taskbar. This brings up the **Pan & Zoom Editor** where you can use a preset pan-and-zoom setting, manually set it, or set advanced settings.

9 Add Narration

After the settings for your slideshow are in place, you might want to narrate it. Click on the **Add Narration** icon in the taskbar to bring up the **Add Narration Wizard**. Select the **Audio Settings** button to check your input device and set the destination folder.

Rewind the slideshow to the point you would like to start narrating and click **Record**. You are given a three-second countdown, and then the slideshow starts, along with the recording. As the slideshow runs, record your narration.

When you are finished, click **Stop**. You can preview the narration along with the slideshow. When you are satisfied with your narration, click the **Done** button to exit the **Add Narration Wizard**.

10 Output Production

After you are satisfied with all of your settings and have narrated your slideshow, you are ready to save it to a file or burn it to a disc. Click **Next** to go to the **Output** window in **Slideshow Assistant**.

In the **Output** menu you have four options: **Save this project**, **Burn To Disc**, **Create video file**, and **Edit in VideoWave**.

Saving the project does not complete the slideshow; it simply saves the project you are working on so you can make changes later. Your project is saved as a **.DMSS file**, which is the file extension for an Easy Media Creator production file.

You can burn your slideshow directly to disc by clicking on the **Burn To Disc** menu option. This brings up **MyDVD Express**. Please see **65** **Burn a Slideshow to a Disc** for step-by-step instructions.

You can also export your slideshow to a video file by clicking on the **Create video file** button. Please see **64** **Export a Slideshow to a Video File** for step-by-step instructions.

53

If you would like to make further changes to your slideshow, you can edit it in **VideoWave**. **VideoWave** has many advanced editing features not found in **Slideshow Assistant**. Click on the **Edit in VideoWave** button to export your project into **VideoWave**.

54 **Add Photos to a Slideshow**	
✔ **BEFORE YOU BEGIN**	→ **SEE ALSO**
72 About the VideoWave Interface	Chapter 10, "Editing Video"

The following tasks take you step-by-step through creating a slideshow in **VideoWave**. Although **VideoWave** is a video-editing application, it can be used to create a slideshow with photos as well. The first step to creating your slideshow is to launch **VideoWave** and import your photos into a new project.

1 Open VideoWave

From the Easy Media Creator **project** pane, select **DVD & Video** to open up the menu. From the **DVD & Video** menu, select **Edit Video**. This launches **VideoWave**.

54

2 Create New Production

When **VideoWave** has launched, you are given the option to create a new production or edit an existing one. Select **Create a new production** and set your aspect ratio. Change the aspect ratio of your slideshow to fit your TV. Standard TVs are 4:3; widescreen TVs are 16:9. Click **OK**.

3 Select Add Photo/Video

After you are inside **VideoWave**, select **Add Photo/Video** to bring up the **Insert photos/videos** window.

4 Browse for Photos

From the **Insert photos/videos** window, you can browse for your albums or folders to find the pictures to create a slideshow. You can select more than one by pressing down the **Shift** key and clicking to select photos in a series or the **Control** key to select more than one individually.

5 Click Open

When you are finished selecting the photos you want, click **Open** to import them into **VideoWave**.

54

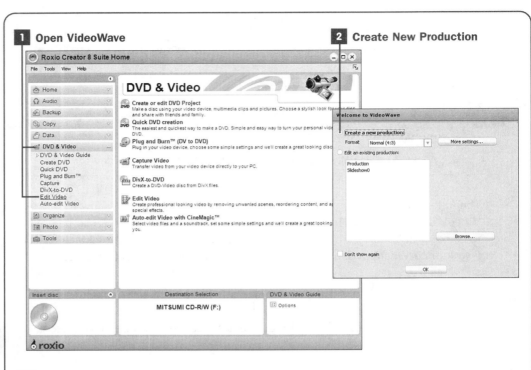

1 Open VideoWave

2 Create New Production

3 Select Add Photo/Video

4 Browse for Photos

5 Click Open

54 Add Photos to a Slideshow

55 Edit and Sort Photos for a Slideshow

✔ BEFORE YOU BEGIN	→ SEE ALSO
54 Add Photos to a Slideshow **72** About the VideoWave Interface	Chapter 6, "Editing Photos" Chapter 10, "Editing Video"

After you have imported your photos into **VideoWave**, you might want to edit some of them individually. You are certainly going to want to sort them and place them in the order you would like them to be in your slideshow. You can rotate your photos, do simple edits, and rearrange the order in **VideoWave**.

1 Select the Photo Panel

Inside **VideoWave**, select the photo you would like to edit by clicking on it inside the *storyline* or *timeline*. The photo is brought up in the **Preview** window so you can see it better.

▶ **KEY TERMS**

Storyline—A view of a video production that only shows the video track. It is defined by a storyboard panel for each scene.

Timeline—A view of a video production that shows all the tracks at once. It is defined by a continuous video line that is clearly marked by time increments.

2 Rotate the Photo

To quickly rotate your photo, click on the **90° rotation** button in the taskbar. If your photo needs rotated 180°, click the button again.

3 Edit the Photo

With your photo selected, click on the **Edit Photo** icon in the taskbar to bring up the **Pocket Editor**. From the **Pocket Editor** you can make basic changes to your photo such as performing an autofix, cropping your photo, fixing red eye, changing the brightness/contrast, color correcting, or rotating your photo. If you would like help using the **Pocket Editor**, refer to Chapter 6, "Editing Photos."

When you have finished editing your photo, close the **Pocket Editor** by clicking **OK**.

55

1 Select the Photo Panel

2 Rotate the Photo

3 Edit the Photo

3 Edit the Photo

4 Adjust the Duration of the Photo Within the Slideshow

5 Drag and Drop the Photo

55

4 Adjust the Duration of the Photo Within the Slideshow

5 Drag and Drop the Photo

55 Edit and Sort Photos for a Slideshow

4 Adjust the Duration of the Photo Within the Slideshow

With your photo selected, click on the **Adjust Duration** icon in the **Production Editor** taskbar. This brings up the **Adjust Duration** window. You can adjust the duration of the selected photo, or apply the adjusted duration to all the still images in the production by checking the appropriate box. Set the duration in seconds and click **OK**.

5 Drag and Drop the Photo

To sort your photos, you might find it easier to use the **Storyline** view. Click on the **Storyline** icon in the **Timeline** menu. This brings up a storyboard view, showcasing each of your photos individually. Expand the **Storyline** window by dragging the top of it as far as it will go, shrinking the **Preview** window.

When you have a good view of your photos, drag and drop them into the order you would like to have them in the slideshow. After you are finished, reduce the **Storyline** window back to its original position.

▶ TIP

If you need to rearrange multiple photos for your slideshow, you should start your project in **Slideshow Assistant**. It is much easier to rearrange your photos from there.

56

56 Add a Blank Slide to a Slideshow	
✔ **BEFORE YOU BEGIN**	→ **SEE ALSO**
54 Add Photos to a Slideshow	Chapter 10, "Editing Video"

You can add a blank slide anywhere in your slideshow to add a menu or a break. Your blank slide can be any color and you can add text, a special effect, or an overlay to it, just as if it were a photo slide.

1 Select Location

Before you add a blank slide to your slideshow, select the photo nearest the location that you would like it to be in. If you do not select a photo, the slide is added to the end of the production.

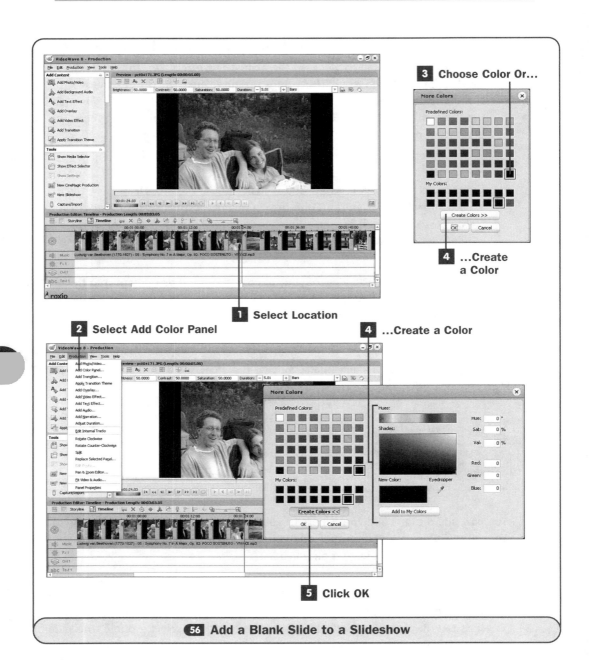

3 Choose Color Or...

4 ...Create a Color

1 Select Location

2 Select Add Color Panel

4 ...Create a Color

5 Click OK

56 Add a Blank Slide to a Slideshow

2 Select Add Color Panel

After you have selected a location, select **Add Color Panel** from the
Production drop-down menu at the top of the screen. This brings up the
More Colors window.

3 **Choose Color Or...**

From the **More Colors** window, choose a color for your blank slide.

4 **...Create a Color**

If you don't see a color you like, click on the **Create Colors** button to expand the window and choose from an infinite number of color choices. You can also use the dropper to select any color showing on your computer screen.

5 **Click OK**

When you have selected the color for your blank slide, click **OK**. The blank slide is inserted after the photo you have selected. From there you can treat it just as any other slide, adding transitions, text, and effects.

---

57 **Add Transitions or a Transition Theme to a Slideshow**

✔ BEFORE YOU BEGIN	→ SEE ALSO
54 Add Photos to a Slideshow	Chapter 10, "Editing Video"

57

A *transition* is how one photo turns into the next within your slideshow. If you do not add transitions, your photos are simply immediately replaced by the next photo in the slideshow. A fade transition darkens the first photo as it lightens the next. A wipe is like using an eraser on a chalkboard to take away the first photo and replace it with the next. You get the idea.

You can either preview the transitions and place them one at a time, or you can apply a transition theme, which randomly places similar transitions throughout your production.

1 **Click Apply Transition Theme Or...**

If you would like to apply a transition theme to your slideshow, click on the **Apply Transition Theme** button in the **tasks** pane. This brings up a theme list. The theme names are descriptive, so although there are no previews, you can get an idea of what each will be like. For example, if you were to select **Wipes**, different transitions would be placed throughout your production, but they would all have one thing in common—the first picture would be wiped out and replaced by the second picture.

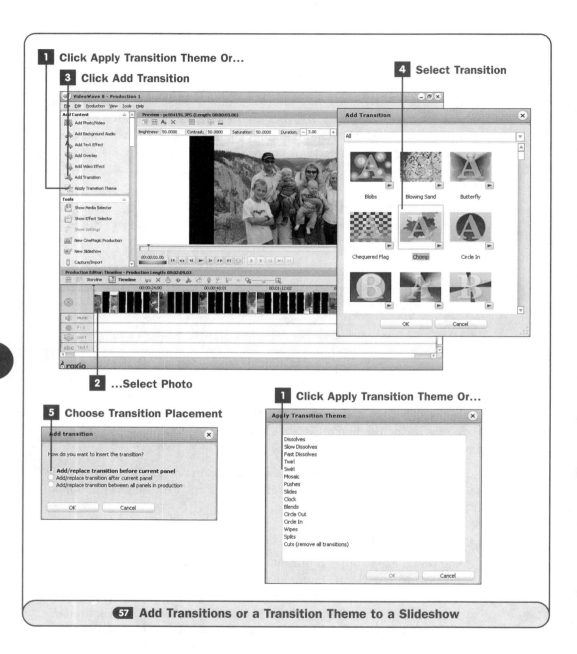

1 Click Apply Transition Theme Or...

3 Click Add Transition

4 Select Transition

2 ...Select Photo

5 Choose Transition Placement

1 Click Apply Transition Theme Or...

57 Add Transitions or a Transition Theme to a Slideshow

▶ **NOTE**

When choosing a transition theme, not all of them consist of more than one transition. The **Circle in** option, for instance, is only one transition, a closing circle that replaces the first picture (inside the circle) with the second picture (outside the circle). If you want more than one transition in your production, choose a theme that is plural, such as **Dissolves** or **Pushes**.

Select a theme and click **OK**. This randomly places several transitions, all belonging to the theme you selected throughout the production. You can always change themes and remove the first theme entirely from the project, and you can also replace individual transitions after you have applied a theme if you have a specific transition you'd like to see in a particular spot.

2 ...Select Photo

Inside **VideoWave**, select the photo that you would like to add a transition to by clicking on it inside the **Storyline** or **Timeline**.

3 Click Add Transition

Click on the **Add Transition** button in the **tasks** pane. This brings up the **Add Transition** window.

4 Select Transition

From the drop-down menu you can select a transition style to narrow your choices. Preview each transition by clicking on the **Play** icon in the corner of each transition. When you have selected the transition you want, click **OK**.

5 Choose Transition Placement

After having clicked **OK**, you are prompted to indicate where you would like the transition to be placed in regard to your photo or inside the production. Click on your desired option and click **OK**.

58

58 Add an Audio Track to a Slideshow	
✔ **BEFORE YOU BEGIN**	→ **SEE ALSO**
54 Add Photos to a Slideshow	Chapter 2, "Importing Audio" Chapter 3, "Editing Audio" Chapter 10, "Editing Video"

To spice up your slideshow, you'll want to add audio to it. You can add any audio file on your computer or you can rip one from a CD. The great thing about importing into your slideshow in **VideoWave** instead of using **Slideshow Assistant** is that you can do some basic editing and place it anywhere inside your production.

1 Select Timeline View

The first thing you are going to want to do when adding audio is make sure your production is in the **Timeline** view. This allows you to see your audio track and edit it more easily. Select the **Timeline** icon from the **Production Editor** taskbar to change the view.

2 Select Add Background Audio

Select **Add Background Audio** from the **tasks** pane to bring up **Media Manager**.

3 Browse for Audio File

From **Media Manager**, you can browse your albums or folders to find audio files to add to your slideshow. You can select more than one by holding down the **Control** key and clicking on files. When you are done selecting your audio, click **OK**.

4 Choose Where to Insert Track

After you have selected your audio, you are asked which track you would like to place it on, the music track or the sound effect track. There is essentially no difference between the two except for their names. Click on the option you would prefer and click **OK**.

58

▶ NOTE

When your audio is dropped into your project, it only lasts as long as your slideshow, no matter how long the audio track is. You can only stretch your audio out if you add more to the video track.

▶ TIP

You can make your slideshow conform to the length of your audio track by selecting **Fit Video & Audio** from the **Production** pull-down menu. This shortens or lengthens each photo (including blank slides) in your production so it is the same length as the audio you have chosen. This only works if your audio and video are relatively close to the same length in the first place.

5 Edit Audio

You can edit your audio in several ways within **VideoWave**. To start, select the audio track and click on the **Edit** icon in the **Preview** taskbar. This brings up the **Audio Trimmer**. Here you can set the start and end points for your audio and loop the audio track. If you have unwanted silence or your audio is too long for your slideshow, this is the place to trim it down to size by clipping off the beginning or the end. When you are finished making your edits, click **OK** to return to **VideoWave**.

2 Select Add Background Audio

3 Browse for Audio File

4 Choose Where to Insert Track

1 Select Timeline View

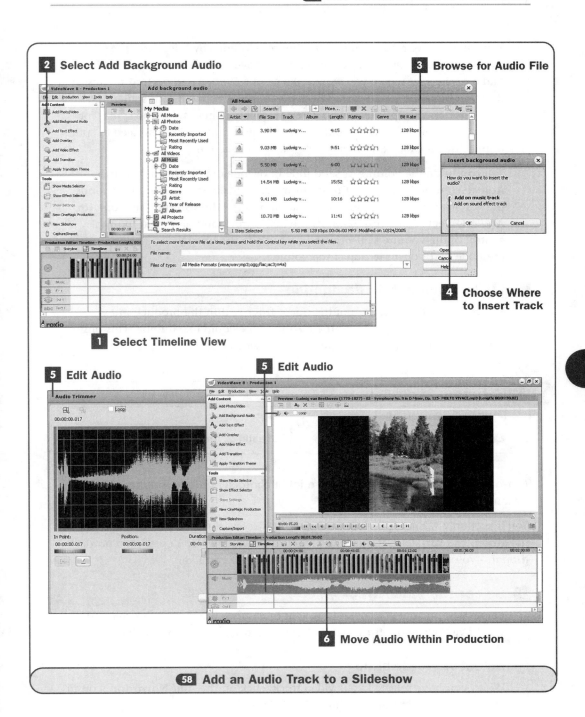

5 Edit Audio

5 Edit Audio

6 Move Audio Within Production

58

You can split your audio into two or more selections by selecting the **Split** icon from the **Production Editor** taskbar. Move the selection line over the audio to the spot where you would like it split. It is very important to be sure that you have the audio track selected; otherwise you will split something else. Click on the **Split** icon. You can now delete either one of the splits. For instance; if you want to edit out the middle of a music clip, you need to split it into three sections and then delete the center section.

You can mute the volume or set a fade in or fade out by clicking on the **Adjust Volume** icon in the **Production Editor** taskbar. You can also change the volume settings manually by clicking on the **Edit Volume Envelope for Audio Objects** icon. This expands the audio track and gives you manual control of the volume indicator. Add a node to the line by clicking on it. Drag the node up or down to adjust the volume.

6 Move Audio Within Production

You can adjust the location of the audio track within the production by selecting it and dragging it to the location you would like it to be. This only works if the audio track is shorter than the video track.

59

59 Narrate a Slideshow

✔ BEFORE YOU BEGIN	→ SEE ALSO
54 Add Photos to a Slideshow	Chapter 2, "Importing Audio"

Narrating a slideshow can really add a lot of character and personality to it. It certainly makes it more fun to watch.

You'll probably want to preview your slideshow a few times as you practice your narration. You can do that inside the **Narration** window. Don't work too hard, though—you can narrate the slideshow in sections if you like.

1 Select the Video Track

Before you narrate your slideshow, you must have the video track selected. If you have your audio track selected, the **Narrate** button is not active.

2 Select Add Narration

When you have selected your video track, click on the **Add Narration** icon in the taskbar to bring up the **Narration Wizard**.

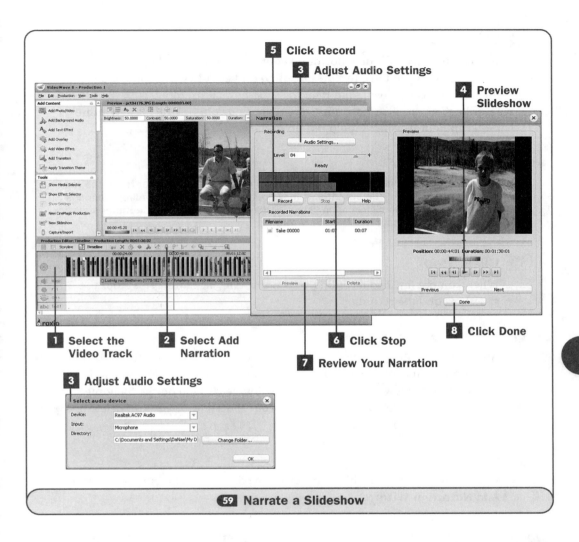

5 **Click Record**

3 **Adjust Audio Settings**

4 **Preview Slideshow**

1 **Select the Video Track**

2 **Select Add Narration**

3 **Adjust Audio Settings**

6 **Click Stop**

7 **Review Your Narration**

8 **Click Done**

59 Narrate a Slideshow

3 Adjust Audio Settings

When the **Narration Wizard** has launched, select the **Audio Settings** button to check your input devices and set the destination folder. Your input devices probably do not need to be changed; they are a microphone and your sound card. You want to double-check the directory that the audio is being stored in. Choose a directory that is easy to remember so you can find your audio later. When you are finished, click **OK**.

4 Preview Slideshow

After your audio settings are correct, use the **playback controls** to preview your slideshow. Practice narrating it while it plays.

5 Click Record

When you are comfortable narrating your slideshow, rewind the slideshow to the point you would like to start narrating and click **Record**. You are given a three-second countdown, and then the slideshow starts, along with the recording. As the slideshow runs, record your narration. Watch the **volume meter indicators**; they should rise up and down with your voice.

▶ TIP

As you narrate your production, the volume meter indicators should never reach the red bands at the upper end of the indicator. If they do, this means your recording volume is too high and there will be distortion in your recording. Set the level so the meter stays in the yellow range throughout most of the recording.

6 Click Stop

When you are finished recording your narration, click **Stop**. This stops the slideshow and the recording.

7 Review Your Narration

After you have stopped the recording, a file appears in the list of recorded narrations. You can review your narration by selecting the filename and clicking the **Preview** button or by simply double-clicking on the filename. You can continue to narrate sections of your slideshow or you can delete a narration and try it again.

8 Click Done

When you are satisfied with your narration, click the **Done** button to exit the **Add Narration Wizard**.

60 Add Text to a Slideshow	
✔ BEFORE YOU BEGIN	→ SEE ALSO
54 Add Photos to a Slideshow	Chapter 6, "Editing Photos" Chapter 10, "Editing Video"

You can add text to your slideshow by adding it to the photos themselves or by placing it on its own track. What you can do with the text largely depends on where you have placed it.

Placed inside the frame, the text is limited to that frame. It appears with the frame and disappears as the frame disappears. It is also subject to the transitions on either side of the frame. This is a good way to add a caption to individual photos.

If you place the text on its own track, you have a lot more control of it. You can stretch or shrink it to any length of time you want, add separate motion, and place it anywhere inside your production.

1 Add Text Effect to a Photo Or...

To add a text effect to a photo, you must first select the photo to which you would like to add text. After you have the photo selected, select **Add Text Effect** from the **Add Content** menu. The **Add Text Effect** window comes up, giving you quite a few text styles from which to choose. Remember that you can edit these in any way you choose later. Choose the style you like and click **OK**. You are then given the option to add your text to the production or to place it on the internal track of the selected panel. Choose to place the text on the internal track of the selected panel. This adds it to the photo itself, making it part of the panel.

▶ TIP

You might find it easier to add text to your photos individually before importing them into a slideshow. Of course, this has its drawbacks, too, because you won't have the entire frame to work with unless you create it ahead of time by changing the dimensions of the canvas to 4:3 or 16:9.

2 ...Add Text Effect to a Text Track

When you add text to its own track within your slideshow, it appears on the text track. You might not be able to see this track unless you stretch your **Production Editor** window up a little bit. Stretch it until you see the track labeled **Text 1**.

You can add text to your slideshow production in three ways:

- Simply click on the **Add Text** icon in the **Preview** taskbar. This immediately drops a text object into the spot you have currently selected in your production.

- Select **Add Text Effect** from the **tasks** pane. The **Add Text Effect** window comes up, giving you quite a few text styles from which to choose. Remember that you can edit these in any way you choose later. Choose the style you like and click **OK**. You are then given the option to add your text to the production or to place it on the internal track of the selected panel. Select **Add Text to the Production**, dropping it into the text track.

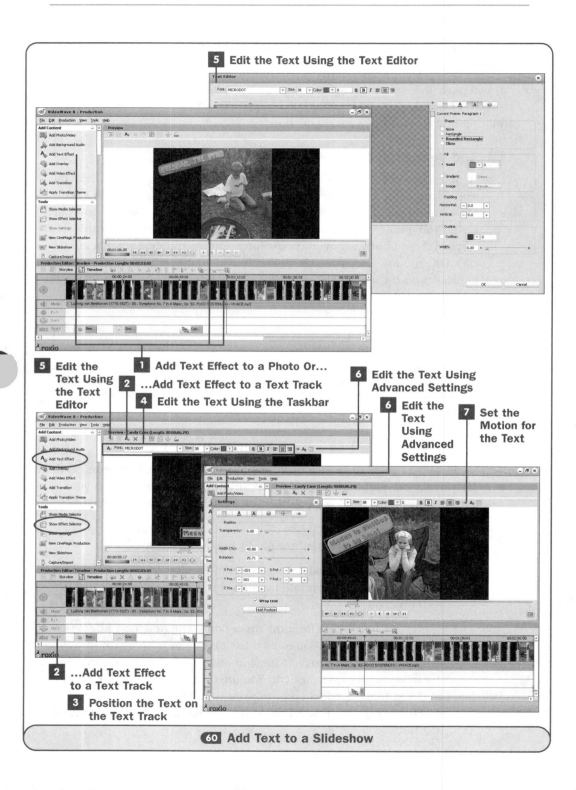

5 Edit the Text Using the Text Editor

5 Edit the Text Using the Text Editor

1 Add Text Effect to a Photo Or...

2 ...Add Text Effect to a Text Track

4 Edit the Text Using the Taskbar

6 Edit the Text Using Advanced Settings

6 Edit the Text Using Advanced Settings

7 Set the Motion for the Text

2 ...Add Text Effect to a Text Track

3 Position the Text on the Text Track

60 Add Text to a Slideshow

- Select the **Show Effect Selector** in the **tasks** pane to bring up the **Effect Selector** window. Click on the **Text** tab in the top of the **Effect Selector** to bring up the text styles. Choose a style and drag and drop it into the desired location on the **Text 1** track.

3 Position the Text on the Text Track

If you have placed your text on its own track, you probably want to place it more precisely where you want it. You can select it and move it anywhere along the text track. By clicking and dragging on the edges you can shrink or stretch it to the desired length. You can also clip it to shorten it by clicking on the **Clip** icon.

▶ TIP

If you add the text to the internal track of a photo, select the photo and click on the **Edit Internal Tracks or Entire Production** icon in either the **Preview** taskbar or the **Production Editor** taskbar. This brings up the internal tracks of the selected photo where you can perform the same edits as if it were on the external text track. Click on the icon again to return to the view of the entire production.

4 Edit the Text Using the Taskbar

60

After you have your text in place, you can position the text itself by dragging the bounding box to the desired location. Use the handles on the edges of the bounding box to change its shape.

Highlight the text to make changes to it. You can make basic changes by using the **Text** taskbar just above the **Preview** window. You can change the font, color, and alignment, among other things.

5 Edit the Text Using the Text Editor

If you want to make more changes than the taskbar allows, click on the **Text Editor** icon in the taskbar to bring your text up in the **Text Editor Wizard**. Here you have four tabs where you can do such things as set a box or shadow on your text or create a 3D effect. When you are finished making changes, click **OK**.

6 Edit the Text Using Advanced Settings

If this is *still* not enough, and sometimes it's not, click on the **More Settings** icon. It might not look like much, but when the **Settings** window comes up, you see that you have all the same capabilities of the **Text Editor**, plus some. You can choose the following tabs:

- **Style**—Here you have all your style settings. Change the font, alignment, and paragraph settings.

- **Color**—Here you can change the color of the face, outline, and shadow of your text.

- **Frame**—Here you can change the settings and colors for a frame around your text.

- **3D**—Give your text or frame a 3D effect by adding a bevel and adjusting its settings.

- **Position**—These are the setting that you can't find anywhere else. From here you can position your text precisely using a measured location, or more usefully, you can rotate it.

- **Motion**—In this window you can choose an entrance and exit style for the text object.

7 Set the Motion for the Text

You can set the motion for your text by selecting your text object and clicking on the **Motion** icon in the **Text** taskbar. You are given several options for a grand entrance for your text. Your text, rather than just appearing on the screen, can fly in or scroll onto your production, giving it a more artistic flair.

61

61   Apply Pan and Zoom to Slideshow Photos

✔ BEFORE YOU BEGIN	→ SEE ALSO
54 Add Photos to a Slideshow	Chapter 10, "Editing Video"

The **Pan & Zoom** feature creates movement within each frame of the slideshow by zooming in or out of the photo and moving the photo back and forth or up and down.

You can add the **Pan & Zoom** feature automatically to the entire production by selecting the **Auto Motion** feature, or you can edit the **Pan & Zoom** feature for each individual photo.

1 Set Auto Motion Or...

To add a randomized **Pan & Zoom** feature to the photos in your slideshow, select the photo or photos to which you would like to add the automatic **Pan & Zoom** feature. Right-click on the selected photo and select **Auto Motion** from the drop-down menu that appears.

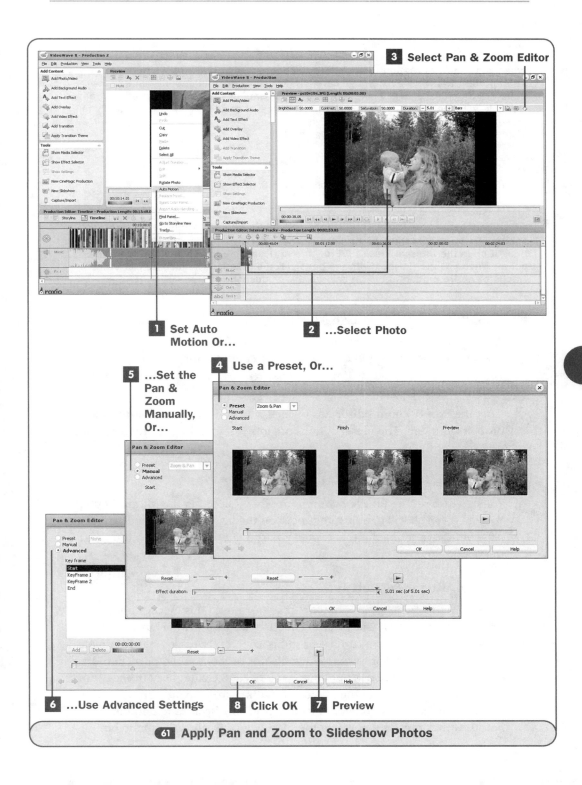

3 Select Pan & Zoom Editor

1 Set Auto Motion Or...

2 ...Select Photo

5 ...Set the Pan & Zoom Manually, Or...

4 Use a Preset, Or...

6 ...Use Advanced Settings

8 Click OK

7 Preview

61

61 Apply Pan and Zoom to Slideshow Photos

▶ **TIP**

When you use **Auto Motion** to apply **Pan & Zoom** presets to all images automatically, it's important to review each image carefully. For all its good intentions, sometimes **VideoWave**'s preset **Pan & Zoom** moves key elements of your images out of the frame's viewable area, and you'll need to apply another preset or edit the motion manually to make sure your photo is properly displayed.

2 ...Select Photo

Select the photo to which to apply a **Pan & Zoom** effect.

▶ **TIP**

The way to make sure that you have your panel selected is to double-click on it and bring it up in the **Internal Tracks Editor**. You are only able to see and edit the selected panel. When you are finished with the panel, click on the icon labeled **Edit internal tracks or entire production** to go back to the production.

3 Select Pan & Zoom Editor

After your photo is selected, click on the **Pan & Zoom Editor** icon in the **Preview** taskbar. This brings up the **Pan & Zoom Editor** window.

61

4 Use a Preset, Or...

After the **Pan & Zoom Editor** has opened, you can choose a preset from the drop-down menu. The preset options are fairly descriptive, but try a few out and see what you like.

5 ...Set the Pan & Zoom Manually, Or...

You can also set the **Pan & Zoom** manually by selecting the **Manual** option. You are given sliders to adjust the zoom on the beginning and ending frame. After you have zoomed into a frame, you can change the pan by dragging the bounding box.

6 ...Use Advanced Settings

If you want to create even more motion, you can do this by clicking the **Advanced** option. Use the slider to choose a *key frame* and change the settings for that frame. You can use as many key frames as you need to create the effect you want. For instance, if you want to zoom into a particular area of a picture and then back out again, you need to create a key frame in the middle of the duration of the photo. At that key frame, you want to zoom into the particular spot on your picture. Leave the beginning and the end points as they are. As you watch the slideshow, this starts the photo out normally, zooms it into the particular spot, and then pans back out as the photo ends.

Change the location of a key frame by moving its marker anywhere inside the timeline.

▶ KEY TERM

Key frame—A frame within a video that sets a definition for the frames around it.

7 Preview

You can preview your **Pan & Zoom** settings by clicking on the **Play** icon under the **Preview** screen inside of the **Pan & Zoom Editor**.

8 Click OK

When you are satisfied with your settings, click **OK**. The effects are applied to your photo and the **Pan & Zoom Editor** closes.

---

62   Add Special Effects to a Slideshow

✔ BEFORE YOU BEGIN	→ SEE ALSO
54 Add Photos to a Slideshow	**63** Add Overlays to a Slideshow

62

You can add a special effect to your slideshow by adding it to the photos themselves or by placing it on its own track.

Placed inside the photo frame, the special effect is limited to that frame. It appears with the frame and disappears as the frame disappears. It is also subject to the transitions on either side of the frame.

If you place the special effect on its own track, you have much more control of it. You can stretch or shrink it to any length of time you want and place it anywhere inside your production.

1 Select Location for the Special Effect

Select the frame or location to which to add the special effect. If you want to add the effect to the internal track of a photo, make sure the photo is selected.

2 Select Add Video Effect

When you have selected the location for the special effect, select **Add Video Effect** from the **Add Content** menu to bring up the **Add Video Effect** window.

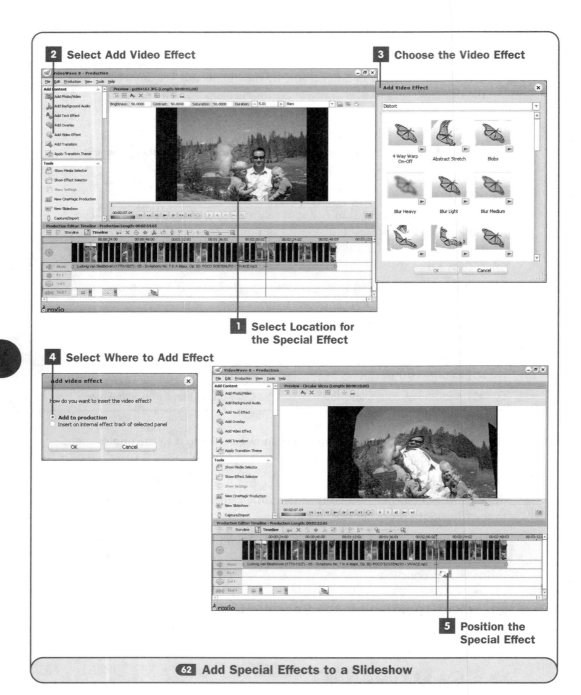

2 Select Add Video Effect

3 Choose the Video Effect

1 Select Location for the Special Effect

4 Select Where to Add Effect

5 Position the Special Effect

62 Add Special Effects to a Slideshow

3 Choose the Video Effect

After the **Add Video Effect** window is open, use the drop-down menu to narrow your choices and select the special effect you want to use. You can preview the special effect by clicking on the **Play** icon in the corner of each. When you have selected the desired effect, click **OK**.

▶ **NOTE**

Because special effects are processor intensive, you might not get a clean preview of the effect because **VideoWave** can't render and preview it at full-quality in real time. Rest assured that as your final production renders, the special effect is applied correctly.

4 Select Where to Add Effect

After you click **OK**, you are asked where you would like to place the special effect. If you would like it added to the photo itself, choose **Insert on internal effect track of selected panel**. If you would prefer to add the special effect to its own track, select **Add to production**.

5 Position the Special Effect

If you added your special effect to its own track, you can now shrink it or stretch it to the desired length. You can also drag and drop it anywhere along the production timeline.

63

63 Add Overlays to a Slideshow	
✔ **BEFORE YOU BEGIN**	→ **SEE ALSO**
54 Add Photos to a Slideshow	**62** Add Special Effects to a Slideshow

An overlay is like a frame or border for your slideshow. The effect is a lot like having a moving scrapbook. You can add an overlay to your slideshow by adding it to the photos themselves or by placing it on its own track.

Placed inside the photo frame, the overlay is limited to that frame. It appears with the frame and disappears as the frame disappears. It is also subject to the transitions on either side of the frame.

If you place the overlay on its own track, you have much more control of it. You can stretch or shrink it to any length of time you want and place it anywhere inside your production.

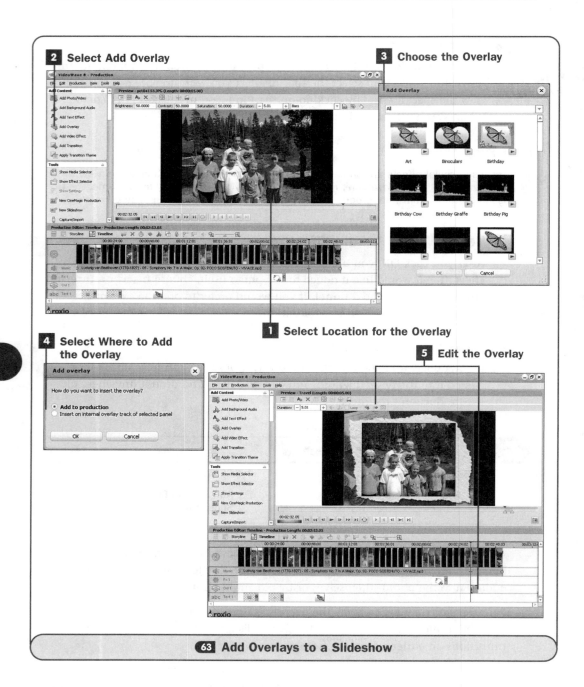

2 Select Add Overlay

3 Choose the Overlay

1 Select Location for the Overlay

4 Select Where to Add the Overlay

5 Edit the Overlay

63 Add Overlays to a Slideshow

1 Select Location for the Overlay

Select the frame or location to which to add the overlay. If you want to add the effect to the internal track of a photo, make sure that the photo is selected.

2 Select Add Overlay

When you have selected the location for the overlay, select **Add Overlay** from the **Add Content** menu to bring up the **Add Overlay** window.

3 Choose the Overlay

After the **Add Overlay** window is open, use the drop-down menu to narrow your choices and select the overlay you want to use. You can preview the overlay by clicking on the **Play** icon in the corner of each. When you have selected the desired overlay, click **OK**.

▶ **NOTE**

Because overlays are processor intensive, you might not get a clean preview of the effect. Rest assured that as your final production renders, the overlay is applied correctly.

4 Select Where to Add the Overlay

After you click **OK**, you are asked where you would like to place the overlay. If you would like it added to the photo itself, choose **Insert on internal overlay track of selected panel**. If you would prefer to add the overlay to its own track, select **Add to production**.

5 Edit the Overlay

If you added your overlay to its own track, you can now shrink it or stretch it to the desired length. You can also drag and drop it anywhere along the production timeline.

You can also set a motion for the overlay by clicking on the **Motion** icon in the **Preview** taskbar. This determines how your overlay is placed into the production.

64

---

64 Export a Slideshow to a Video File

✔ BEFORE YOU BEGIN	→ SEE ALSO
Chapter 1, "Start Here" (Review information on video file formats) **54** Add Photos to a Slideshow	**65** Burn a Slideshow to a Disc Chapter 12, "Authoring DVDs"

When you have completely edited your slideshow, it's time to export it. Whether or not you want to burn it to a disc, it is an excellent idea to create a video file of the production. That way you can save it to your computer or burn the file itself to a CD or DVD to be viewed, edited, or burned later. You can also export it to a digital camcorder, play it to a TV or VCR, or email it.

1 Select Output As

To export your slideshow into a video file, select the **Output As** icon from the **Preview** taskbar.

2 Save Production

When you have clicked on the **Output As** icon, you are prompted to save your production. You are strongly encouraged to do so. After you have saved your production, the **Make Movie** window opens.

3 Select Destination

After the **Make Movie** window is open, select your destination by clicking on the appropriate button.

4 Change Settings

After you have selected your destination, your window might have changed, but you can change the format and file settings for your video file in any one of them. NTSC is the standard for North America. PAL is standard everywhere else.

You can also change the file extension and quality from the **Video file quality** drop-down menu. You are able to choose from a full range of file options only in the **Video File** window. If you are unsure which option to choose, review the video file information in Chapter 1, "Start Here."

5 Name the File

After you have set your options, you can change the name of your file and set a destination. The default name for your file is the name of your production, but you can change it. Browse to find the location to which you would like to save it.

6 Click Create Video File

When you are ready, click either the **Create Video File** or the **Start Output** option (for the DV camera, TV/VCR, and email destinations) at the bottom of the screen. You are able to preview the production as it is rendered and stored or exported as a video file. This process takes several minutes. When it is finished, click **Done**.

1 Select Output As   **2** Save Production

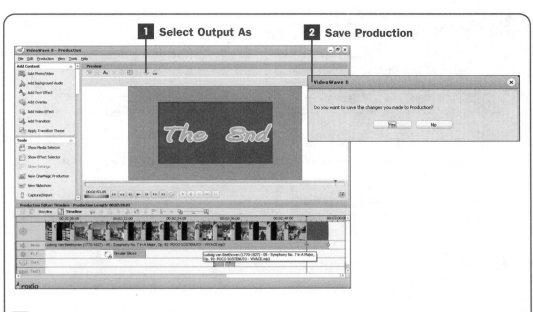

4 Change Settings

3 Select Destination

6 Click Create Video File

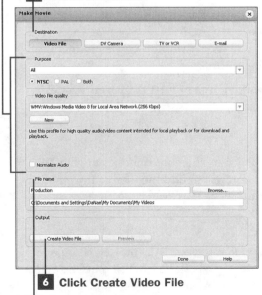

6 Click Create Video File

5 Name the File

65   Burn a Slideshow to a Disc

✔ BEFORE YOU BEGIN	→ SEE ALSO
Chapter 1, "Start Here" (Review information on video file formats)	64 Export a Slideshow to a Video File
54 Add Photos to a Slideshow	Chapter 12, "Authoring DVDs"

With just a few quick steps you can export your slideshow directly to a DVD, complete with menus, so you can enjoy watching it for years to come or share your special memories with others.

You might want to export your creation to a video file as well as burning it to a DVD so you will always have the option to view it on your computer or import it into a new project as a video file. *Or good tv: my DVD Express*

1   Select Burn with MyDVD Express

When you are ready to burn your production to a DVD, click on the **Burn with MyDVD Express** icon in the **Preview** taskbar. This opens **MyDVD Express**.

2   Choose the Disc Format

After **MyDVD Express** has launched, choose your disc format from the drop-down menu. DVDs are so inexpensive anymore that it is rare that you would want to use an alternative disc format. If you do want to create another disc format, however, you can choose from several.

Be sure and set the disc type at the bottom of the **MyDVD Express** window so your available space indicator is correct.

3   Add New Movie

You can add additional slideshow or video productions and files to your DVD. Select the **Add New Movie** button and browse to find the files you want to add. When you have selected your files, click **OK**.

4   Change Menu Style

After you have added any additional videos to your DVD project, change the menu style by selecting the **Change Menu Style** button to bring up the **Select Menu Style** window. From this window you are able to select from several styles for your menu. Preview the styles by clicking on them to bring them up into the larger windows. When you have selected the style you like best, click **OK**. After you are back in **MyDVD Express**, you can preview the menu style by clicking the **Play** icon in the taskbar.

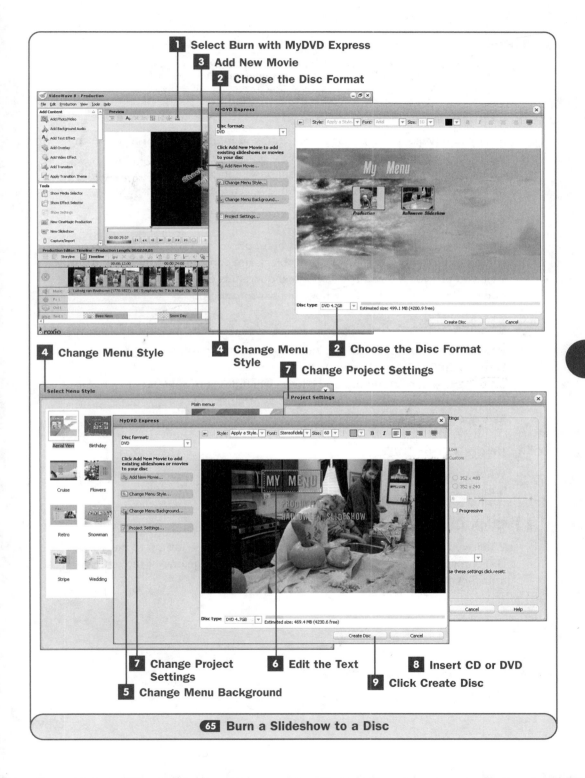

1 Select Burn with MyDVD Express

3 Add New Movie

2 Choose the Disc Format

4 Change Menu Style

4 Change Menu Style

2 Choose the Disc Format

7 Change Project Settings

7 Change Project Settings

6 Edit the Text

5 Change Menu Background

8 Insert CD or DVD

9 Click Create Disc

► **TIP**

You can preview the way your menu will operate on a DVD by clicking on the **Preview** icon in the taskbar. The **Preview** icon looks like a miniature TV.

5 Change Menu Background

After you have set the style for your menu, you might want to use your own photo for the menu background to give it a personal touch. Click on the **Change Menu Background** button and browse for the photo you would like to have as a background. When you have selected a photo, click OK.

6 Edit the Text

After you have put in your own background photo, you can do some basic editing of the text. Although the text objects are constrained to the menu style you picked, you can retype the text as well as change the font, color, and size by using the taskbar above the background photo.

7 Change Project Settings

When you are satisfied with the look of your menu, select the **Project Settings** button. In the **Project Settings** window you can change the aspect ratio, set the video standard, and choose whether you would like the production to be interlaced or progressive, among other things. When your settings look good, click OK.

8 Insert CD or DVD

When you are ready to burn the disc, insert the disc you are using into your burner.

9 Click Create Disc

When you have inserted your disc, click the **Create Disc** button to burn your DVD project. The **Burn DVD** window comes up. Change any of the options and click **Burn**.

65

9

Capturing Video

IN THIS CHAPTER:

One of the most useful features of Roxio Easy Media Creator is the capability to capture video from home videos, camcorders, webcams, and other sources. This feature gives you the ability to back up priceless memories that you've captured on home video. It also allows you to store the video as digital files that you can edit and use to create your own home productions.

After you have imported your video, you are introduced to a completely new world of amazing things that you can do with your video to make it interesting to watch. Admit it; you haven't pulled out those dusty VHS tapes in a while, right? Well, get ready to gather around the TV—you're going to have some fun.

In this chapter you learn how to capture video from digital camcorders, DVDs, webcams, VCRs, cable, satellite, TiVo, and other devices.

66 Capture Video from a Digital Camcorder

✔ BEFORE YOU BEGIN	→ SEE ALSO
Chapter 1, "Start Here" (Review information on video file formats)	67 Capture Video from a Digital Camcorder Using Smart Scan
	68 Capture Streaming Video from a Webcam or Video Capture Card

The first task in editing your video or burning it to disc is to capture it. A few camcorders record directly to a DVD, and compact hard disks are also available that connect to DV camcorders and record video as it is shot, but most digital camcorders record to a miniDV tape. Using a *FireWire* cable to connect your digital camcorder to your computer, you can easily download your video and edit it into a fun-to-watch production.

▶ KEY TERM

FireWire—The common cable format used for transferring video from one device to another.

1 Plug Your Camcorder into the Computer

The first step in capturing video from your camcorder is to attach the camcorder to the computer using a FireWire or USB cable. After the camcorder is plugged into the computer, turn it on. It should be recognized by the system as a new device.

▶ TIP

Plug the camcorder into a power supply to save battery life.

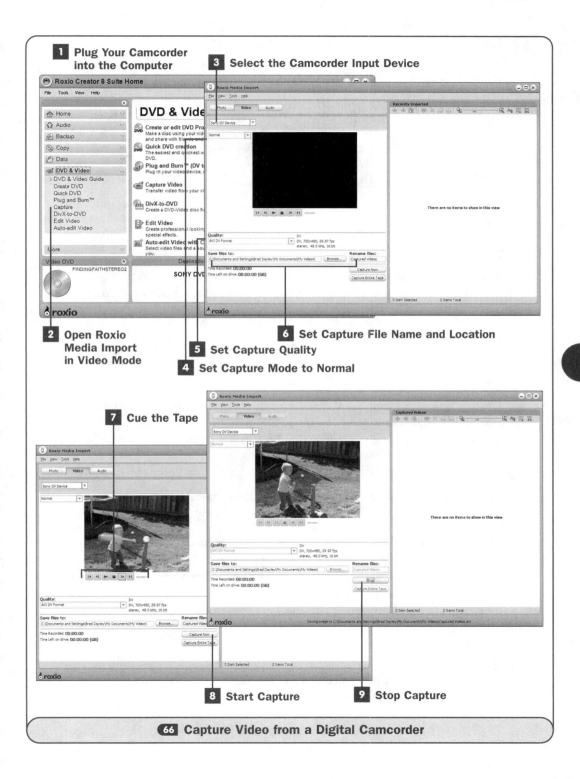

1 Plug Your Camcorder into the Computer

3 Select the Camcorder Input Device

2 Open Roxio Media Import in Video Mode

6 Set Capture File Name and Location

5 Set Capture Quality

4 Set Capture Mode to Normal

7 Cue the Tape

8 Start Capture

9 Stop Capture

2 Open Roxio Media Import in Video Mode

After the camcorder has been attached to the computer, you can start **Roxio Media Import** in one of two ways, depending on which is easiest for you. If you have the Easy Media Creator **Home** page up, simply click on **Video** and then select **Capture** from the **DVD & Video** submenu. You can also open **Roxio Media Import** by selecting **Programs, Roxio Easy Media Creator 8, DVD and Video, Media Import** from the **Start** menu in Windows.

3 Select the Camcorder Input Device

From **Roxio Media Import**, select the camcorder from the device drop-down menu.

4 Set Capture Mode to Normal

After you have selected the camcorder, the camcorder capture controls appear. Set the capture mode to **Normal** in the **Capture** mode drop-down list.

5 Set Capture Quality

66

After you have set the **Capture** mode, set the quality for your captured video. You can capture either at AVI DV or MPEG-2.

The advantage of using the *MPEG-2* format is that the size of the captured video file is significantly smaller. If you are going to view the files on the computer or send them via email, use the MPEG-2 format.

▶ KEY TERM

MPEG-2—The video file format used for DVD videos. This file format is more compressed than the AVI DV formats and therefore slightly inferior.

The advantage of using the *AVI DV* format is that the quality is better. Unless you are pressed for storage space, it is always best to capture and edit in the highest quality possible; each time your editing program has to convert and compress your video, you lose quality. If you plan to use the video to make a movie and export it to a DVD, use the AVI DV format.

▶ KEY TERM

AVI DV—The largest and highest quality video file format. Captured on a MiniDV tape as a DV file and imported into the computer as an AVI file.

6 Set Capture File Name and Location

Video files are extremely large and take a lot of time to copy from one hard disk to another. Set the destination location in the **Save files to** box to the location in which you want to keep the captured file permanently, so you do not have to take the time to move the file from one location to another.

▶ **TIP**

Save the captured files to a drive other than C: if you are planning to use the video file in **VideoWave** or another editor. Most editors use the C: drive to store temporary files when they are rendering or doing other intensive tasks. Having the video files on a different drive improves performance and speeds up rendering times.

After you have set the destination location, set the prefix you want to use for the captured files in the **Rename files** text box. The captured file names will begin with that prefix and end in a number. For example, if you are capturing using the AVI DV format and specify MyVideo for the prefix, the captured files would be named **MyVideo001.avi**, **MyVideo002.avi**, and so on.

7 Cue the Tape

After you have set the destination location and the captured filename prefix, you need to cue the tape before capturing the video. You can cue the tape by using the controls on the camcorder itself or by using the controls on the capture screen of **Roxio Media Import**.

8 Start Capture

When the tape is cued, click the **Capture Now** button to begin capturing video.

▶ **TIP**

When using the **Normal** mode, the camcorder automatically starts and stops when you start and stop the capture.

9 Stop Capture

When you have captured as much video as you want, click the **Stop** button.

66

67   Capture Video from a Digital Camcorder Using Smart Scan

✔ BEFORE YOU BEGIN	→ SEE ALSO
Chapter 1, "Start Here" (Review information on video file formats)	66 Capture Video from a Digital Camcorder 68 Capture Streaming Video from a Webcam or Video Capture Card

Most home video tapes have several sessions on them, recorded at different times for different events. **Roxio Media Import** provides an extremely useful tool to help you capture each session individually. Instead of having to import the entire tape or cue up each individual session, you can use the *Smart scan* feature to scan the tape and identify each session for you, creating thumbnails for each one. You can then choose which sessions to import.

▶ KEY TERM

Smart scan—The ability of **Roxio Media Import** to detect individual recording sessions on the same tape and create separate thumbnails for each allowing you to choose the sessions to import.

The following steps describe how to import individual recording sessions from a digital camcorder using **Roxio Media Import**.

1 Plug Camcorder into the Computer

The first step in capturing video from your camcorder is to attach the camcorder to the computer using a FireWire or USB cable. After the camcorder is plugged into the computer, turn it on and it should be recognized by the system as a new device.

2 Open Roxio Media Import in Video Mode

After the camcorder has been attached to the computer, you can start **Roxio Media Import** in one of two ways, depending on which is easiest for you. If you have the Roxio **Home** page up, simply click on **Video** and then select **Capture** from the **DVD & Video** submenu. You can also open **Roxio Media Import** by selecting **Programs**, **Roxio Easy Media Creator 8**, **DVD and Video**, **Media Import** from the **Start** menu in Windows.

3 Select the Camcorder Input Device

From **Roxio Media Import**, select the camcorder from the device drop-down menu.

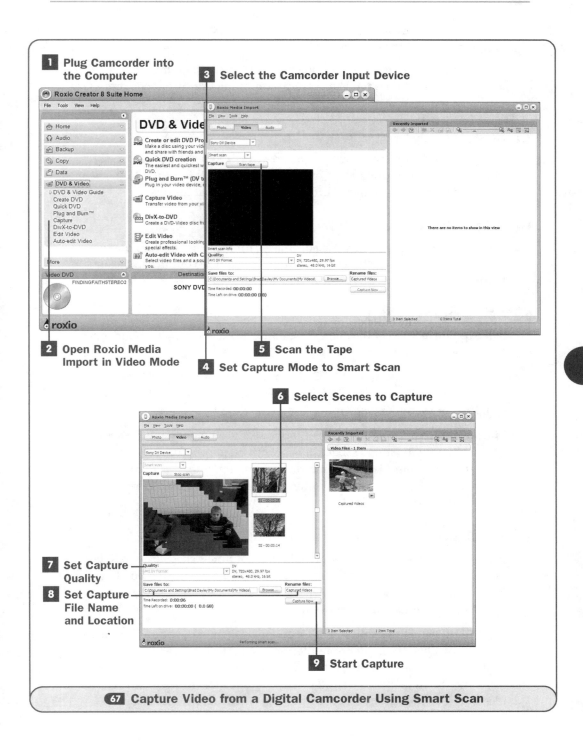

1 Plug Camcorder into the Computer

3 Select the Camcorder Input Device

2 Open Roxio Media Import in Video Mode

4 Set Capture Mode to Smart Scan

5 Scan the Tape

6 Select Scenes to Capture

7 Set Capture Quality

8 Set Capture File Name and Location

9 Start Capture

67

4 Set Capture Mode to Smart Scan

After you have selected the camcorder, the camcorder capture controls appear. Set the capture mode to **Smart scan** in the **Capture** mode drop-down list.

5 Scan the Tape

After you set the **Capture** mode to **Smart scan**, you see the **Scan tape** button. Click the **Scan tape** button and your camcorder is rewound to the beginning and scanned for scenes. This process takes several minutes.

6 Select Scenes to Capture

After the scenes have been detected, you see thumbnails showing the first frame of the scene. Select the thumbnails you want to capture by clicking on them while holding down the **Control** key.

7 Set Capture Quality

After you have selected the scenes to capture, set the quality for your captured video. You can capture either at AVI DV or MPEG-2.

The advantage of using the MPEG-2 format is that the size of the captured video file is significantly smaller. If you are going to view the files on the computer or send them via email, use the MPEG-2 format.

The advantage of using the AVI DV format is that the quality is better. Unless you are pressed for storage space, it is always best to capture and edit in the highest quality possible; each time your editing program has to convert and compress your video, you lose quality. If you plan to use the video to make a movie and export it to a DVD, use the AVI DV format.

8 Set Capture File Name and Location

Video files are extremely large and take a lot of time to copy from one hard disk to another. Set the destination location in the **Save files to** box to the location in which you want to keep the captured file permanently, so you do not have to take the time to move the file from one location to another.

After you have set the destination location, set the prefix you want to use for the captured files in the **Rename files** text box. The captured file names will begin with that prefix and end in a number. For example, if you are capturing using the AVI DV format and specify MyVideo for the prefix, the captured files would be named **MyVideo001.avi**, **MyVideo002.avi**, and so on.

67

9 **Start Capture**

After the destination and prefix has been set, click the **Capture Now** button to capture the scenes.

▶ **NOTE**

You must have the date and time set properly on your camcorder for **Smart scan** to work. The date and time must also be embedded into the tape you are trying to scan.

---

68 **Capture Streaming Video from a Webcam or Video Capture Card**

✔ BEFORE YOU BEGIN	→ SEE ALSO
Chapter 1, "Start Here" (Review information on video file formats)	**66** Capture Video from a Digital Camcorder
	67 Capture Video from a Digital Camcorder Using Smart Scan

You can capture streaming (live) video from your camcorder, your webcam, or a video capture card. This saves you a step or two in the capture process. Of course, you are limited on what you can capture; no hiking shots while your camcorder is hooked to the computer.

A more practical use for capturing with a video capture card is connecting your VCR to capture those old VHS tapes. You can also connect your TV or capture recorded programs from your TiVo recorder.

1 **Plug Input Device into the Computer**

The first step in capturing streaming video is to attach the input device to the computer. In the case of a webcam or camcorder, simply connect the device to the computer using a FireWire or USB cable. In the case of using a video capture card, connect the cable, satellite, antenna, DVD, TiVo, VCR, or other video input into the appropriate video capture port. After the input device is plugged into the computer, turn it on if necessary.

▶ **TIP**

Most digital camcorders come with an RCA input that allows you to plug a VCR, TiVo, satellite, or other device into them. You can use this plug to capture video if you do not have a video capture card. Just connect the device to the camcorder and then the camcorder to the computer.

68

1 Plug Input Device into the Computer

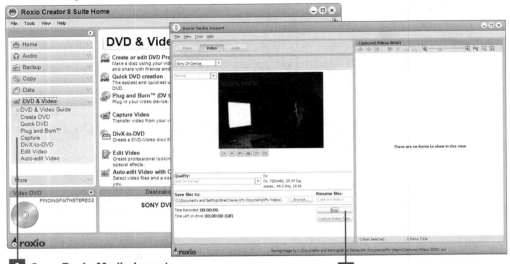

2 Open Roxio Media Import in Video Mode

9 Stop Capture

68

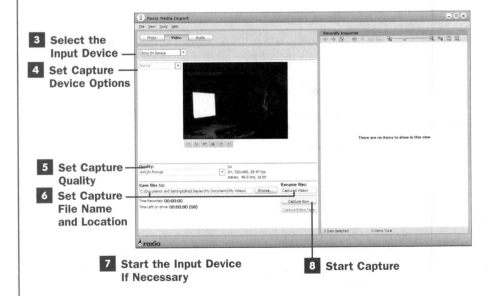

3 Select the Input Device

4 Set Capture Device Options

5 Set Capture Quality

6 Set Capture File Name and Location

7 Start the Input Device If Necessary

8 Start Capture

68 Capture Streaming Video from a Webcam or Video Capture Card

② Open Roxio Media Import in Video Mode

After the input device has been attached to the computer, you can start **Roxio Media Import** in one of two ways, depending on which is easiest for you. If you have the Roxio **Home** page up, simply click on **Video** and then select **Capture** from the **DVD & Video** submenu. You can also open **Roxio Media Import** by selecting **Programs, Roxio Easy Media Creator 8, DVD and Video, Media Import** from the **Start** menu in Windows.

③ Select the Input Device

From **Roxio Media Import**, select the camcorder, webcam, or video capture card from the device drop-down menu.

④ Set Capture Device Options

Depending on the device you select, you might be given different options to set for the device. For example, if you select a cable TV tuner, you are able to set the channel, brightness, and contrast. Set any needed settings specific for the device.

⑤ Set Capture Quality

After you have selected the scenes to capture, set the quality for your captured video. You can capture either at AVI DV or MPEG-2.

The advantage of using the MPEG-2 format is that the size of the captured video file is significantly smaller. If you are going to view the files on the computer or send them via email, use the MPEG-2 format.

The advantage of using the AVI DV format is that the quality is better. Unless you are pressed for storage space, it is always best to capture and edit in the highest quality possible; each time your editing program has to convert and compress your video, you lose quality. If you plan to use the video to make a movie and export it to a DVD, use the AVI DV format.

⑥ Set Capture File Name and Location

Video files are extremely large and take a lot of time to copy from one hard disk to another. Set the destination location in the **Save files to** box to the location in which you want to store the captured file permanently, so you do not have to take the time to move the file from one location to another.

After you have set the destination location, set the prefix you want to use for the captured files in the **Rename files** text box. The captured file names will begin with that prefix and end in a number. For example, if you are

68

capturing using the AVI DV format and specify MyVideo for the prefix, the captured files would be named **MyVideo001.avi**, **MyVideo002.avi**, and so on.

7 Start the Input Device If Necessary

After you are ready to begin capturing, start the playback device if necessary. For example, if you have a VCR, TiVo, or DVD attached to the video capture device, you need to press **Play** on the device to begin the playback in order to capture. What you see in the **Preview** window is what will be captured.

▶ TIP

You might want to swap steps 7 and 8 and actually begin capturing before starting playback on the device if you want to make absolutely certain that you capture the very beginning of the playback.

8 Start Capture

After the playback has begun, click the **Capture Now** button to begin capturing video.

9 Stop Capture

When you have captured as much streaming video as you want, click the **Stop** button.

---

69   Import Video from a DVD

✔ BEFORE YOU BEGIN	→ SEE ALSO
Chapter 1, "Start Here" (Review information on video file formats)	2 Extract Audio Tracks from a DVD

A completely different way to capture video is to extract it from a previously recorded DVD. This is handy if you would like to take a previously recorded project and add to it or make changes. You might also have files that are backed up on a DVD that you would like to edit.

If you have a camcorder that records directly to a DVD, you want to use this process to extract the files from the DVD.

▶ NOTE

Of course, you would never import copyrighted material from a licensed DVD, but just in case you were thinking of it, be aware that most of them are encrypted and you will find it impossible.

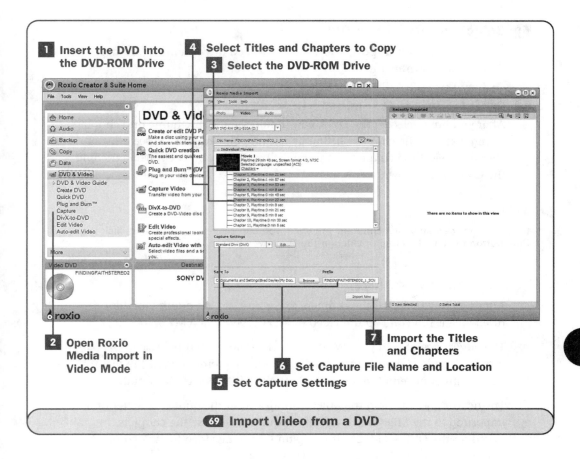

1 Insert the DVD into the DVD-ROM Drive
4 Select Titles and Chapters to Copy
3 Select the DVD-ROM Drive

2 Open Roxio Media Import in Video Mode

7 Import the Titles and Chapters
6 Set Capture File Name and Location
5 Set Capture Settings

69 Import Video from a DVD

1 Insert the DVD into the DVD-ROM Drive

The first step in capturing video from a DVD is to insert the DVD into the DVD-ROM drive of the computer.

2 Open Roxio Media Import in Video Mode

After the DVD has been inserted into the computer, you can start **Roxio Media Import** in one of two ways, depending on which is easiest for you. If you have the Roxio **Home** page up, simply click on **Video** and then select **Capture** from the **DVD & Video** submenu. You can also open **Roxio Media Import** by selecting **Programs**, **Roxio Easy Media Creator 8**, **DVD and Video**, **Media Import** from the **Start** menu in Windows.

❸ Select the DVD-ROM Drive

From **Roxio Media Import**, select the DVD-ROM drive capture card from the device drop-down menu.

❹ Select Titles and Chapters to Copy

After you have selected the DVD, you should see the disc name and chapters listing. Expand the chapters listing by clicking on **Chapters** to see a list of chapters. Select the chapters from the list by clicking on them while holding the **Control** key down.

▶ **TIP**

If you are not certain which chapters you want, you can select a chapter and click the **Play** button to view the chapter video in the **Preview** window.

❺ Set Capture Settings

After you have selected the chapters to capture, set the quality for your captured video. You can capture video in MPEG, DivX, or WMV.

The advantage of using the WMV or DivX format is that the size of the captured video file is significantly smaller. If you are going to view the files on the computer or send them via email, use the WMV or DivX format.

The advantages of using the MPEG format is that the quality is better and importing to the MPEG format is much quicker because the chapters are stored on the DVD as MPEG. If you plan to use the video to make a movie and export it to a DVD, use the MPEG format.

❻ Set Capture File Name and Location

Video files are extremely large and take a lot of time to copy from one hard disk to another. Set the destination location in the **Save to** box to the location in which you want to store the captured file permanently, so you do not have to take the time to move the file from one location to another.

After you have set the destination location, set the prefix you want to use for the captured files in the **Prefix** text box. The captured file names will begin with that prefix.

❼ Import the Titles and Chapters

After the destination and prefix has been set, click the **Import Now** button to capture the titles and chapters.

69

10

Editing Video

IN THIS CHAPTER:

If you've never edited your video using a computer before, you might be a little reluctant to start. You might be afraid that editing video is an advanced skill that just isn't up your alley. Here is your big chance to give it a try! Roxio Easy Media Creator 8 includes a video-editing application called **VideoWave** that is simple to use and yet gives you many of the capabilities of some of the best professional video-editing applications.

Some of the features of **VideoWave** include the capability to add music, sound effects, and narration to your video; add text to your video; and even special effects, including using a chroma key, or green screen, to layer your video for a special effect.

A video production is one possible culmination of all the media projects within Easy Media Creator. Now you can take the audio you've imported and edited and the photos you've cleaned, cropped, and added text to and add them to your video clips to create a fantastic production you can enjoy for years to come.

70	**Create a CineMagic Production**	
✔ **BEFORE YOU BEGIN**		→ **SEE ALSO**
Chapter 5, "Importing Photos" Chapter 9, "Capturing Video"		**83** Export a Video Production to a Video File

Like many of the applications within Easy Media Creator, **CineMagic Assistant** is a step-by-step wizard that allows you to create a video production quickly and easily, even if you have never done it before.

CineMagic Assistant is very limited on capability, however. You won't be able to edit your individual video files or photos in any way. Although you can change a production style, you can't choose the special effects or the pictures or video clips on which to use them. The advantage of using **CineMagic Assistant** is that if you have some video clips that don't add up to much of a storyline, you can create an appealing music video from them with very little effort. Editing *video clips* to the tempo and beat of music can be time-consuming, but **CineMagic Assistant** analyzes an audio track you select and does it for you, with transitions and pacing that suit the style you choose. What it won't do that you as a video editor can do is create an edited production that reflects the content of your video.

▶ **KEY TERM**

Video clip—A portion of video that has been captured continuously as one file or object. You can create more than one clip within a video file by splitting the file into two or more clips.

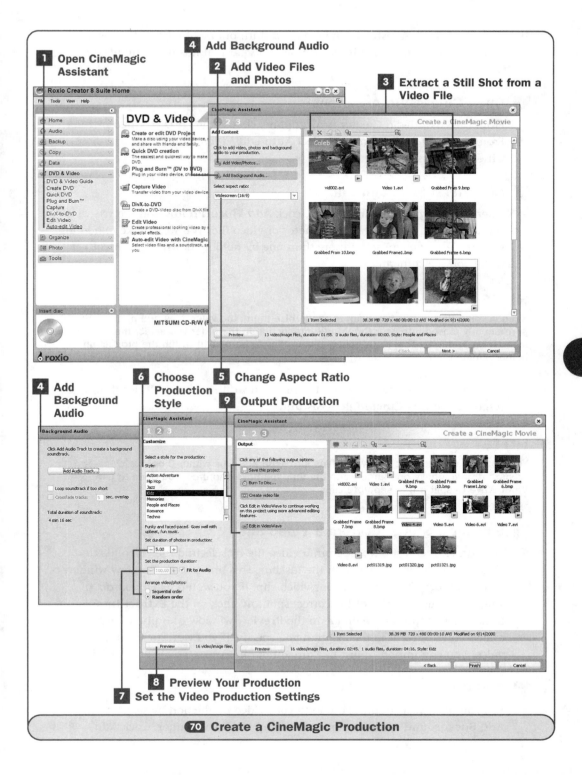

1 Open CineMagic Assistant

4 Add Background Audio

2 Add Video Files and Photos

3 Extract a Still Shot from a Video File

4 Add Background Audio

6 Choose Production Style

5 Change Aspect Ratio

9 Output Production

8 Preview Your Production

7 Set the Video Production Settings

In short, **CineMagic Assistant** can be a good start, but please don't stop here. You will find that **VideoWave** is also simple to use, and it has much more capability.

1 Open CineMagic Assistant

From the Easy Media Creator **project** pane, choose the **DVD & Video** menu. From the **DVD & Video** menu, select **Auto-edit Video**. This brings up **CineMagic Assistant**.

2 Add Video Files and Photos

After **CineMagic Assistant** is open, click **Add Video/Photos** and browse through Media Manager for the photos or video files you would like to add to your project. You can select more than one by holding down the **Control** key while you select them.

▶ **NOTE**

Keep in mind that unless you want to randomize them, the video files and photos are permanently placed into your **CineMagic** production in the order you select them. Take some time to decide how you would like your files to be placed within the production before adding them.

When you are finished selecting the files you want, click **Add Video/Photo** to import them into **CineMagic Assistant**.

▶ **NOTE**

You won't be able to split your video files into separate clips within **CineMagic Assistant**. If you have one large video file that you have captured, you need to use **VideoWave** to split it into separate clips.

3 Extract a Still Shot from a Video File

You can extract a still frame from a video file by selecting the video file and clicking on the **Preview** icon in the taskbar. This brings up a **Preview** window where you are able to watch your video clip. If you would like to extract a still shot, pause the clip at the correct spot and click on the **Extract Image** button. This captures the image in the **Preview** window as a photo and allows you to save it to the location you specify. If you want to use it in your video, you can import it, just like any other photo.

4 Add Background Audio

You can add music or other audio to your video production by selecting the **Add Background Audio** button to bring up **Media Manager**. Click **Add**

70

Audio Track and browse for the audio file you would like to add. Choose more than one by holding down the **Control** key as you select the files. After you have selected your tracks, click **Add Audio** to go back to the **Background Audio** window.

From the **Background Audio** window, you have the option to loop the tracks if they are too short or to crossfade more than one track. When you are finished setting your options, click **OK**.

5 Change Aspect Ratio

Change the aspect ratio of your video production to fit your TV. Standard TVs are 4:3; widescreen TVs are 16:9. Select the correct option from the **Select aspect ratio** drop-down menu.

When you have finished making changes to your project, click **Next** to move on to the **Customize** window.

▶ TIP

You can preview your video production at any time by clicking on the **Preview** button in the **CineMagic Assistant**.

70

6 Choose Production Style

From the **Customize** window in **CineMagic Assistant**, you can choose one of several production styles. Adding a style to your production adds transitions, overlays, and special effects to your video relevant to the style you choose. Click on each from the **Style** menu to see a short description.

7 Set the Video Production Settings

After you have chosen your production style, set the length to play each photo in the video production, choose whether to fit the video production to audio, and choose to play your files in sequential order or to randomize them.

8 Preview Your Production

When you are satisfied with the settings for your video production, you want to preview it before exporting it. Click on the **Preview** button to bring up the **Preview** window, and enjoy your production!

Keep in mind that because video files are so big, the preview won't be the quality that it will be after the final rendering.

9 Output Production

After you are satisfied with your video production, you are ready to save it to a file or burn it to a disc. Click **Next** to take you to the **Output** window in **CineMagic Assistant**.

You have four options in the **Output** window: **Save this project**, **Burn To Disc**, **Create video file**, and **Edit in VideoWave**.

Saving the project does not complete the video production; it simply saves the project you are working on so you can make changes later. Your project is saved as a **.dmsm** file, which is the file extension for an Easy Media Creator **VideoWave** production file.

▶ NOTE

You can't return to **CineMagic** and open a file you have saved. After you have saved a **CineMagic** project, the only way you can further edit it or export it is to open it in **VideoWave**.

You can burn your video production directly to disc by clicking on the **Burn to Disc** option. This brings up **MyDVD Express**. Please see **84 Burn a Video Production to a Disc Using MyDVD Express** for step-by-step instructions.

You can also export your video production to a video file by clicking on the **Create video file** button. Please see **83 Export a Video Production to a Video File** for step-by-step instructions.

If you would like to make further changes to your video production, you can edit it in **VideoWave**. **VideoWave** has many advanced editing features not found in **CineMagic Assistant**. Click on the **Edit in VideoWave** button to export your project into **VideoWave**.

71 Launch VideoWave and Change the Production Settings

→ SEE ALSO

72 About the VideoWave Interface

73 Add Video Files and Photos to VideoWave

Although the settings for a **VideoWave** production are few and fairly simple, they can change the whole look and feel of your production, not to mention save you an immeasurable amount of time when you decide you want your still shots to last for six seconds rather than five.

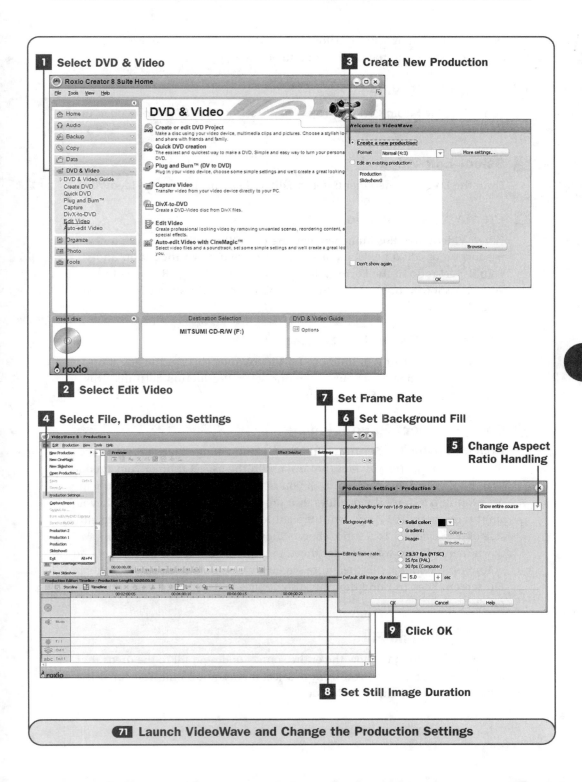

1 Select DVD & Video

3 Create New Production

2 Select Edit Video

7 Set Frame Rate

6 Set Background Fill

4 Select File, Production Settings

5 Change Aspect Ratio Handling

9 Click OK

8 Set Still Image Duration

It is best to change your settings before you start to add files to the production so there is no question that the settings are universally applied.

1 Select DVD & Video

From the Easy Media Creator **project** pane, select **DVD & Video** to open up the menu.

2 Select Edit Video

LAUNCH VIDEOWAVE

From the **DVD & Video** menu, select **Edit Video**. This launches **VideoWave**.

3 Create New Production

When **VideoWave** has launched, you are given the option to create a new production or edit an existing one. Select **Create a new production** and set your aspect ratio in the **Format** drop-down menu. Change the aspect ratio of your slideshow to fit your TV. Standard TVs are 4:3; widescreen TVs are 16:9. Click **OK**.

4 Select File, Production Settings

After you are in the main interface for **VideoWave**, click on the **File** drop-down menu at the top of your screen and select **Production Settings**. This opens the **Production Settings** window.

5 Change Aspect Ratio Handling

From the **Production Settings** window, you can change four settings. The first is to change the way files that are not in the aspect ratio of your production are handled. In other words, if you selected a 16:9 aspect ratio but you are planning to import video files that are in a 4:3 aspect ratio, how do you want them handled? If you want the entire image to show, with bars to either side of it to create a 16:9 ratio, choose **Show entire source** from the drop-down menu. If you would prefer the 4:3 image to be cropped on the top and bottom so the image fills the entire screen with no bars to either side, choose **Fill screen**. Keep in mind that this also applies to any photos you add to the production.

6 Set Background Fill

If you are planning to show the entire source, adding a fill to the areas that the image doesn't cover, you want to select a background fill. You can select a solid color, a gradient, or an image.

71

▶ **TIP**

If you have an everyday photo in mind, adding an image as a background fill seems silly. But if you take a picture of a group of flowers, a piece of wood, or any other interesting color or texture, you have a very nice background fill.

7 Set Frame Rate

Set your *frame rate* to NTSC for North America and PAL anywhere else.

▶ **KEY TERM**

Frame rate—The number of frames that appear in every second of video.

8 Set Still Image Duration

When you import photos and add color panels to your production, they are given a duration time inside the production. Set the duration to the number of seconds you would like each still shot to be on the screen.

▶ **NOTE**

The transitions you add to your production shave about half a second from each side of your images, but the transition itself lasts half a second. So if you have three images together, all set to a five-second duration, the first is four-and-a-half seconds long and has a half-second transition into the next image, which is four seconds long and followed by a half-second transition. The last panel is four-and-a-half seconds long.

9 Click OK

When you are done with your settings, click **OK** to take you back to the **VideoWave** interface. You are ready to add files.

72	**About the VideoWave Interface**
✔ **BEFORE YOU BEGIN**	→ **SEE ALSO**
71 Launch VideoWave and Change the Production Settings	**73** Add Video Files and Photos to VideoWave
	74 Position Video Clips and Photos Inside VideoWave
	78 Add Transitions or a Transition Theme to a Video Production
	79 Add Audio Files to a Video Production
	81 Add Text to a Video Production

Task Pane   Preview Window

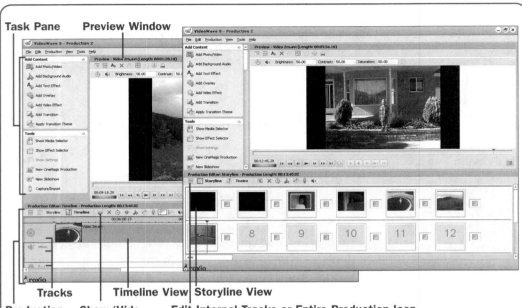

Tracks   Timeline View Storyline View

Production   Show/Hide   Edit Internal Tracks or Entire Production Icon
Editor   Tracks Icon

Adding Tracks

Effect Selector, Docked

Settings, Docked

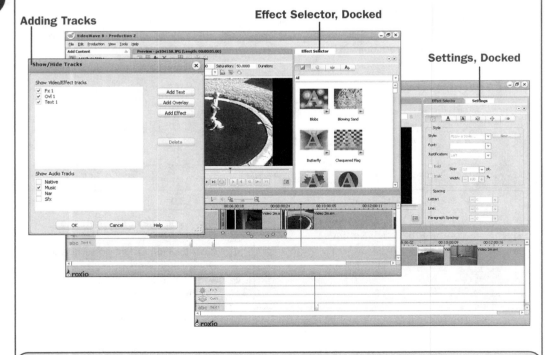

72 About the VideoWave Interface

The **VideoWave** window is a little more complicated than most project windows, but after you get used to it you will find that it is very simple to understand and use. It is actually quite a bit simpler than the windows in professional video-editing programs, but it has many of the same capabilities.

The largest window is the **Preview** window. It contains elements such as the screen, where you can preview all or part of your video production, and the taskbar relevant to the items on the screen. You will learn how to use the tools in this taskbar as you perform the tasks in this chapter.

On the left side of the window you have the **task** pane, containing the **Add Content** menu and the **Tools** menu. You can close either of these menus to create more room by clicking on the arrow next to the menu title.

At the bottom of your screen you see the **Production Editor**. Here is where all the work takes place. You can stretch this window to fill more than half the screen by clicking on the top and dragging it. This is useful in **storyline view** if you need to take a look at more of your images or in **timeline view** if you have multiple tracks.

Speaking of the storyline and timeline views, you'll want to understand the benefits of each view.

The _storyline view_ shows a storyboard view of your production, placing each of your video and photo elements in its own panel. The storyline view only contains your video and transitions. This means you can't view or edit the other elements of your production, such as the audio and special effects.

The storyline view is very useful if you want to sort your files. You can easily drag or drop them into place. It is also easy to organize your transitions in this view because they too have their own window and can be dragged into new locations.

The _timeline view_ is the one you'll want to use most of the time, particularly after you have added additional tracks to your production. It is easier to maneuver in and you have a full view of all of your tracks. There is one last view you can use while editing. By clicking on the **Edit Internal Tracks or Entire Production** icon, the object you have selected appears by itself in the timeline. From here you can edit any _internal tracks_ you have placed on the selected object. Whenever you place an effect, you are given the option to add it to the production (external tracks) or to the selected file (internal tracks). After you have chosen to edit the internal tracks, they appear on the track lines, and you are able to manipulate them within the object.

72

▶ **TIP**

You can also double-click on any video or photo file to open the view of its internal tracks. Click on the **Edit Internal Tracks or Entire Production** icon to change the view back to the entire production.

▶ **KEY TERM**

Internal track—A text or a special effect that is linked to a specific video or photo file.

In the timeline view, you have several tracks for the elements you might want to add to your production. You can add or delete these tracks from the view to streamline your editing process. Click on the **Show/Hide Tracks** icon in the **Production Editor**. This brings up a window that allows you to check the tracks you would like to use and see. Keep in mind that just because you can't see a track doesn't mean it is not in use. So if you are satisfied with the text you have added to your production, you can hide the text track in order to make your track view cleaner and easier to work with. This does not affect the text in any way.

There are two more windows of which you need to be aware. The first is the **Effect Selector** window and the second is the **Settings** window.

The **Effect Selector** allows you to add an effect to your production just by selecting it. When you click on the **Effect Selector**, it comes up as a separate window—which doesn't make it any more useful than clicking on the **Add Text Effect** or **Add Video Effect** options. You can dock your **Effect Selector**, though, and that makes it quite a bit more useful because now you can select your effect just by clicking on it rather than taking two steps, one to open the effect window and a second to select the effect. After your **Effect Selector** window is up, click on the **View** drop-down menu at the top of your screen and select **Dock Effect Selector**. This places your **Effect Selector** to the right of your **Preview** window, where you can grab your effects at will.

▶ **NOTE**

When you try to dock either the Effect Selector or the Settings window, you might get an error message reading, "It is not possible to dock the (settings dialog) at the current display resolution." This means that your monitor is not set to a resolution that is compatible with the docking capabilities of **VideoWave**. Reset your screen resolution until you find one that allows you to dock the **Settings** window and the **Effect Selector** and works for your personal preferences as well.

The **Settings** window can also be docked. The **Settings** window allows you to change the settings of your text objects. It actually has quite a few capabilities, which are covered in ⁸¹ **Add Text to a Video Production**. Open your settings window and dock it along with the **Effect Selector** to the right of your **Preview** window. Now you can toggle between the two by clicking on the tab for each.

Now that you are a little more familiar with the **VideoWave** interface, you are ready to get started on that production.

---

73 | **Add Video Files and Photos to VideoWave**

✔ **BEFORE YOU BEGIN**

71 Launch VideoWave and Change the Production Settings

72 About the VideoWave Interface

The first step to creating a complete video production is to import your video files and photos into a new project. After you have done that, the magic can begin.

1 Select Add Photo/Video

After you are inside **VideoWave**, select **Add Photo/Video** to bring up **Media Manager**.

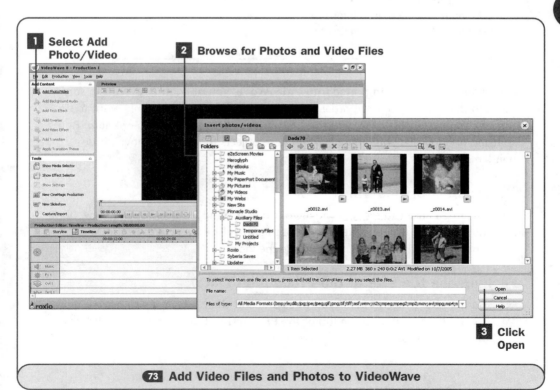

1 Select Add Photo/Video

2 Browse for Photos and Video Files

3 Click Open

2 Browse for Photos and Video Files

From **Media Manager**, you can browse your albums or folders to find the video files and pictures to create a video production. You can select more than one file or picture by holding down the **Control** key as you select them.

▶ **TIP**

You will probably use several files to create a video production. You will find it much easier to work with these files if they are in a folder or album together.

3 Click Open

When you are finished selecting the files you want, click **Open** to import them into **VideoWave**.

74	Position Video Clips and Photos Inside VideoWave
✔ BEFORE YOU BEGIN	**→ SEE ALSO**
71 Launch VideoWave and Change the Production Settings **72** About the VideoWave Interface **73** Add Video Files and Photos to VideoWave	**75** Trim or Split a Video Clip or Photo

74

After you get your files imported into **VideoWave**, you are going to want to sort them so they are in the right order for your production. You probably want to do this in conjunction with the next task, **75 Trim or Split a Video Clip or Photo**. By splitting a video file, you create two separate objects that can be moved independently.

1 Select Storyline View

It is much easier to see and move your files around in the storyline view. If you are in the timeline view, click on the **Storyline View** icon in the **Production Editor** taskbar to change the view.

2 Increase the Size of the Production Editor

You are able to see more of your files and sort them easier if you have a larger view. Click and drag the top of the **Production Editor** window until it is as far up as it goes.

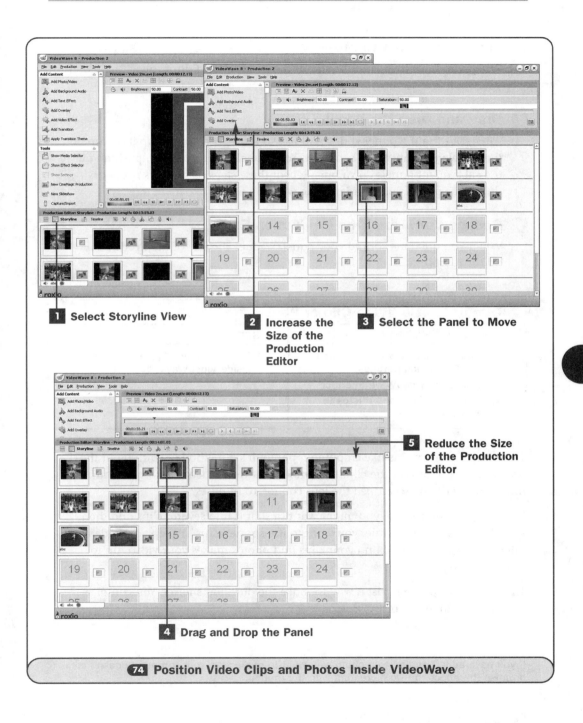

1 Select Storyline View

2 Increase the Size of the Production Editor

3 Select the Panel to Move

5 Reduce the Size of the Production Editor

4 Drag and Drop the Panel

74 Position Video Clips and Photos Inside VideoWave

3 Select the Panel to Move

When you have increased the size of the **Production Editor**, select the panel you would like to move.

4 Drag and Drop the Panel

After selecting the panel you would like to move, drag and drop it on top of the panel you want to be behind it. Your panel falls into place, pushing all the subsequent panels down one. Repeat these steps as often as necessary until your production is ordered the way you would like it.

5 Reduce the Size of the Production Editor

When you are done sorting your panels, reduce the size of the **Production Editor** to normal.

---

75 Trim or Split a Video Clip or Photo

✔ BEFORE YOU BEGIN	→ SEE ALSO
71 Launch VideoWave and Change the Production Settings	74 Position Video Clips and Photos Inside VideoWave
72 About the VideoWave Interface	
73 Add Video Files and Photos to VideoWave	

Trimming a video clip is like cropping a photo. It's a method of cutting out the unnecessary portions of the clip. Remember that time when you forgot to turn off the camcorder and videotaped the lens cap for 10 minutes?

If you have a longer clip, you might want to split it into several clips and then trim them. As a general rule, you want to use shorter clips to keep your video interesting. Creatively mixing your clips and photos makes your video fun to watch.

Trimming your photo is just a way to make the duration shorter. You can also split a photo to use it in two places.

▶ TIP

If you have added motion to a photo, you want to make sure your trimming doesn't compromise the effect you were creating with the motion.

1 Select the File to Trim

Highlight the video clip or photo you would like to trim by clicking on it.

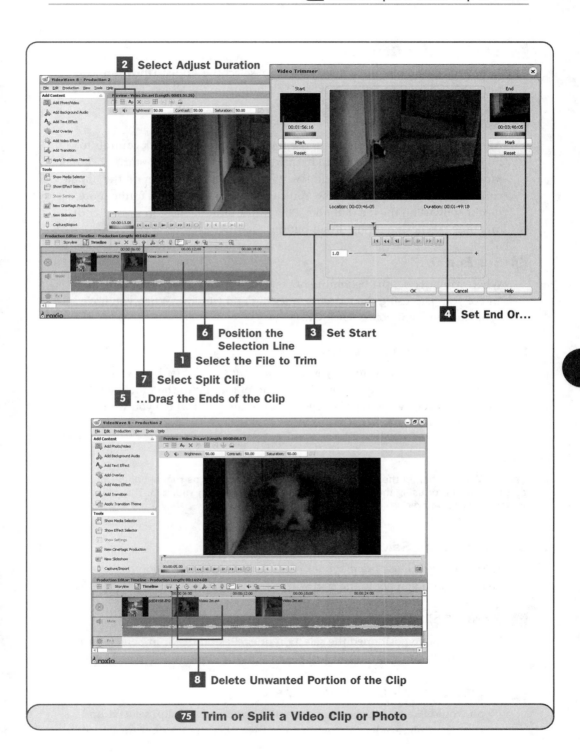

2 Select Adjust Duration

6 Position the Selection Line

3 Set Start

4 Set End Or...

1 Select the File to Trim

7 Select Split Clip

5 ...Drag the Ends of the Clip

8 Delete Unwanted Portion of the Clip

75 Trim or Split a Video Clip or Photo

2 Select Adjust Duration

After you have highlighted your video clip, select the **Adjust Duration** icon from the **Production Editor** taskbar. This brings up the **Video Trimmer**.

3 Set Start

After the **Video Trimmer** is open, use the slider or the playback controls to find the point on your video clip from which you would like to start. Click the **Mark** button under the **Start** window; this sets the start marker on the image currently in the **Preview** window. You can now adjust the start frame more precisely by using the jog dial above the **Mark** button. You can start over at any time by clicking on the **Reset** button.

4 Set End Or...

When you have set the beginning of your clip, do the same thing to set the end of your clip using the buttons under the **End** window. When you have set your start and end points, click **OK**.

5 ...Drag the Ends of the Clip

For a less precise but faster way to trim your clips, click and hold your mouse key down as you drag the beginning or end of the clip in the timeline view. Watch the **Preview** window closely to choose the point where you want to stop dragging.

75

▶ TIP

Use the **Zoom** option in the taskbar to make your clip as long as manageable when dragging to trim or using the selection line to find a position in your clip. This makes it much easier to be precise.

6 Position the Selection Line

To split your clip, use the playback controls or drag the selection line over your clip until you get to the spot where you would like your clip to be split.

7 Select Split Clip

When you have positioned the selection line, click on the **Split Selected Item** icon in the **Production Editor** taskbar to split the clip into two pieces.

8 Delete Unwanted Portion of the Clip

If you would like to delete one of the split portions of the clip, select it and click on the **Delete Selected Item** icon in the either the **Production Editor** or **Preview** taskbar.

▶ **TIPS**

Deleting an unwanted portion of a video clip is also a convenient way of trimming the clip.

After you have trimmed or split a video clip, you can easily retrieve the missing portions of it by dragging the end of the clip in the timeline view with the left mouse button held down.

---

76 | **Extract a Still Shot from a Video Clip**

✔ BEFORE YOU BEGIN	→ SEE ALSO
71 Launch VideoWave and Change the Production Settings	**31** Capture Still Shots from a Video
72 About the VideoWave Interface	
73 Add Video Files and Photos to VideoWave	

Taking a still shot from a video file is handy in several situations. You might want to end your production by freezing the video at the last frame. You can also create the effect of a photo being taken inside a video clip. Or you can save the image to print or use in a photo project.

Most digital camcorders enable you to take a still shot while you are video taping. Using **VideoWave** to extract them is an ideal way to capture those shots as photo files rather than as video files.

▶ **NOTE**

The resolution of a video file is not nearly as high as that of most photo files. The pictures you capture from a video file are not very big and won't look very good printed out. Captured pictures are great to add to a video production or slideshow, however.

1 **Use the Timeline to Locate Image**

You can locate your image on the timeline in a number of ways. You can use the jog dial to gradually make your way through the video, you can drag the selection line through the video until you come to the right spot, or you can play the video back and stop it at the right spot. You can take as many photos out of the video as you want, so your choice might depend on whether you are looking for something specific or just trying to capture photos of an experience.

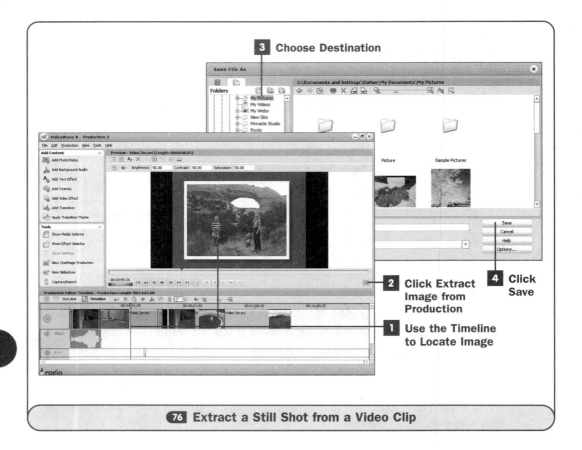

3 Choose Destination

2 Click Extract Image from Production

4 Click Save

1 Use the Timeline to Locate Image

76 Extract a Still Shot from a Video Clip

2 Click Extract Image from Production

After your image is displayed in the **Preview** window, click on the **Extract Image from Production** button (the camera icon) in the lower right of the video **Preview** window. This brings up the **Save File As** window.

3 Choose Destination

After you have brought up the **Save File As** window, browse to the destination path on your computer to which to save the images. The destination path is a location on a hard disk or any directly writable device, such as an SD card, USB drive, and so forth. Make this a folder that is conveniently accessible and easy to remember. When it comes time to add these photos to a project, you'll want to be able to find them again.

4 **Click Save**

After you have chosen a destination for your image, click **Save**. This takes you back to **VideoWave**.

▶ **NOTE**

If you want to add the photo to your current **VideoWave** production, you have to follow the steps in **73** Add Video Files and Photos to VideoWave.

---

77 **Insert a Color Panel into a Video Production**

✔ BEFORE YOU BEGIN	→ SEE ALSO
71 Launch VideoWave and Change the Production Settings	**56** Add a Blank Slide to a Slideshow
72 About the VideoWave Interface	
73 Add Video Files and Photos to VideoWave	

You can add a *color panel* anywhere in your video production to add a menu or a break. You can choose any color and add text, a special effect, or an overlay to it, just as if it were a photo.

The color panel is set at the duration you have set for your still images.

▶ **KEY TERM**

Color panel—A still frame in a video production or slideshow that is created by choosing a solid color for the background. It can be used to break up portions of the production or as a menu. A color panel has all the attributes of a still shot. It's also called a blank slide.

▶ **TIP**

At the very least, you should add a color panel to the beginning and end of your production; this creates the lead time needed to give the production a finished look.

1 **Select Location**

Before you add a color panel to your video production, select the photo or video clip nearest the location you would like it to be in. If you do not select a clip, the color panel is added to the end of the production.

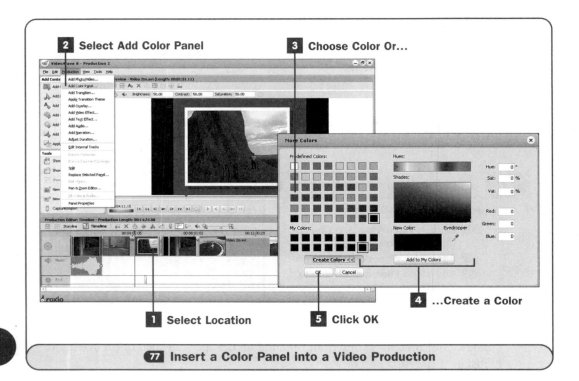

2 Select Add Color Panel   **3** Choose Color Or...

4 ...Create a Color

1 Select Location   **5** Click OK

77 Insert a Color Panel into a Video Production

2 Select Add Color Panel

After you have selected a location, select **Add Color Panel** from the
Production drop-down menu at the top of the screen. This brings up the
More Colors window.

3 Choose Color Or...

From the **More Colors** window, choose a color for your color panel.

4 ...Create a Color

If you don't see a color you like, click on the **Create Colors** button to expand
the window and choose from an infinite number of color choices. You can
also use the dropper to select any color showing on your computer screen.

5 Click OK

When you have selected the color for your blank slide, click **OK**. The color
panel is inserted after the clip you have selected. From there you can treat it
just as any other clip, adding transitions, text, and effects.

78   Add Transitions or a Transition Theme to a Video Production

✔ BEFORE YOU BEGIN	→ SEE ALSO
71 Launch VideoWave and Change the Production Settings **72** About the VideoWave Interface **73** Add Video Files and Photos to VideoWave	**57** Add Transitions or a Transition Theme to a Slideshow

A *transition* is what happens between one clip and the next in your video production. If you do not add transitions, the end of the clip is simply immediately replaced by the start of the next clip. This is called a *cut*. A fade transition darkens the end of the first clip as it lightens the beginning of the next. A wipe is like using an eraser on a chalkboard to take away the first clip and replace it with the next. You get the idea.

VideoWave offers a range of transition options, ranging from simple fades to many more playful and theme-specific options. Using attention-grabbing transitions such as star wipes and flying cubes is fun, but it can also detract from the video production if done too frequently.

You can either preview the transitions and place them one at a time, or you can apply a transition theme, which randomly places similar transitions throughout your production.

1   Select Video Clip or Photo

Inside **VideoWave**, select the clip you would like to add a transition to by clicking on it inside the storyline or timeline.

2   Click Add Transition

Click on the **Add Transition** button in the **tasks** pane. This brings up the **Add Transition** window.

3   Select Transition

From the drop-down menu you can select a transition style to narrow your choices. Preview each transition by clicking on the **Play** icon in the corner of each. When you have selected the transition you want, click **OK**.

4   Choose Transition Placement Or...

After you have clicked **OK**, you are prompted to indicate where you would like the transition to be placed in regard to your clip or inside the production. Click on your desired option and click **OK**.

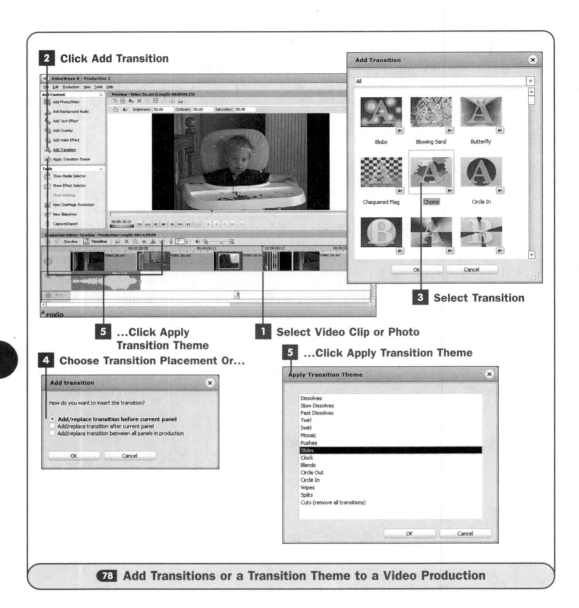

2 **Click Add Transition**

3 **Select Transition**

5 **...Click Apply Transition Theme**

4 **Choose Transition Placement Or...**

1 **Select Video Clip or Photo**

5 **...Click Apply Transition Theme**

78 **Add Transitions or a Transition Theme to a Video Production**

5 **...Click Apply Transition Theme**

If you would like to apply a transition theme to your video production, click on the **Apply Transition Theme** button in the **tasks** pane. This brings up a theme menu. The theme names are descriptive, so although there are no previews, you can get an idea of what each will be like. Select a theme and click **OK**. This randomly places several transitions, all belonging to the theme you selected, throughout your production. You can always go back and change individual transitions as desired.

79 Add Audio Files to a Video Production

✔ BEFORE YOU BEGIN	→ SEE ALSO
71 Launch VideoWave and Change the Production Settings	Chapter 2, "Importing Audio"
72 About the VideoWave Interface	Chapter 3, "Editing Audio"
73 Add Video Files and Photos to VideoWave	**58** Add an Audio Track to a Slideshow

To spice up your video production, you'll want to add audio to it. You can add any audio file on your computer or you can rip one from a CD. Although you can do some basic editing of your audio—such as splitting or clipping the track and adjusting the volume—within **VideoWave**, you'll want to do any major editing in **Sound Editor** before importing your audio into a video production.

1 Select Timeline View

The first thing you are going to want to do when adding audio is make sure your production is in the timeline view. This allows you to see your audio track and edit it more easily. Select the **Timeline** icon from the **Production Editor** taskbar to change the view.

2 Select Add Background Audio

Select **Add Background Audio** from the **tasks** pane to bring up the **Add background audio** window.

3 Browse for Audio File

From the **Add background audio** window, you can browse your albums or folders to find audio files to add to your video production. You can select more than one file by holding down the **Control** key while clicking. When you are done selecting your audio, click **Open**.

4 Choose Where to Insert Track

After you have selected your audio, you are asked which track you would like to place it on: the music track or on the sound effect track. There is essentially no difference between the two except for their name. Click on the option you would prefer and click **OK**.

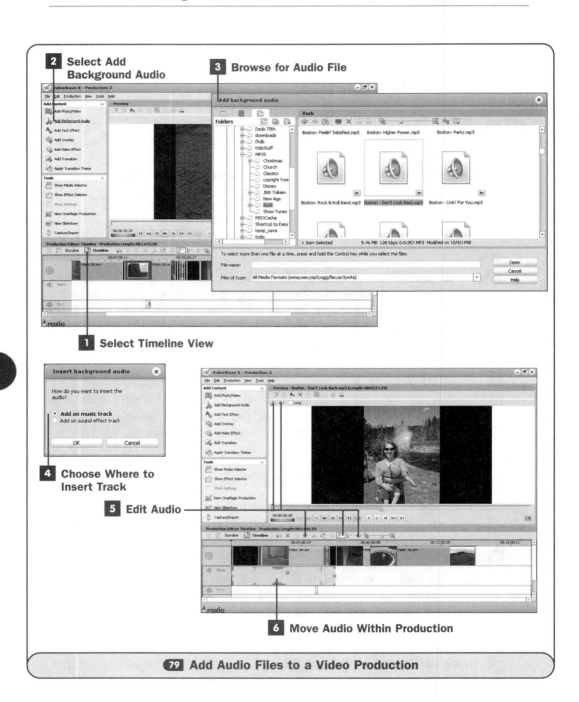

2 Select Add Background Audio

3 Browse for Audio File

1 Select Timeline View

4 Choose Where to Insert Track

5 Edit Audio

6 Move Audio Within Production

79 Add Audio Files to a Video Production

79

▶ **NOTE**

When your audio is dropped into your project, it lasts only as long as your video production, no matter how long the audio track is. You can only lengthen your audio if you add more time to the video track.

5 Edit Audio

You can edit your audio in several ways within **VideoWave**. To start, select the audio track and click on the **Edit** icon in the **Preview** taskbar. This brings up the **Audio Trimmer**. Here you can set the start and end points for your audio and loop the audio track. If your audio is too long for your video production, this is the place to trim it down to size by clipping off the beginning or the end.

You can split your audio into two or more selections by selecting the **Split** icon from the **Production Editor** taskbar. Move the selection line over the audio to the spot where you would like it clipped. It is very important to be sure that you have the audio track selected; otherwise you will clip something else. Click on the **Split** icon.

▶ **NOTE**

You can delete the center portion of your audio by splitting it into three sections and deleting the center section.

You can mute the volume or set a fade in or fade out by clicking on the **Adjust Volume** icon in the **Production Editor** taskbar. You can also change the volume settings manually by clicking on the **Edit Volume Envelope for Audio Objects** icon. This expands the audio track and gives you manual control of the volume indicator. Add a node to the line by clicking on it. Drag the node up or down to adjust the volume. For more information about adjusting the volume of your audio, see **82** **Change the Audio Volume of a Video Production**.

6 Move Audio Within Production

You can adjust the location of the volume within the production by selecting it and dragging it to the location you would like it to be. This only works if the audio track is shorter than the video track.

79

80 Narrate a Video Production

✔ BEFORE YOU BEGIN

71 Launch VideoWave and Change the Production Settings

72 About the VideoWave Interface

73 Add Video Files and Photos to VideoWave

→ SEE ALSO

Chapter 2, "Importing Audio"

59 Narrate a Slideshow

Narrating a video production can really add a lot of character and personality to it. It certainly makes it more fun to watch.

You'll probably want to preview your video production a few times as you practice your narration. You can do that inside the **Narration** window. Don't work too hard, though; you can narrate the video production in sections if you like.

80

1 Select the Video Track

Before you narrate your production, you must have the video track selected. If you have your audio track selected, the **Add Narrate** icon is not active.

2 Select Add Narration

When you have selected your video track, click on the **Add Narration** icon in the taskbar to bring up the **Add Narration Wizard**.

3 Adjust Audio Settings

When the **Add Narration Wizard** has launched, select the **Audio Settings** button to check your input devices and set the destination folder. Your input devices probably do not need to be changed; they are a microphone and your sound card. You want to double-check the directory in which the audio is being stored. Choose a directory that is easy to remember so you can find your audio later. When you are finished, click **OK**.

4 Preview Video Production

After your audio settings are correct, use the playback controls to preview your video production. Practice narrating it while it plays.

5 Click Record

When you are comfortable with your narration, rewind the video production to the point you would like to start narrating and click **Record**. You are given a three-second countdown, and then the video production starts, along with the recording. As the video runs, record your narration. Watch the volume meter indicators, located above the **Record** button; they should rise and fall with your voice.

▶ TIP

As you narrate your production, the volume meter indicators should never reach the red bands at the upper end of the indicator. If they do, this means your recording volume is too high and there will be distortion in your recording. Set the level so the meter stays in the yellow range throughout most of the recording.

6 Click Stop

When you are finished recording your narration, click **Stop**. This stops the video preview and the recording.

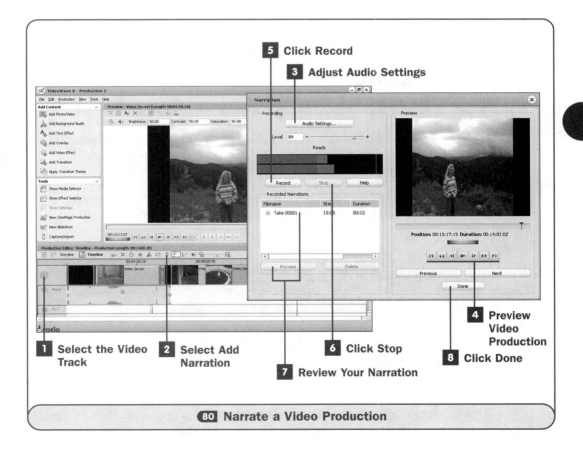

5 Click Record

3 Adjust Audio Settings

80

4 Preview Video Production

1 Select the Video Track

2 Select Add Narration

6 Click Stop

8 Click Done

7 Review Your Narration

7 Review Your Narration

After you have stopped the recording, a file appears in the list of recorded narrations. Review your narration by double-clicking on the file or by selecting it and clicking the **Preview** button. You can continue to narrate sections of your video production, or you can delete a narration and try it again.

8 Click Done

When you are satisfied with your narration, click the **Done** button to exit the **Add Narration Wizard**.

---

81   Add Text to a Video Production

✔ BEFORE YOU BEGIN

71 Launch VideoWave and Change the Production Settings
72 About the VideoWave Interface
73 Add Video Files and Photos to VideoWave

→ SEE ALSO

41 Add Text to a Photo
60 Add Text to a Slideshow

You can add text to your video production by adding it to the clips themselves or by placing it on its own track. What you can do with the text largely depends on where you have placed it.

Placed inside your clips, the text is limited to those clips. It appears with the clip and disappears as the clip disappears. It is also subject to the transitions on either side of the clip. This is a good way to add a caption to individual photos or create a title menu.

 If you place the text on its own track, you have much more control of it. You can stretch or shrink it to any length of time you want, add separate motion, and place it anywhere inside your production.

1 Add Text Effect to a Video Clip or Photo

To add a text effect to a clip, you must first select the clip to which you would like to add text. After you have the photo selected, select **Add Text Effect** from the **tasks** pane. The **Add Text Effect** window comes up, giving you quite a few text styles from which to choose. Remember that you can edit these in any way you choose later. Choose the style you like and click **OK**. You are then given the option to add your text to the production or to place it on the internal track of the selected panel. Choose to place the text on the internal track of the selected panel. This adds it to your clip itself, making it part of the panel.

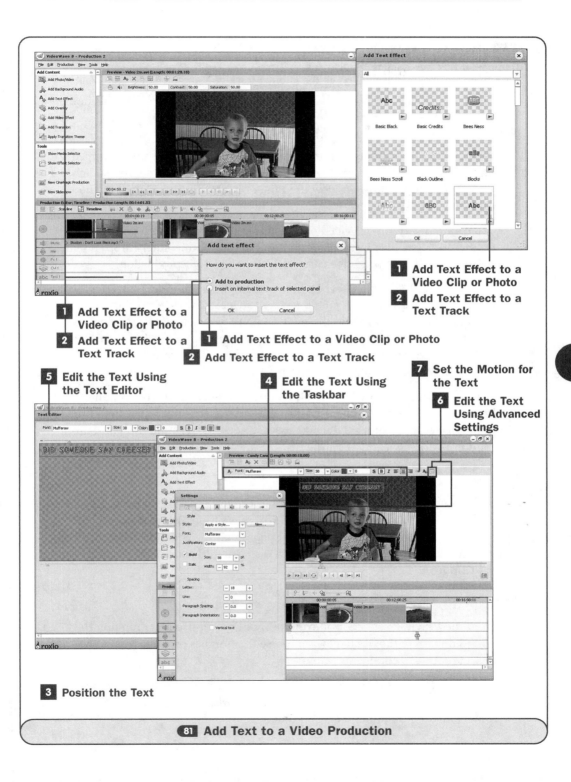

1 Add Text Effect to a Video Clip or Photo
2 Add Text Effect to a Text Track

1 Add Text Effect to a Video Clip or Photo
2 Add Text Effect to a Text Track

1 Add Text Effect to a Video Clip or Photo
2 Add Text Effect to a Text Track

5 Edit the Text Using the Text Editor

4 Edit the Text Using the Taskbar

7 Set the Motion for the Text

6 Edit the Text Using Advanced Settings

81

3 Position the Text

▶ **TIP**

Remember that by selecting the **Edit Internal Tracks or Entire Production** icon, you have the capability to edit the text on the internal track of a photo or video clip. You have all the same text editing options as if you had placed it on the external track.

2 **Add Text Effect to a Text Track**

When you add text to its own track within your video production, it appears on the text track. You might not be able to see this track unless you stretch your **Production Editor** window up a little bit. Stretch it until you see the track labeled **Text 1**.

You can add text to your video production in three ways. First, simply click on the **Add Text** icon in the **Preview** taskbar. This immediately drops a text object into the spot you have currently selected in your production.

Second, select **Add Text Effect** from the **tasks** pane. The **Add Text Effect** window comes up, giving you quite a few text styles from which to choose. Remember that you can edit these later in any way you choose. Choose the style you like and click **OK**. You are then given the option to add your text to the production or to place it on the internal track of the selected panel. Select **Add to production**, dropping it into the text track.

The final method is to select the **Show Effect Selector** in the **tasks** pane to bring up the **Effect Selector** window. Click on the **Text** tab in the top of the **Effect Selector** to bring up the text styles. Choose a style and drag and drop it into the desired location on the text track.

3 **Position the Text**

If you have placed your text on its own track, you probably want to place it more precisely where you want it. You can select it and move it anywhere along the text track. By clicking and dragging on the edges you can shrink or stretch it to the desired length. You can also clip it to shorten it by clicking on the **Clip** icon.

4 **Edit the Text Using the Taskbar**

From the **Preview** window, you can position the text itself by dragging the bounding box to the desired location. Use the handles on the edges of the bounding box to change its shape.

Highlight the text to make changes to it. You can make basic changes by using the **Text** taskbar just above the **Preview** window. You can change the font, color, and alignment, among other things.

81

5 Edit the Text Using the Text Editor

If you want to make more changes than the taskbar allows, click on the **Text Editor** icon in the taskbar to bring up your text in the **Text Editor Wizard**. Here you have four tabs where you can do such things as set a box or shadow on your text or create a 3D effect. When you are finished making changes, click **OK**.

6 Edit the Text Using Advanced Settings

If this is *still* not enough (and sometimes it's not), click on the **More Settings** icon. It might not look like much, but when the **Settings** window comes up, you will see that you have all the same capabilities of the **Text Editor**, plus some. You can choose the following tabs:

- **Style**—Here you have all your style settings. Change the font, alignment, and paragraph settings.

- **Color**—Here you can change the color of the face, outline, and shadow of your text.

- **Frame**—Here you can change the settings and colors for a frame around your text.

- **3D**—Give your text or frame a 3D effect by adding a bevel and adjusting its settings.

- **Position**—These are the settings you can't find anywhere else. From here you can position your text precisely using a measured location, or more usefully, you can rotate it.

- **Motion**—In this window you can choose an entrance and exit style for the text object.

► **TIP**

Remember that you can dock the **Settings** window to make the text-editing process easier. With the **Settings** window up, select **View, Dock Settings**. This places the **Settings** window to the right of your **Preview** window.

7 Set the Motion for the Text

You can set the *motion* for your text by selecting your text object and clicking on the **Motion** icon in the **Text** taskbar. You are given several options for a grand entrance for your text.

81

► **KEY TERM**

Motion—The term used to denote the entrance style of a text effect or overlay. For instance, if you choose to set a flying motion, your text flies into the frame rather than just appearing or being subject to the transition.

---

82   **Change the Audio Volume of a Video Production**

✔ BEFORE YOU BEGIN	→ SEE ALSO
71 Launch VideoWave and Change the Production Settings **72** About the VideoWave Interface **73** Add Video Files and Photos to VideoWave	**79** Add Audio Files to a Video Production

---

By now, you are probably carrying several tracks of audio in your production. Not only do you have the native, embedded audio, but you might have added music, sound effects, and narration. You're probably wondering how you are going to manage all the audio and make it sound good together.

We've already covered the basics of editing an audio track in **79** **Add Audio Files to a Video Production**, but this task goes a little farther and shows you how to manage several tracks.

1 **Select Show/Hide Tracks**

From the **Production Editor** taskbar, select the **Show/Hide Tracks** icon. This brings up the **Show/Hide Tracks** window.

2 **Check Audio Tracks**

Within the **Show/Hide Tracks** window, select all the audio tracks you are using in your production, including native. This allows you see all of the tracks you need to edit. If you are not using one or more tracks, uncheck the box next to it.

3 **Deselect All Other Tracks**

After you have selected the audio tracks, uncheck the boxes next to all the other tracks. This hides them in the timeline view so you can focus on the audio.

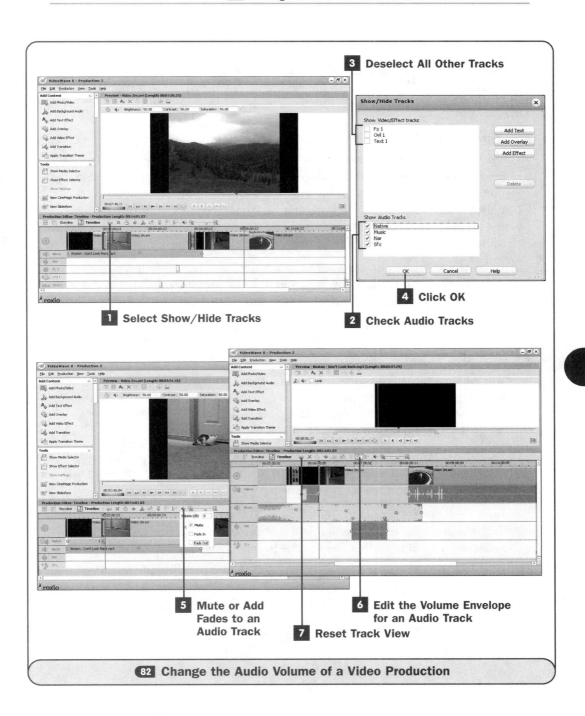

3 Deselect All Other Tracks

1 Select Show/Hide Tracks

2 Check Audio Tracks

4 Click OK

5 Mute or Add Fades to an Audio Track

6 Edit the Volume Envelope for an Audio Track

7 Reset Track View

82 Change the Audio Volume of a Video Production

4 Click OK

When you are done selecting the audio tracks you want to edit, click **OK**. This closes the **Show/Hide Tracks** window and takes you back to **VideoWave** where you can have up to four tracks of audio in your view.

5 Mute or Add Fades to an Audio Track

Your native audio is not always the best audio to leave with the track. If you are planning to create a music video or you just want to narrate your video production and don't want to use any of the native audio, you can mute the native audio track. Select the track and click on the **Adjust Volume** icon in the **Production Editor** taskbar to bring up the volume adjustment. Check the **Mute** box. Your audio track turns grey, indicating that it is dormant.

If you would like to fade the volume of the track you have selected, check either the **Fade In** or **Fade Out** box. You can also adjust the volume of the entire track by typing in a decibel level or using the slider.

Click anywhere inside **VideoWave** to exit the volume adjustment.

6 Edit the Volume Envelope for an Audio Track

You might want to adjust the volume of a small portion of an audio track for a variety of reasons. For instance, if you are occasionally narrating a production to which you have added a music track, you probably want to fade the music down during the narration.

Click the **Edit Volume Envelope** icon in the **Production Editor**. This increases the width of all of your audio tracks. If you need to, stretch the **Production Editor** up so you can see all of your tracks.

From here, you can easily make volume adjustments. Click on any volume line to add a node or handle that you can drag to any volume setting. Two nodes are needed to change the volume in a relatively short amount of time.

Make the needed changes throughout your production. Preview your changes as you make them by using the playback controls in the **Preview** window. That way, you can make sure your volume levels don't clash.

When you are finished making changes, click on the **Volume Envelope** icon once again to shrink the tracks to their smaller size.

▶ TIP

You might want to click on the **Edit the Volume Envelope** icon before you make any adjustments to your audio so you can get a better view of what you are doing.

7 Reset Track View

After you have reset the tracks to their normal size, click on the **Show/Hide Tracks** icon once again and follow the steps to restore the track view that you would prefer. At this point, you might want to hide all of your audio tracks and focus on the other tracks.

---

83 Export a Video Production to a Video File

✔ BEFORE YOU BEGIN	→ SEE ALSO
Chapter 1, "Start Here" (Review information on video file formats)	Chapter 12, "Authoring DVDs"
71 Launch VideoWave and Change the Production Settings	**84** Burn a Video Production to a Disc Using MyDVD Express
72 About the VideoWave Interface	
73 Add Video Files and Photos to VideoWave	

When you have completely edited your video production, it's time to export it. Whether or not you want to burn it to a disc, it is an excellent idea to create a video file of the production. That way you can save it to your computer or burn the file itself to a CD or DVD to be viewed, edited, or burned later.

You can also export it to a digital camcorder, play it to a TV or VCR, or email it.

1 Select Output As

To export your video production into a video file, select the **Output As** icon from the **Preview** taskbar.

2 Save Production

When you have clicked on the **Output As** icon, you are prompted to save your production. You are strongly encouraged to do so. After you have saved your production, the **Make Movie** window opens.

3 Select Destination

After the **Make Movie** window is open, select your destination by clicking on the appropriate button.

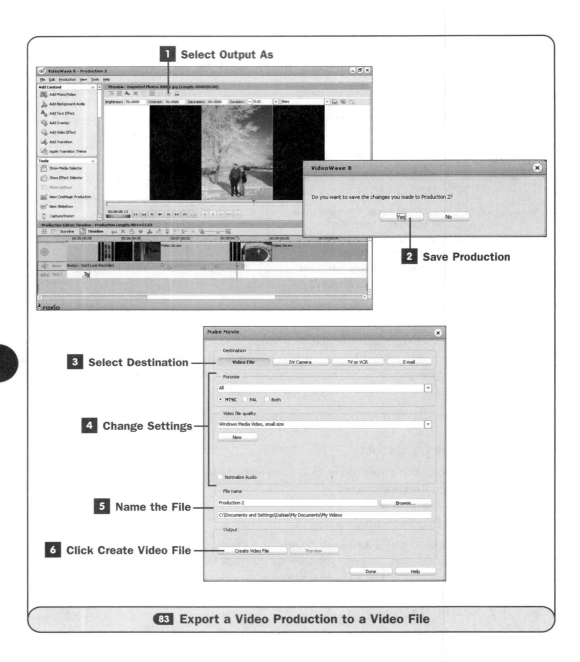

83

83 Export a Video Production to a Video File

4 Change Settings

After you have selected your destination, your window might have changed, but you can change the format and file settings for your video file in any

[handwritten: ⊘ MY TEMPLATE]

version of the window. **NTSC** is the standard for North America. **PAL** is standard everywhere else.

[handwritten: ⊘ MPEG-2 FOR DVDS]

You can also change the file extension and quality from the **Video file quality** drop-down menu. You are able to choose from a full range of file options only in the **Video File** window. If you are unsure which option to choose, review the video file information in Chapter 1, "Start Here."

[handwritten: BEST QUALITY]

[handwritten: ⊘ file Type: MPEG]

5   Name the File

After you have set your options, you can change the name of your file and set a destination. The default name for your file is the name of your production, but you can change it. Browse to find the location to which you would like to save it.

[handwritten: ⊘ Normalize audio ✓]

6   Click Create Video File

When you are ready, click either the **Create Video File** or the **Start Output** option (available in the **DV Camera**, **TV or VCR**, and **Email** options) at the bottom of the screen. You are able to preview the production as it is rendered and stored or exported as a video file. This process takes several minutes. When it is finished, click **Done**.

84

---

84   **Burn a Video Production to a Disc Using MyDVD Express**

✔ BEFORE YOU BEGIN	→ SEE ALSO
Chapter 1, "Start Here" (Review information on video file formats)	Chapter 12, "Authoring DVDs"
71 Launch VideoWave and Change the Production Settings	**83** Export a Video Production to a Video File
72 About the VideoWave Interface	
73 Add Video Files and Photos to VideoWave	

With just a few quick steps you can export your video production directly to a DVD, complete with menus, so you can enjoy watching it for years to come or share your special memories with others.

You might want to export your creation to a video file, as well as burning it to a DVD, so you always have the option to view it on your computer or import it into a new project as a video file.

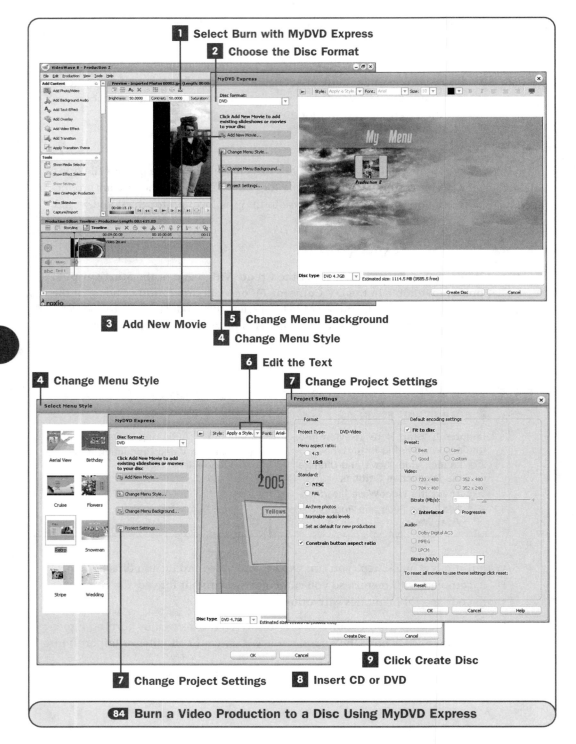

1 Select Burn with MyDVD Express

2 Choose the Disc Format

3 Add New Movie

5 Change Menu Background

4 Change Menu Style

6 Edit the Text

4 Change Menu Style

7 Change Project Settings

7 Change Project Settings

8 Insert CD or DVD

9 Click Create Disc

84 Burn a Video Production to a Disc Using MyDVD Express

► **NOTE**

MyDVD Express is a simplified version of the more robust **MyDVD**, a full DVD-authoring application that can give you several more options for creating a DVD menu than the Express version. Take a look at Chapter 12, "Authoring DVDs."

1 **Select Burn with MyDVD Express**

When you are ready to burn your production to a DVD, click on the **Burn with MyDVD Express** icon in the **Preview** taskbar. This opens **MyDVD Express**.

2 **Choose the Disc Format**

After **MyDVD Express** has launched, choose your disc format from the **Disc format** drop-down menu. DVDs are so inexpensive now that it is rare that you would want to use an alternative disc format. If you do want to create another disc format, such as Video CD, which burns video in a standardized format to an ordinary CD, you can choose from several.

Be sure and set the disc type at the bottom of the **MyDVD** window so your available space indicator is correct.

84

3 **Add New Movie**

You can add additional video productions and files to your DVD. Select the **Add New Movie** button and browse to find the files you want to add. When you have selected your files, click **OK**.

4 **Change Menu Style**

After you have added any additional videos to your DVD project, change the menu style by selecting the **Change Menu Style** button to bring up the **Change Menu Style** window. From this window you are able to select from several styles for your menu. Preview the styles by clicking on them to bring them up into the larger windows. When you have selected the style you like best, click **OK**. After you are back in **MyDVD Express**, you can preview the menu style by clicking the **Play** icon in the taskbar.

► **TIP**

You can preview the way your menu will operate on a DVD by clicking on the **Preview** icon in the taskbar. The **Preview** icon looks like a miniature TV.

5 **Change Menu Background**

After you have set the style for your menu, you might want to use your own photo for the menu background to give it a personal touch. Click on the **Change Menu Background** button and browse for the photo you would like to have as a background. When you have selected a photo, click **OK**.

6 **Edit the Text**

After you have put in your own background photo, you can do some basic editing of the text. Although the text objects are constrained to the menu style you picked, you can retype the text as well as change the font, color, and size by using the taskbar above the background photo.

7 **Change Project Settings**

When you are satisfied with the look of your menu, select the **Project Settings** button. In the **Project Settings** window you can change the aspect ratio, set the video standard, and choose whether you would like the production to be interlaced or progressive, among other things. When your settings look good, click **OK**.

84

8 **Insert CD or DVD**

When you are ready to burn the disc, insert the disc you are using into your burner.

9 **Click Create Disc**

When you have inserted your disc, click the **Create Disc** button to burn your DVD project. The **Burn DVD** window comes up. Change any of the options and click **Burn**.

11

Advanced Video Editing Techniques

IN THIS CHAPTER:

The techniques discussed in this chapter are only considered advanced because they are not necessarily used on your average home video. As a matter of fact, some of these techniques are the easiest to apply, so don't be afraid to jump right in and have some fun.

You can really spice up your video by adding special effects to key points or adding motion to your still shots. Create a feeling of romance or suspense by slowing your video down or create a comedy by speeding it up.

You can even create your own monster movie by layering your video and applying a chroma key effect. Your creations can be as diverse and fun as your imagination allows.

85

85 **Synchronize Audio and Video**	
✔ **BEFORE YOU BEGIN**	→ **SEE ALSO**
71 Launch VideoWave and Change the Production Settings **72** About the VideoWave Interface **73** Add Video Files and Photos to VideoWave **79** Add Audio Files to a Video Production	**75** Trim or Split a Video Clip or Photo

When you have imported all of your audio, video, and photo files, there will probably be some discrepancy between the duration of your video track and your audio track. Your audio might play just a few seconds longer than your video or vice-versa. Normally you could solve this problem by individually increasing or decreasing the duration of your still shots by a fraction to get the video to match the audio. This is very time consuming and the results are not always satisfactory. If you are in this situation, there is an easier way—**VideoWave** can do it for you, assuming that your audio and video last pretty close to the same amount of time. **VideoWave** resets the length of your video track to exactly match the audio.

It is very important to synchronize your audio and video in the correct sequence of tasks. Your transitions, for instance, shorten your video track, so you need to have added them before you synchronize. On the other hand, you want to narrate your production after you synchronize it, so you don't throw the narration off by stretching or shrinking your video track. Think carefully through the steps you are taking to create your production before you perform this task.

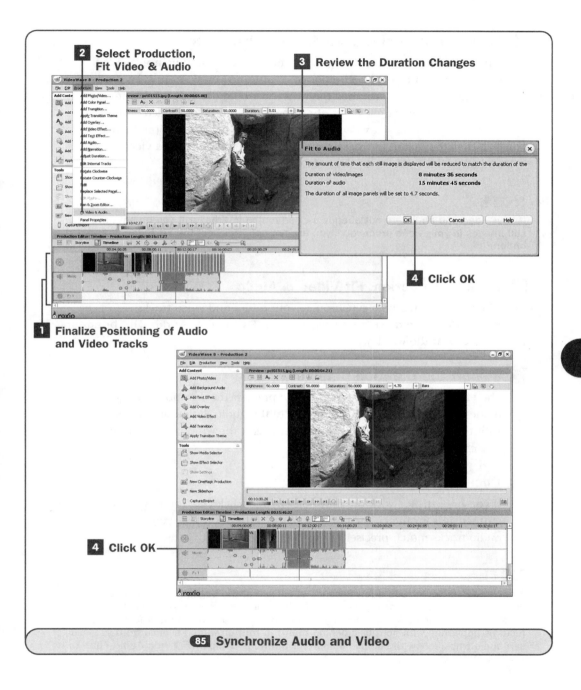

2 Select Production, Fit Video & Audio

3 Review the Duration Changes

Fit to Audio

The amount of time that each still image is displayed will be reduced to match the duration of the

| Duration of video/images | **8 minutes 36 seconds** |
| Duration of audio | **15 minutes 45 seconds** |

The duration of all image panels will be set to 4.7 seconds.

OK   Cancel   Help

4 Click OK

1 Finalize Positioning of Audio and Video Tracks

4 Click OK

1 Finalize Positioning of Audio and Video Tracks

This is the most important step of this task. Before you synchronize your tracks, make sure you have imported everything you want in your production and that each clip is trimmed the way you would like it to appear in your video. Make any changes that affect the duration of your video or audio track, such as setting a video clip to play in fast or slow motion. Remember that the other external tracks are not linked to the audio and video tracks, and any effects placed on them do not move with the video.

▶ NOTE

If your video and audio are not already a close match in time, or if you do not have any still images in your video production, you are not able to select the **Fit Video & Audio** option.

2 Select Production, Fit Video & Audio

When you are ready to synchronize your audio and video tracks, select the **Production** drop-down menu and click on **Fit Video & Audio**. This brings up the **Fit to Audio** window.

3 Review the Duration Changes

The **Fit to Audio** window allows you to preview the duration change that is made to each still shot to fit the video to the audio. If you are not satisfied with the duration change, click **Cancel** to exit the window without making any changes.

4 Click OK

If you are satisfied with the duration change, click **OK**. You have to wait several seconds for the change to take place, but after it has, your video and audio tracks match precisely.

▶ NOTE

Many audio tracks include a few seconds of silence at the beginning and end. Be sure to check for extended periods of silence at the beginning and end of your audio track before choosing **Fit Audio & Video** if you don't want to have your first or last couple of pictures appearing with no music behind them. To trim unwanted silence from your chosen audio track, follow the steps outlined for trimming a clip in 79 **Add Audio Files to a Video Production.**

85

86 Set a Video Clip to Play in Fast or Slow Motion

✔ BEFORE YOU BEGIN	→ SEE ALSO
71 Launch VideoWave and Change the Production Settings **72** About the VideoWave Interface **73** Add Video Files and Photos to VideoWave	**75** Trim or Split a Video Clip or Photo

You've seen it done in movies and in commercials. Changing the speed of a film can help relay emotion. Playing film in slow motion gives it a nostalgic or romantic feel. Video that has been sped up has a slapstick or hectic feel. Within **VideoWave**, changing the speed of your video clip couldn't be simpler.

1 Select the Video Clip

Highlight the video clip you would like to play in fast or slow motion.

▶ **TIP**

If you would like to change the speed of just a portion of a video clip, you need to split the clip so the section in which you want to adjust the speed is separate from the rest of the clip.

86

2 Select Adjust Duration

After you have highlighted your video clip, select the **Adjust Duration** icon from the **Production Editor** taskbar. This brings up the **Video Trimmer**.

3 Set Speed

After the **Video Trimmer** is open, you'll see a slider at the bottom of the window. Use this slider to adjust the speed of your clip. If you would like your clip to play in slow motion, set the slider to a value less than one. The value .5 plays your clip at half the normal speed.

If you want your video to play in fast motion, set the slider to a value higher than one. The value **2** plays your video twice as fast.

▶ **NOTE**

You can't preview your speed settings in the **Audio Trimmer**. You are able to see the effect in the **Preview** window in **VideoWave**, however.

3 Set Speed

2 Select Adjust Duration

4 Click OK

1 Select the Video Clip

86 Set a Video Clip to Play in Fast or Slow Motion

4 Click OK

When you are finished setting the speed of your video clip, click **OK**.

▶ NOTE

When you change the speed of a video clip, it won't be just the video that changes. Your native audio also plays at a different speed. This creates an effect that will probably make you laugh, but that you probably don't want in your production. See **82 Change the Audio Volume of a Video Production** for help on muting your native audio.

Pan and Zoom Within a Video

✔ BEFORE YOU BEGIN	→ SEE ALSO
71 Launch VideoWave and Change the Production Settings **72** About the VideoWave Interface **73** Add Video Files and Photos to VideoWave	**61** Apply Pan and Zoom to Slideshow Photos

The **Pan & Zoom** feature can only be used on a photo within your video production. It creates movement by zooming in or out of the photo and moving it around as you are viewing it. This can create the feeling that the photo is part of the video and add interest to the photos in your video production.

1 **Set Auto Motion Or...**

To add a randomized **Pan & Zoom** feature to the photos in your slideshow, select the photo or photos to which you would like to add the automatic **Pan & Zoom** feature. Right-click on the selected photo and select **Auto Motion** from the context menu that appears.

▶ **TIP**

When you use Auto Motion to apply **Pan & Zoom** presets to all images automatically, it's important to review each image carefully. For all its good intentions, sometimes **VideoWave**'s preset **Pan & Zoom** moves key elements of your images out of the frame's viewable area, and you'll need to apply another preset or edit the motion manually to make sure your photo is properly displayed.

2 **...Select Photo or Panel**

Select the photo or panel to which to apply a **Pan & Zoom** effect.

3 **Select Pan & Zoom Editor**

After your photo is selected, click on the **Pan & Zoom Editor** icon in the **Preview** taskbar. This brings up the **Pan & Zoom Editor** window.

4 **Use a Preset, Or...**

After the **Pan & Zoom Editor** has opened, you can choose a preset from the drop-down menu. The preset options are fairly descriptive, but try a few out and see what you like.

87

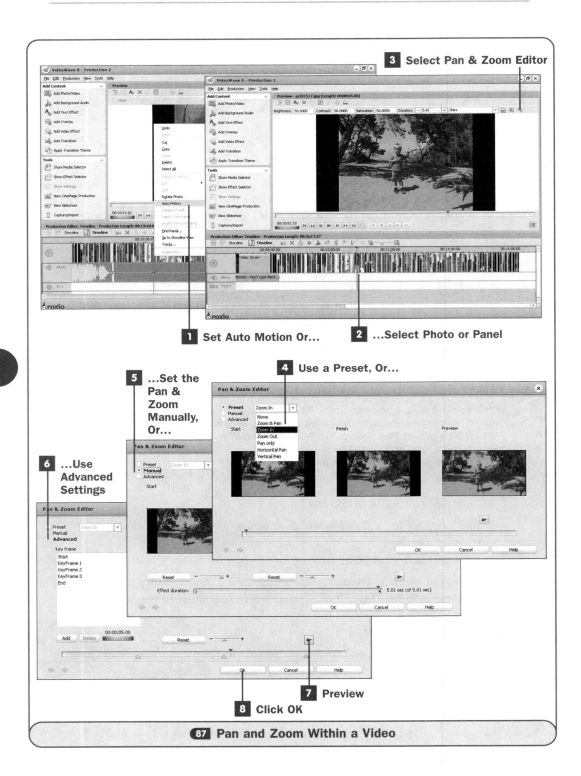

3 Select Pan & Zoom Editor

1 Set Auto Motion Or...

2 ...Select Photo or Panel

4 Use a Preset, Or...

5 ...Set the Pan & Zoom Manually, Or...

6 ...Use Advanced Settings

7 Preview

8 Click OK

87 Pan and Zoom Within a Video

5 ...Set the Pan & Zoom Manually, Or...

You can also manually set the **Pan & Zoom** by selecting the **Manual** option. You are given sliders to adjust the zoom on the beginning and ending frame. After you have zoomed into a frame, you can change the pan by dragging the bounding box. Use this approach to modify any pan and zoom moves applied using presets as well.

6 ...Use Advanced Settings

If you want to create even more motion, you can do this by clicking the **Advanced** option. Use the slider to choose a key frame and change the settings for that frame. You can use as many key frames as you need to create the effect you want.

Change the location of a key frame by moving its marker anywhere inside the timeline.

7 Preview

You can preview your **Pan & Zoom** settings by clicking on the **Play** icon under the **Preview** screen inside of the **Pan & Zoom Editor**. If you have added an audio track to your production, the audio plays as you preview your video.

8 Click OK

When you are satisfied with your settings, click **OK**. The effects are applied to your photo and the **Pan & Zoom Editor** closes.

---

88 | **Change Color/Brightness of a Video**

✔ BEFORE YOU BEGIN	→ SEE ALSO
71 Launch VideoWave and Change the Production Settings	**34** Color Correct a Photo
72 About the VideoWave Interface	
73 Add Video Files and Photos to VideoWave	

When you adjust something such as the brightness or contrast on a video clip, your change has to be made to about 29 images per second of video. It's not hard to see why there are not as many capabilities for editing video as there are for editing photos.

88

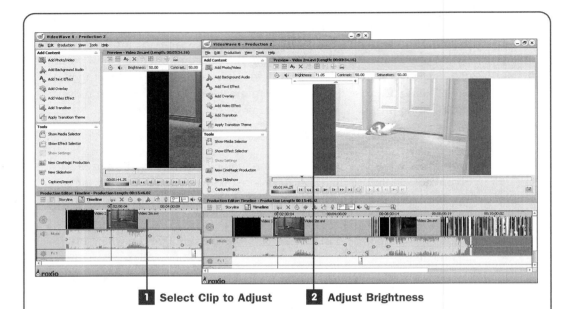

1 **Select Clip to Adjust**   2 **Adjust Brightness**

3 **Adjust Contrast**

4 **Adjust Saturation**

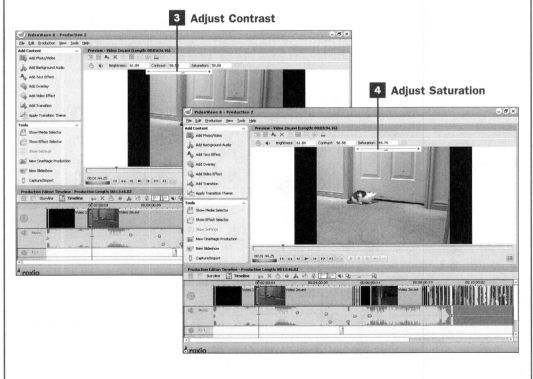

88 Change Color/Brightness of a Video

You can change the brightness, contrast, and saturation of your video, which can really make a difference to your dark or washed-out video clips.

▶ **TIP**

Instead of desaturating your video, you can change it to black and white or even sepia by using a special effect on it.

▣ Select Clip to Adjust

You've probably noticed by now that the taskbar in the **Preview** window changes depending on what kind of clip you have selected. You can adjust the color of either a video clip or a still shot inside your production. The taskbar looks slightly different for each one. Select the clip you want to change.

▣ Adjust Brightness

Click on the **Brightness** value to bring up the slider. Adjust the slider until you are satisfied with the result in the **Preview** window. You can close the slider by clicking anywhere inside the **VideoWave** window.

▣ Adjust Contrast

Usually, you want to adjust the brightness before you adjust the contrast. Sometimes you'll want to tweak your settings by going back and forth. That's why the brightness and contrast options almost always come together. Click on the **Contrast** value to bring up the slider. Adjust the slider until you are satisfied with the result in the **Preview** window.

88

▶ **TIP**

As you adjust the brightness and contrast, watch the whites in your picture. When they start looking washed out, you've gone too far.

▶ **NOTE**

If your picture is extremely light or dark, it might not have enough pixels in the light or dark areas to correct sufficiently.

▣ Adjust Saturation

After your brightness and contrast are set, you might want to adjust the saturation. The *saturation* of a picture is the amount of color it contains. You can adjust the color up or down. Click on the **Saturation** value to bring up the slider. Adjust the slider until you are satisfied with the result in the **Preview** window.

89   Add Special Effects to a Video

✔ BEFORE YOU BEGIN	→ SEE ALSO
71 Launch VideoWave and Change the Production Settings	**62** Add Special Effects to a Slideshow
72 About the VideoWave Interface	**91** Use a Chroma Key or Green Screen to Create Special Effects
73 Add Video Files and Photos to VideoWave	

You can add a special effect to your video production by adding it to the clips themselves or by placing it on its own track.

Placed on the internal track of the clip, the special effect is limited to that clip. It appears with the clip and ends with the clip. It is also subject to the transitions on either side of the clip.

If you place the special effect on its own track, you have much more control of it. You can stretch or shrink it to any length of time you want and place it anywhere inside your production.

89

1 Select Location for the Special Effect

Select the frame or location to add the special effect. If you want to add the effect to the internal track of a clip, make sure the clip is selected. If you want to add the special effect to its own track, drag the selection line to the right location.

2 Select Add Video Effect

When you have selected the location for the special effect, select **Add Video Effect** from the **tasks** pane to bring up the **Add Video Effect** window.

▶ TIP

If you have your **Effect Selector** docked, you can drag and drop your special effect to the special effects track. If you want your special effect to be on an internal track, select the **Edit the Internal Track or Entire Production** icon and drag and drop it into the internal track.

3 Choose the Video Effect

After the **Add Video Effect** window is open, use the drop-down menu to narrow your choices and select the special effect you want to use. You can preview the special effect by clicking on the **Play** icon in the corner of each. When you have selected the desired effect, click **OK**.

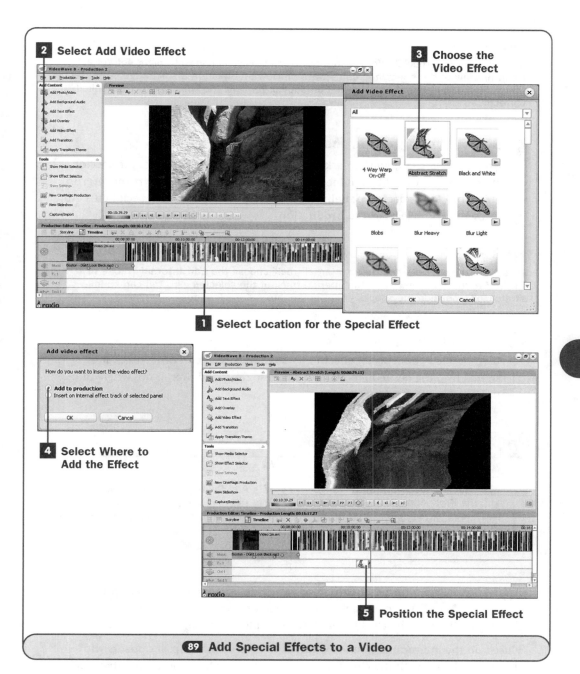

2 Select Add Video Effect

3 Choose the Video Effect

1 Select Location for the Special Effect

4 Select Where to Add the Effect

5 Position the Special Effect

89 Add Special Effects to a Video

▶ **NOTE**

Because applying special effects is a processor-intensive action, you might not get a clean preview of the effect. You can always preview an effect on a still image or paused frame. Rest assured that as your final production renders, the special effect is applied correctly.

4 Select Where to Add the Effect

After you click **OK**, you are asked where you would like to place the special effect. If you would like it added to the photo itself, choose **Insert on internal effect track of selected panel**. If you would prefer to add the special effect to its own track, select **Add to production**.

▶ **NOTE**

If you add the special effect to an internal track, choose the **Edit Internal Tracks or Entire Production** icon to edit the internal track of the selected clip. You can shrink, stretch, or reposition the special effect in the internal track editor.

5 Position the Special Effect

If you added your special effect to its own track, you can now shrink it or stretch it to the desired length. You can also drag and drop it anywhere along the production timeline.

90

---

90   Add Overlays to a Video

✔ BEFORE YOU BEGIN	→ SEE ALSO
71 Launch VideoWave and Change the Production Settings	**63** Add Overlay to a Slideshow
72 About the VideoWave Interface	**91** Use a Chroma Key or Green Screen to Create Special Effects
73 Add Video Files and Photos to VideoWave	

An overlay is like a frame or border for your video production. The effect is much like having a moving scrapbook. You can add an overlay to your video production by adding it to the clips themselves or by placing it on its own track.

Placed on the internal track, the overlay is limited to that clip. It appears with the clip and ends with the clip. It is also subject to the transitions on either side of the clip. If you place the overlay on its own track, you have much more control of it. You can stretch or shrink it to any length of time you want and place it anywhere inside your production.

2 Select Add Overlay

3 Choose the Overlay

1 Select Location for the Overlay

4 Select Where to Add the Overlay

5 Edit the Overlay

90

1 Select Location for the Overlay

Select the clip or location to which to add the overlay. If you want to add the effect to the internal track of a clip, make sure the clip is selected. If you want to add the overlay to its own track, drag the selection line to the correct location.

2 Select Add Overlay

When you have selected the location for the overlay, select **Add Overlay** from the **tasks** pane to bring up the **Add Overlay** window.

▶ **TIP**

If you have your **Effect Selector** docked, you can drag and drop your overlay to the overlay track. If you want your overlay to be on an internal track, select the **Edit the Internal Track or Entire Production** icon and drag and drop it into the internal track.

3 Choose the Overlay

After the **Add Overlay** window is open, use the drop-down menu to narrow your choices and select the overlay you want to use. You can preview the overlay by clicking on the **Play** icon in the corner of each. When you have selected the desired overlay, click **OK**.

90

▶ **NOTE**

Because applying overlays is a processor-intensive action, you might not get a clean preview of the effect. You can always preview an effect on a still image or paused frame. Rest assured that as your final production renders, the overlay is applied correctly.

4 Select Where to Add the Overlay

After you click **OK**, you are asked where you would like to place the overlay. If you would like it added to the clip itself, choose **Insert on internal effect track of selected panel**. If you would prefer to add the overlay to its own track, select **Add to production**.

5 Edit the Overlay

If you added your overlay to its own track, you can now shrink it or stretch it to the desired length. You can also drag and drop it anywhere along the production timeline.

You can also set a motion for the overlay by clicking on the **Motion** icon in the **Preview** taskbar. This determines how your overlay is placed into the production.

You can also choose the **Settings** window to apply several advanced effects to your overlay. These are covered in **91** **Use a Chroma Key or Green Screen to Create Special Effects**. Creating a green screen effect is simply a matter of applying a chroma key to an existing overlay.

▶ **NOTE**

If you add the overlay to an internal track, choose the **Edit Internal Tracks or Entire Production icon** to edit the internal track of the selected clip. You can shrink, stretch, or reposition the overlay in the internal track editor.

---

91 **Use a Chroma Key or Green Screen to Create Special Effects**

✔ BEFORE YOU BEGIN	→ SEE ALSO
71 Launch VideoWave and Change the Production Settings	**89** Add Special Effects to a Video
72 About the VideoWave Interface	**90** Add Overlays to a Video
73 Add Video Files and Photos to VideoWave	

A *chroma key* works by deleting all the pixels of a certain color out of a picture or video clip. By using a solid color, such as bright green, for the background, you can make the background transparent. Now you, too, can make your own B-rated monster movies!

▶ **KEY TERM**

Chroma key—A transparency effect based on color, or the exact color that is used for the transparency effect.

Creating a special effect using a chroma key is actually done by applying the **Chroma Key** setting to an overlay. This creates the layered effect needed to use the chroma key effectively.

With a little imagination, the chroma key can be a very useful tool. With a clip art border that is filled with the same solid color, you can create your own frame to use as an overlay. You can even do this with a photograph of a frame or texture by either photographing it with a solid color or placing the solid color in after the fact in **PhotoSuite**.

A bright or neon green is the most popular solid color to use because it is a naturally uncommon color. If you want something green to show up, a bright blue is also a popular color.

91

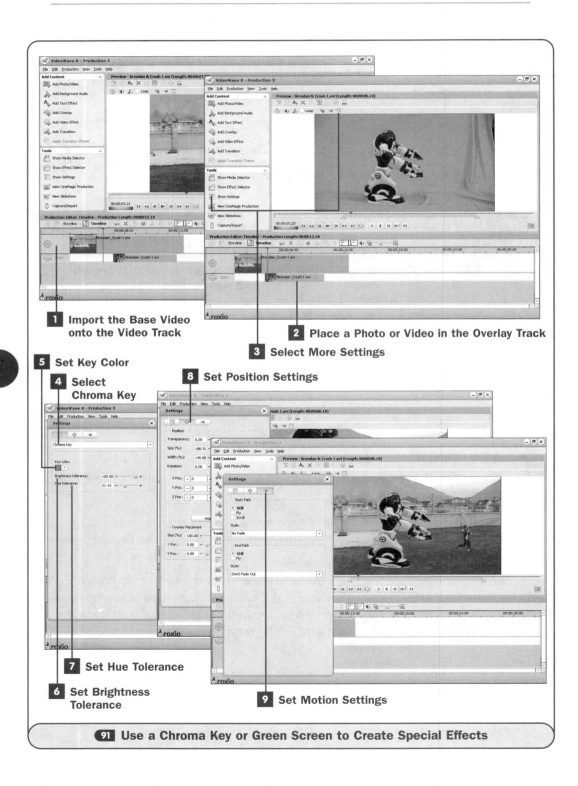

1 Import the Base Video onto the Video Track

2 Place a Photo or Video in the Overlay Track

3 Select More Settings

5 Set Key Color

8 Set Position Settings

91

4 Select Chroma Key

7 Set Hue Tolerance

6 Set Brightness Tolerance

9 Set Motion Settings

91 Use a Chroma Key or Green Screen to Create Special Effects

① Import the Base Video onto the Video Track

To create a **Chroma Key** effect, you need two layers of video. The bottom or base layer is the main video. This will probably be the setting for action in your video. Anything placed in the overlay track covers this layer. Only by making portions of the overlay transparent are you able to see the base layer.

② Place a Photo or Video in the Overlay Track

Whenever you place video in your production, you are always given the option of placing a second or subsequent video or photo in the overlay track. You can make any of your video files or photos into an overlay. To make the **Chroma Key** effect work, you need to place a video or picture that has quite a bit of the same solid color in it. Import the file and select the option to place it on the overlay track.

③ Select More Settings

After you have placed a video or photo in the overlay track, it is the only picture you are able to see in the **Preview** window. Make sure it is highlighted and click on the **More Settings** icon in the **Preview** window to bring up the **Settings** window.

91

▶ TIP

If your **Settings** window is docked, you are able to see these options any time your overlay is selected.

④ Select Chroma Key

The drop-down menu in the **Settings** window has several options. Select the **Chroma Key** option.

▶ NOTES

When you have an overlay selected, the settings window is set specifically for the effects you can apply to your overlay. Any one of the options in the drop-down menu can be selected and applied to your overlay. After you have been over the basics of the **Chroma Key** option, you should be able to apply and play with the other options with ease.

The *luma key* is similar to the chroma key because it creates transparency in your overlay. It differs because instead of using a color to create the transparency, it uses the lighter or darker areas of your overlay. For instance, by using the luma key on the robot in the example, I can make all the black or all the white on him disappear.

▶ KEY TERM

Luma key—A transparency effect based on luminance, or the exact luminance used for the transparency effect.

5 Set Key Color

When you have selected **Chroma Key** from the drop-down menu, you are shown the settings for the chroma key. Because the color is literally the key to the way this effect works, choosing the right color is important. The best way to do it is to use the eyedropper to sample the color from your overlay. After you have changed the color, everything in the overlay that is the key color becomes transparent. Well, almost everything. At this point, there are probably a few spots gone that you didn't want gone or maybe there are a few spots of color that weren't zapped by the chroma key. That's what the other settings are for.

▶ TIP

It is very difficult to prevent a "shadow" of color around the parts of the overlay that are left after applying the chroma key. Two things can help a lot: First, make sure your solid color is as uniform as possible. If you are using cloth, make sure there aren't any wrinkles and try to get the lighting as consistent as possible. Second, when you use the dropper, try to get a mid-range portion of the color so the tolerance doesn't need to be set very high.

91

6 Set Brightness Tolerance

The brightness tolerance determines how light or dark the color has to be to be made transparent. The higher the tolerance, the more color disappears. The downside of this is that as you set the tolerance higher, you start to lose portions of the overlay that you want to keep. Play with this and the hue tolerance together until you have the best possible setting.

7 Set Hue Tolerance

The hue tolerance determines how different the colors in the overlay can be from the key color and still go transparent. As you get higher up the scale, the colors radiating from your key color (in respect to the color wheel) start to disappear until your overlay is gone entirely. Watch your **Preview** window carefully to find the best setting.

8 Set Position Settings

After you have set the **Chroma Key** settings as best you can, click on the **Position** icon in the **Settings** taskbar to bring up the **Position** settings. Here you can set several variables to adjust the position of your overlay relative to the base image. If your proportion is not what you expected, you can shrink or enlarge your overlay. You can also stretch it; in this case, I stretched the overlay slightly to cut out part of the overlay that wasn't covered by the green screen when I filmed. You can also stretch a border to exactly fit your aspect ratio.

▶ **TIP**

Remember that these settings can be applied to any overlay, even the predesigned over-lays within **VideoWave**. You can use a 4:3 border and stretch it to fit a 16:9 aspect ratio.

9 **Set Motion Settings**

When you have positioned your overlay, you can adjust the **Motion** settings by clicking on the **Motion** icon in the **Settings** taskbar. Select the way you would like the overlay to appear and disappear from your video. When you are satisfied with your settings, close the **Settings** window.

91

12

Authoring DVDs

IN THIS CHAPTER:

Creating a DVD of your edited home movies with a personalized menu is an accomplishment comparable to creating an elaborate scrapbook for your photos. The difference is that you can make as many copies of your DVD as you want and distribute them to friends and family.

You have several options: You can burn your camcorder tapes straight to a DVD to watch them on TV or to back them up; you can quickly create a DVD with your DivX files; or you can create an elaborate menu for your video (edited or not) with customized videos, photos, and music.

You can also create a quick menu using **MyDVD Express**. After you have used **MyDVD**, **MyDVD Express** will be easy for you. If you would like to use **MyDVD Express** instead, refer to task **84** **Burn a Video Production to a Disc Using MyDVD Express**.

---

92 | Add Movies to a DVD Project

✔ BEFORE YOU BEGIN	→ SEE ALSO
Chapter 9, "Capturing Video"	**84** Burn a Video Production to a Disc Using MyDVD Express

92

You can add as many files to a DVD project as the DVD will hold. Each of these files appears as a different menu object and you are able to customize them in several ways.

1 Open MyDVD

To open **MyDVD**, select **Create DVD** from the **DVD & Video** menu.

▶ NOTE

You can also open all of the Roxio Easy Media Creator applications by going into the **Start** menu and selecting **Programs, Roxio Easy Media Creator 8**. From there select the project folder that your application is stored in, in this case, **DVD and Video**. The applications are listed inside the folder. Select **MyDVD**.

2 Set Project Settings

When **MyDVD** has launched, the first thing you want to do is to set the project settings. Select **File, Project Settings** to bring up the **Project Settings** window. From here you can set the aspect ratio for your menu, which is an important step because if you set this after you have customized your menu, all customizations are lost.

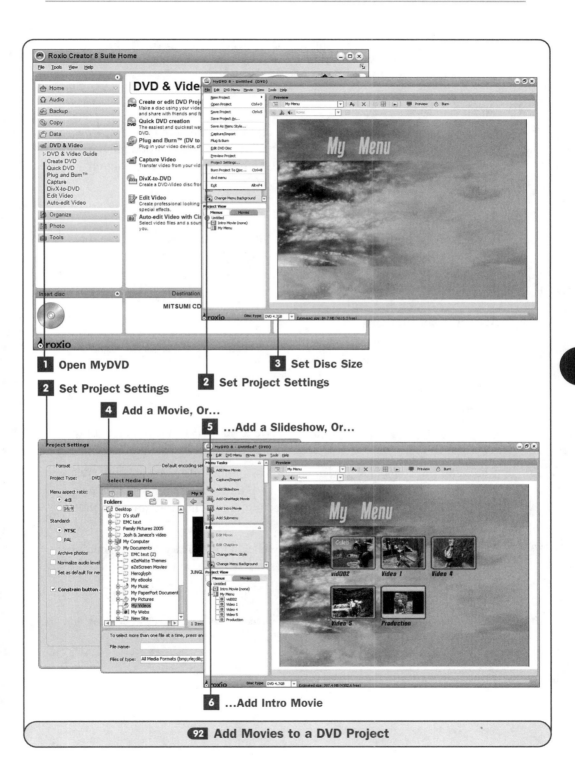

1 Open MyDVD

2 Set Project Settings

3 Set Disc Size

2 Set Project Settings

4 Add a Movie, Or...

5 ...Add a Slideshow, Or...

6 ...Add Intro Movie

92

92 Add Movies to a DVD Project

You can also set the video standard (NTSC for North America, PAL for every-where else) and quality settings for your video and audio. Make sure your settings are correct and then click **OK**.

3 Set Disc Size

After you have opened **MyDVD**, set the disc size in the **Disc type** drop-down list so you can keep track of the amount of free space as you add movies and slide shows. Set the disc size by selecting the type of recordable media on which you will burn the DVD project.

4 Add a Movie, Or...

After you have set the disc size, you can begin adding movies to your project by clicking **Add New Movie**. Use the **Media Manager** to select the movies that you want to add to the project. The movies that you add are displayed in the **Preview** window of the **Project** window.

5 ...Add a Slideshow, Or...

You can also add slideshows directly to the project by clicking on **Add Slideshow** to bring up the **Slideshow Assistant**. See **53** **Use Slideshow Assistant to Create a Slideshow** for more information.

6 ...Add Intro Movie

You might also want to add an intro movie to your DVD. Intro movies play when the DVD is placed in the player before the menu actually comes up.

Adding an intro movie is a great way to personalize the content of the DVD. For example, if you are creating a DVD with home videos on it to send as a gift, you could record a personalized greeting on a camcorder and add that as an intro to the DVD.

You can add intro movies to the DVD by clicking **Add Intro Movie**. Then use the **Media Manager** to select the movies you want to add to the project.

▶ NOTE

You can capture video directly into **MyDVD**, but typically you want to edit your video first or use **Plug and Burn** to record it directly to disc.

92

93 Add and Organize Submenus on a DVD Menu

✔ BEFORE YOU BEGIN	→ SEE ALSO
92 Add Movies to a DVD Project	**94** Add Chapters to a Movie
	95 Set the DVD Menu Style
	96 Set the DVD Menu Background or Add a Motion Background
	97 Add Text to a DVD Menu
	98 Add Music to a DVD Title Menu

A DVD holds a lot of video. When you start adding edited video onto the menu, you will probably find that you have several files—let's just say for example, three years' worth. Instead of placing all those files onto the main menu, you can create submenus to handle them by category. You could create a submenu by year or perhaps by event, such as a Christmas submenu or a family vacation submenu.

1 Add Submenus to DVD Menus

To add submenus to the DVD, select a menu or submenu in the **Project View** area and click **Add Submenu**. The new submenu appears in both the **Preview** window and the project view.

2 Select Menu, Menu Title, or Movie Link

When you add submenus to DVD projects, both the submenu title and the menu link are automatically named **My Menu**. The movie links are named whatever filename they have on disk. You want to change these names to make them more meaningful. To change the name of a menu or movie link, click on it in either the **Project View** area or in the **Project** window.

3 Replace Text

After you have selected the menu or link, it should be highlighted with a red box in the **Preview** window. Select the text for the menu, title, or movie and type in the new name.

4 Drag and Drop Movies and Submenus

After you have added all the tracks and submenus you need and appropriately named them, you can organize them by dragging and dropping them to different locations in the **Project View** area.

93

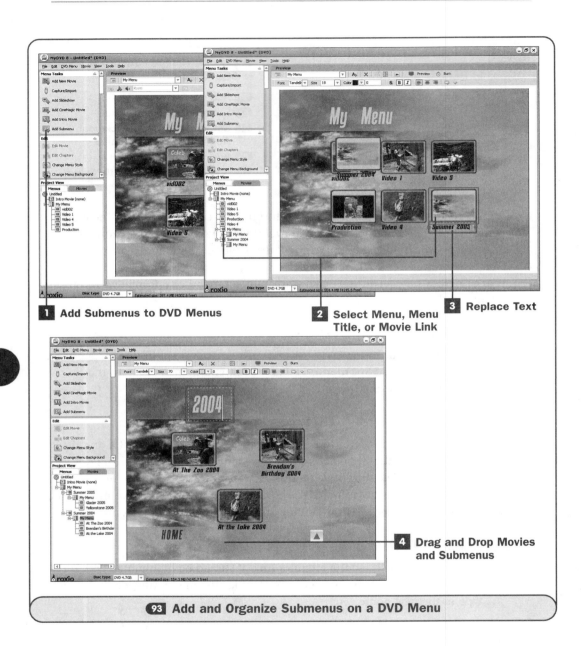

1 Add Submenus to DVD Menus

2 Select Menu, Menu Title, or Movie Link

3 Replace Text

4 Drag and Drop Movies and Submenus

93

93 Add and Organize Submenus on a DVD Menu

▶ TIPS

You can drag and drop movies and submenus at any time if you decide to change things later in the project.

To change the order of movies in a menu, click on the **Movies** tab in the **Project View** area and use the up and down buttons at the bottom of the **Project View** area to change the order in which the movies will be played.

94 Add Chapters to a Movie

✔ BEFORE YOU BEGIN	→ SEE ALSO
92 Add Movies to a DVD Project	**93** Add and Organize Submenus on a DVD Menu
	95 Set the DVD Menu Style
	96 Set the DVD Menu Background or Add a Motion Background
	97 Add Text to a DVD Menu
	98 Add Music to a DVD Title Menu

You can add chapters to a longer movie to make finding a particular spot in your video more manageable. This is also an alternative to creating several menus. You might combine all your video from 2005, for example, and just use chapters to sort through it. That way you also have the option of watching it as a whole.

1 Select Movie

First select the movie in the **Project View** area and make sure it is highlighted in the **Preview** window.

94

2 Click Edit Chapters

After you have selected the movie, click **Edit Chapters** to bring up the **Edit Chapters Wizard**.

3 Manually Add Chapters Or...

You can add chapters to the movie manually by using the slider, jog dial, or playback controls to set the position in the movie and then clicking the **Add chapter here** button. You can create as many chapters as you like.

4 ...Automatically Create Chapters

You can also use the **Automatically create chapters** features to automatically add chapters to your movie. This useful tool allows you to easily add chapters in three ways.

You can add chapters to your movie automatically by selecting the **Use scene detection** option. After you have selected this option, set the sensitivity from 0 to 100. The sensitivity determines how different one scene must be from the next to warrant a new chapter.

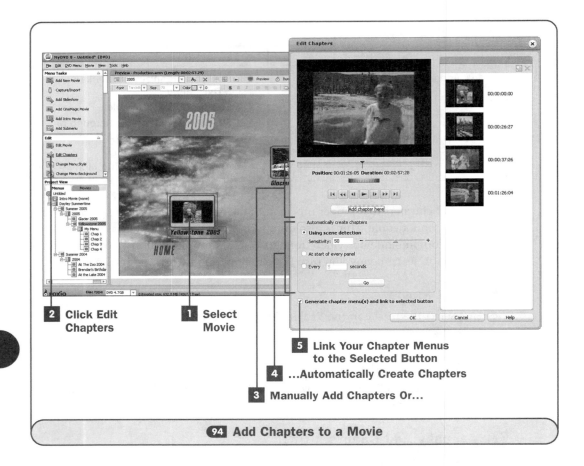

2 Click Edit Chapters

1 Select Movie

5 Link Your Chapter Menus to the Selected Button

4 ...Automatically Create Chapters

3 Manually Add Chapters Or...

94 Add Chapters to a Movie

You can also add chapters to your movie by selecting the **At the start of every panel** option. This adds a new chapter for each panel in the movie. If you have many still images or short video clips, however, this creates too many chapters to manage, so this might not be the best choice.

You can also add chapters to your movie by selecting the **Every (number) seconds** option. A new chapter is created every number of seconds that are specified in the option. This creates uniform chapters, but might split a scene in two.

After you have selected the automatic option and adjusted the setting, click **Go** to generate the chapters automatically.

5 Link Your Chapter Menus to the Selected Button

After you have generated the chapters for the movie, check the box labeled **Generate chapter menu(s) and link to selected button** at the bottom of the

Edit Chapters window. When this option is set, new menus are created and a new link is created in the project for each chapter.

Adding the links and menus to the project can be useful if you need to jump to specific scenes. If this option is not checked, the links and menus won't be created but the chapters still exist in the movie, and you can use the DVD remote to jump from one chapter to the next.

---

95 Set the DVD Menu Style

✔ BEFORE YOU BEGIN	→ SEE ALSO
92 Add Movies to a DVD Project	**93** Add and Organize Submenus on a DVD Menu
	94 Add Chapters to a Movie
	96 Set the DVD Menu Background or Add a Motion Background
	97 Add Text to a DVD Menu
	98 Add Music to a DVD Title Menu

Rather than individually change each element of the menu, you can set a predefined menu style within MyDVD and then change only the elements you want. Of course, you start out with the default menu style, and if you like it, there is no need to change it.

You can set a menu style for each menu individually or you can set the style for the entire project. You want to set the menu style before you add any of your own elements because a new style replaces any background photos or audio options you have set.

▶ NOTE

The menu style changes the font and style of the text objects, the number and placement of the video preview windows, and the color and style of the background.

1 Select Menu or Submenu

To set the menu style, select a menu or submenu in the **Project View** area.

2 Click Change Menu Style

After you have selected a menu or submenu, click **Change Menu Style** to bring up the **Select Menu Style** window.

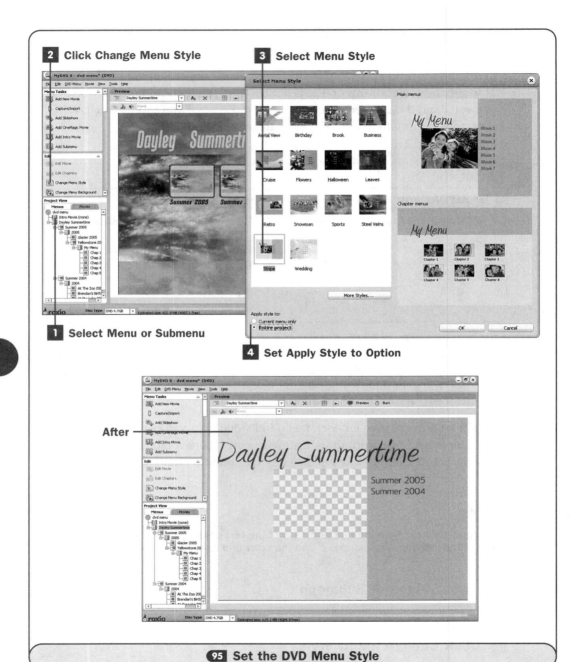

2 Click Change Menu Style

3 Select Menu Style

1 Select Menu or Submenu

4 Set Apply Style to Option

After

95

95 Set the DVD Menu Style

3 Select Menu Style

From within the **Select Menu Style** window, select the style you want to use for the menu.

4 Set Apply Style to Option

After you have selected a style, you have the option of applying that style to the current menu only or to the entire project. Selecting **Entire project** is very useful to change the style of the entire DVD at once. However, if you only want to set the style for one specific menu, select **Current menu only**. After you have set the apply option, click the **OK** button to apply the style to the project.

---

96 Set the DVD Menu Background or Add a Motion Background

✔ BEFORE YOU BEGIN	→ SEE ALSO
92 Add Movies to a DVD Project	**93** Add and Organize Submenus on a DVD Menu
	94 Add Chapters to a Movie
	95 Set the DVD Menu Style
	97 Add Text to a DVD Menu
	98 Add Music to a DVD Title Menu

96

The styles within **MyDVD** are very nice, but you can personalize your menus by adding your own photos or even a video clip to the background. By adding your own photo or video, you are replacing the preset background entirely. You might only want to set the main background, leaving the other menu backgrounds with the preset style.

1 Select Menu or Submenu

To set the menu background, select a menu or submenu in the **Project View** area.

2 Click Change Menu Background

After you have selected a menu or submenu, click **Change Menu Background** to bring up the **Select Media File** window.

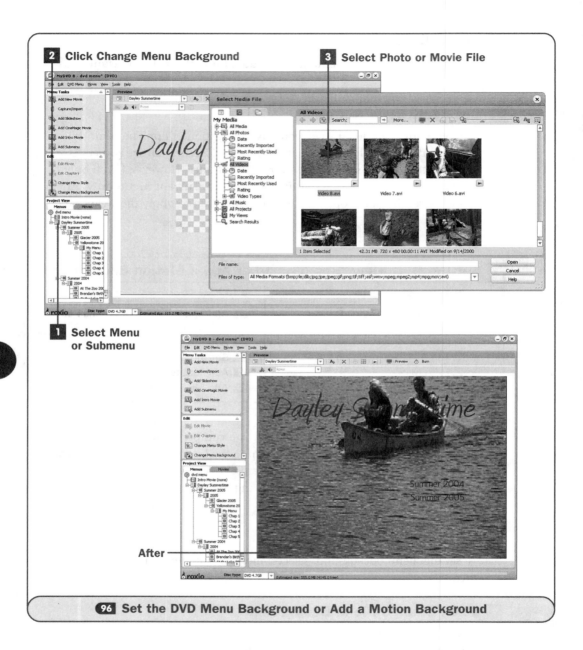

2 Click Change Menu Background

3 Select Photo or Movie File

1 Select Menu or Submenu

After

96 Set the DVD Menu Background or Add a Motion Background

3 Select Photo or Movie File

Use the **Select Media File** window to find a photo or movie to add as the background for the menu. If you select a movie file, the background is a motion background that plays the movie over and over as long as the menu is up. After you have selected the background, click **OK** to apply the background.

▶ TIPS

After you have added your own background, you can delete the placeholders in the menu style that obstruct the view of the background. You can also change the color and placement of the font if your background makes the text hard to read.

You might want to create a specific movie for the background that is just a short sequence of the beginning of another movie file. This reduces the amount of disc space needed to hold the menus.

---

97 **Add Text to a DVD Menu**

✔ BEFORE YOU BEGIN	→ SEE ALSO
92 Add Movies to a DVD Project	**93** Add and Organize Submenus on a DVD Menu
	94 Add Chapters to a Movie
	95 Set the DVD Menu Style
	96 Set the DVD Menu Background or Add a Motion Background

97

You can add as many text objects to your menus as you need. You can also edit any text within your menus, whether you added it or not.

1 Select Menu or Submenu

To add text to a menu, select a menu or submenu in the **Project View** area.

2 Click Add Text

After you have selected a menu or submenu, click the **Add Text** button to add a new text box to the menu.

3 Select New Text Box

When the new text box is added to the window, it contains the default text *Type your text here*. Click on the text to highlight the red text box.

4 Replace Text

After you have highlighted the text box, select the text inside the box and type over it using the keyboard.

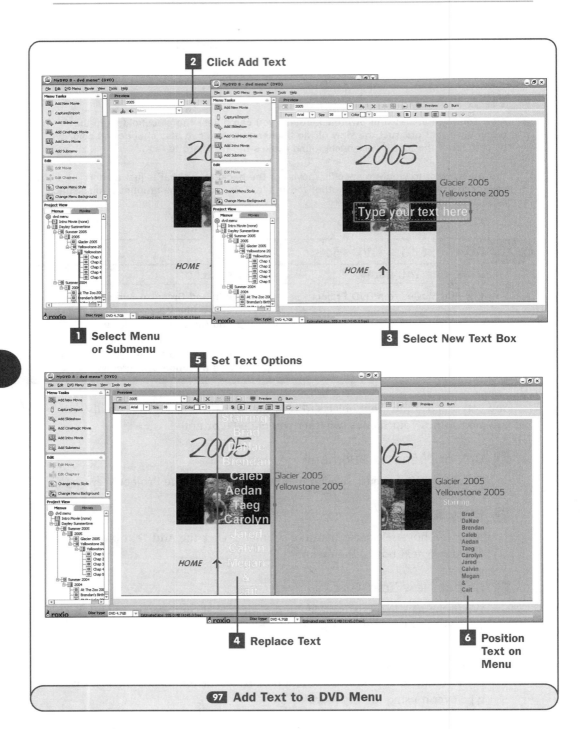

2 Click Add Text

1 Select Menu or Submenu

3 Select New Text Box

5 Set Text Options

4 Replace Text

6 Position Text on Menu

97 Add Text to a DVD Menu

5 Set Text Options

After you are done typing, you can set the font, size, color, alignment, and style using the text controls on the top of the **Preview** window.

▶ NOTE

The text options within **MyDVD** are quite a bit more limited than the text options in other areas of Easy Media Creator. Because of this, it is probably a good idea to choose a menu style and edit the text options provided with the style.

6 Position Text on Menu

When you have set the text options, reposition the text by moving the mouse over the edge of the red text box until the mouse cursor becomes a crosshair with arrows at each point. Then click and hold the mouse button and drag the text to the desired location.

---

98 Add Music to a DVD Title Menu

✔ BEFORE YOU BEGIN	→ SEE ALSO
92 Add Movies to a DVD Project	**93** Add and Organize Submenus on a DVD Menu
	95 Set the DVD Menu Style
	96 Set the DVD Menu Background or Add a Motion Background

98

You can add background music to any or all of your DVD menus to add yet more personal flavor to the menu. In fact, the background audio doesn't have to be music—it can be any audio file.

If you have added a preset menu style to your DVD menu, it came with its own music. Preview it by clicking on the **Animate Preview** icon in the **Preview** window. The music you add to the menu replaces this default music. Even if you don't plan on adding your own music, be sure to preview the default audio. If you'd prefer to have no music instead of the music that accompanies the menu style, open the **DVD Menu** drop-down menu and select **Remove Menu Audio**.

1 Select Menu

To add background music to a menu, select a menu or submenu in the **Project View** area.

2 Click Change Menu Audio

3 Select Audio File

1 Select Menu

98 Add Music to a DVD Title Menu

2 Click Change Menu Audio

After you have selected a menu or submenu, click **Change Menu Audio** to bring up **Media Selector**.

3 Select Audio File

Use **Media Selector** to find an audio file to use for background music that plays while the menu is active. The audio file plays over and over as long as the menu is up. Whether you choose the same audio file or a different one to play behind your submenus, any time your viewers jump to a submenu, the chosen track for that submenu starts at the beginning.

▶ TIP

You might want to create a specific audio file for the background that is just a short sequence of the beginning of a full audio file. This reduces the amount of disc space needed for the menus.

99 Burn DVD to Disc

✔ BEFORE YOU BEGIN	→ SEE ALSO
92 Add Movies to a DVD Project	**93** Add and Organize Submenus on a DVD Menu
	94 Add Chapters to a Movie
	95 Set the DVD Menu Style
	96 Set the DVD Menu Background or Add a Motion Background
	97 Add Text to a DVD Menu
	98 Add Music to a DVD Title Menu

Now that your menu is complete, you can burn your DVD and create something to enjoy for years to come. You can burn multiple copies to give to your friends and family or you can create a disc image so you can burn a disc at any time.

1 Preview the DVD Menu

Before you make your DVD project permanent by burning it, you want to preview it to make sure it is just the way you want it. Click on the **Preview Project** icon in the **Preview** window taskbar. This brings up a **Preview Project** window that contains the complete DVD menu along with a simulated remote control so you can operate your menu just as you would from your DVD player.

Scroll through your menus and even play your videos to make sure you are happy with the result. When you are done previewing, close the window.

2 Click Burn

When you are satisfied that your project is ready to burn, click the **Burn** icon in the **Preview** window to bring up the **Burn Project** dialog.

3 Select Drive

After the **Burn Project** dialog is open, select the DVD burner you want to use and place a blank disc into the drive.

4 Burn Disc Or...

When you have inserted your recordable DVD, click the **Burn** button at the bottom of the window. Your DVD takes several minutes to burn depending on the speed of your burner. When your disc is complete, your DVD is automatically ejected.

99

1 Preview the DVD Menu

2 Click Burn

4 Burn Disc Or...

5 ...Create Disc Image

3 Select Drive

99 Burn DVD to Disc

5 **...Create Disc Image**

Instead of burning a DVD, you can create a disc image. This is like taking a picture of your DVD project and saving it. A disc image, or **.iso** file, is a standard disc image format that can be used by other applications. You can use the **.iso** file to burn a replica of your DVD at any time. Check the **Save disc image file** option and set a destination for the file. Click the **Burn** button at the bottom of the window.

100 Burn DivX to DVD

✔ BEFORE YOU BEGIN	→ SEE ALSO
66 Capture Video from a Digital Camcorder **69** Import Video from a DVD	**101** Plug and Burn from a Camcorder

The **DivX-to-DVD** utility is an extremely fast and easy way to create a DVD from DivX files you have stored on your computer. You must have captured your files in the DivX format to use this utility.

If you use this utility, you are not able to create a custom menu. You are given a few options for your menu and you can use a predefined style, but if you would like to create an elaborate customized menu for your DVD, follow the preceding tasks **92** Add Movies to a DVD Project through **99** Burn DVD to Disc to do so.

1 Open Disc Copier

In the Easy Media Creator **project** pane, select the **DVD & Video** menu. When the **DVD & Video** menu is displayed, select **DivX-to-DVD**. A disclaimer comes up telling you that it is illegal to copy copyrighted material. Click **OK**. This launches **Disc Copier**.

2 Select Video Compilation

After **Disc Copier** has launched, click the **Video Compilation** tab to add DivX files to the project.

3 Set Disc Size

After you have selected the **Video Compilation** tab, set the disc size in the **Disc Size** drop-down list so you can keep track of the amount of free space as you add movies to the disc. Set the disc size by selecting the type of recordable media you are using.

4 Add DivX Movies

Add your DivX movies by clicking on the **Add Movies** button and browsing through **Media Selector** for the files you would like to add. You can add more than one file at a time by holding down the **Control** key while you select them.

100

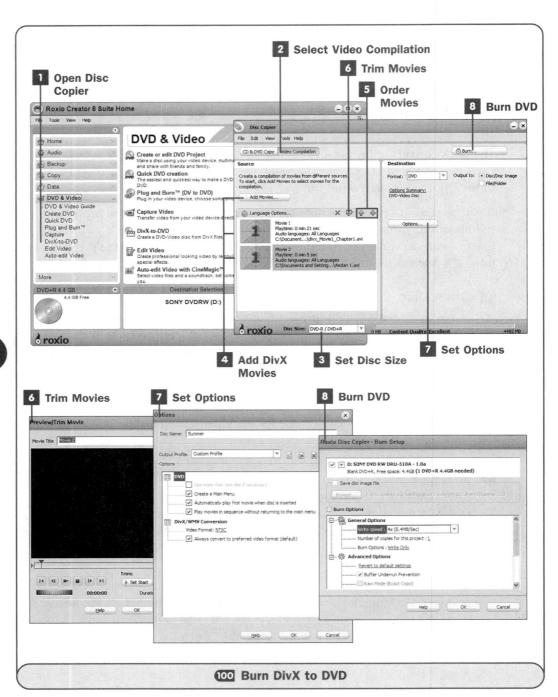

1 Open Disc Copier

2 Select Video Compilation

6 Trim Movies

5 Order Movies

8 Burn DVD

4 Add DivX Movies

3 Set Disc Size

7 Set Options

6 Trim Movies

7 Set Options

8 Burn DVD

100 Burn DivX to DVD

5 Order Movies

When your movies have been imported into the **Disc Copier** window, you can sort them by selecting them one at a time and clicking on the up or down arrows in the taskbar.

6 Trim Movies

You can also preview and trim your movies by clicking on the **Preview/Trim Movie** icon in the taskbar. This brings up the **Preview/Trim Movie** windows.

Use the **Preview/Trim Movie** windows to set a new start and end point for the movie. Only the portion of the movie between the start and end point is added to the DVD. To set the start point, use the play controls or jog dial to adjust the movie to the point where you want the movie to begin, and then click the **Set Start** button. To set the end point, use the play controls or jog dial to adjust the movie to the point where you want the movie to end, and then click the **Set End** button. When you have finished, click the **OK** button to return to the project.

7 Set Options

After you have set the start and end points for the movie, set the project options by clicking on the **Options** button to bring up the **Options** dialog box. Select the options that you would like to include on your DVD. The options include using multiple discs, creating a main menu, auto-playing the first movie, and playing all movies in sequence.

You can also set the option to always convert the files to the preferred video format. This option is checked by default and you shouldn't change it unless you have a specific reason. Click **OK**.

100

8 Burn DVD

After you have finished setting the project options, click the **Burn** button to bring up the **Burn Setup** window. The **Burn Setup** window allows you to specify which drive to use when burning the data project to disc, as well as the write speed, number of copies, and several advanced features.

Select the destination drive from the drive list and then set any options you would like in the **Burn Options** area. When the options are all set correctly, click the **OK** button to burn the disc.

---

101 Plug and Burn from a Camcorder

✔ BEFORE YOU BEGIN	→ SEE ALSO
100 Burn DivX to DVD	66 Capture Video from a Digital Camcorder

The *Plug and Burn* feature of Easy Media Creator allows you to burn movies directly from a camcorder to a DVD burner. If you know that you don't want to edit the video, this is an extremely useful feature because it saves you much time and disk space on the computer, compared to the traditional method of capturing the video to a file, editing it, and then burning it to DVD. This is the perfect option if you just want to burn a backup copy of your tapes to DVD.

▶ KEY TERM

Plug and Burn—Burning a DVD directly from a camcorder without having to store the movie on a hard disk.

101

1 Open Plug and Burn

In the Easy Media Creator **project** pane, select the **DVD & Video** menu. When the **DVD & Video** menu is displayed, select **Plug and Burn** to launch the **Plug and Burn** utility.

2 Set Menu Style

After you have opened **Plug and Burn**, you can select the **Add a Menu** option and click the **Style** button to add a menu to the DVD, or you can select **No Menu** to have no menu on the DVD.

3 Select the DVD Burner and Insert the Disc

After you have set the menu option, select the DVD burner from the **Drive** list and insert a blank disc.

▶ TIP

If you are using rewritable media, you can erase the disc first by clicking on the **Erase** button.

4 Set Disc Type

After you have inserted the disc into the drive, select the disc type from the **Disc type** drop-down list. Then click the **Next** button to move to step two in the **Plug & Burn** window.

1 Open Plug and Burn

1 Open Plug and Burn

2 Set Menu Style

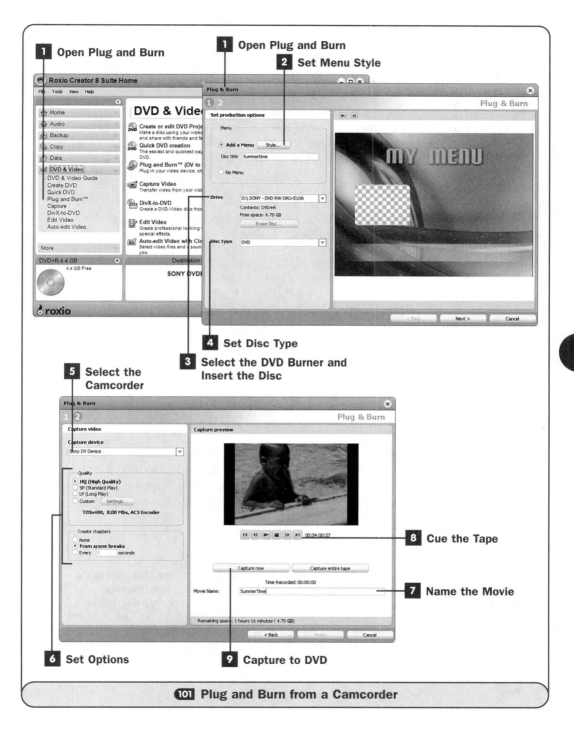

4 Set Disc Type

3 Select the DVD Burner and Insert the Disc

5 Select the Camcorder

8 Cue the Tape

7 Name the Movie

6 Set Options

9 Capture to DVD

101 Plug and Burn from a Camcorder

5 Select the Camcorder

In the **Capture video** area, first select the camcorder from the **Capture device** drop-down list.

6 Set Options

After you have selected the camcorder, set the quality and chapter options for the DVD. You can choose from the **HQ (High Quality)**, **SP (Standard Play)**, or **LP (Long Play)** options. **HQ** is the best option to use; however, it also takes up the most disc space. You can also customize the quality by selecting **Custom** and then clicking on the **Settings** button.

You can also have chapters automatically added to the DVD by selecting either the **From scene breaks** or **Every (number) seconds** option.

7 Name the Movie

After you have set the DVD options, type in a name for your movie in the **Movie Name** text box. This name is displayed on the DVD menu if you include one in the project.

8 Cue the Tape

After you have given the movie a name, you can use the playback controls to cue the tape to where you want to start capturing the video.

9 Capture to DVD

After the tape is cued to the correct starting point, click the **Capture now** button. The camcorder starts playing and the DVD drive starts burning simultaneously. After you have finished capturing, click the **Stop Capture** button to end capturing. After the DVD has finalized, it is ready to play in a DVD player.

▶ **TIP**

Some DVD players choke and sputter on burned discs that are recorded at too high a video bitrate. If you experience this problem with your player, go to **File, Project Settings** to change your project settings to record at a lower bitrate. You can switch from the **Best** to **Good** preset, or manually change the bitrate to 7 or 7.5 megabits per second, which most DVD players can handle.

13

Creating Data Discs

IN THIS CHAPTER:

This chapter discusses using Roxio Easy Media Creator 8 to create *data discs* and *disc images*. Creating a data disc is the process of taking data files on your computer that are important to you and placing them on recordable discs.

► KEY TERMS

Data disc—A CD or DVD with files on it that can be read using a CD or DVD drive in a computer.

Disc image—The contents of an entire CD or DVD that has been turned into a single image file.

This feature is becoming more important all the time because as technology advances, computers are being used for a wider range of tasks. Not too many years ago, word processing documents were about all you needed to worry about backing up. Now you can store video, photos, emails, tax records, bank records, music, and much more on your computer and back it all up on CD and DVD.

This chapter helps you understand how to make the most of Roxio Easy Media Creator's capabilities to create data discs that you can use to archive, transfer, and share your files with others.

102

102 **About Creating Data Discs**	
✔ BEFORE YOU BEGIN	→ SEE ALSO
Chapter 16, "Media Manager Tools"	Chapter 14, "Backing Up Data"

This task helps you understand some of the concepts of data discs so you will be more comfortable with the terminology as you use the data disc utilities.

About Data Discs

The basic concept of a data disc is pretty simple. You take files and burn them on a CD or DVD. What can become confusing are the settings that you are faced with in burning the data to a disc. This section discusses the most common terms and concepts that you come up against when burning data discs:

- **Multi-disc projects**—A multi-disc project is one where you need to burn more data than can fit on a single disc. You can still burn the data, but you need to span multiple discs. This can sometimes present problems when you try to access the data later and so it should be avoided if possible.

Drag to Disc

102 About Creating Data Discs

- **Multi-session/track**—When you hear the terms *session* and *track* in the context of burning, they are the same thing. A track is basically a spiral line of data that goes around a CD from the center to the outside. If you have a single track/session CD, there is one line that starts at the center and spirals out until there is no more data left. Multi-session means that there is more than one track on the disc. This happens if you burn more than once to the same disc. It is okay to have a multi-session disc as long as your CD-ROM drive supports it. Just keep in mind that some CD-ROM drives don't, and your disc will not work on every computer. Also keep in mind that burning multiple sessions to a disc creates overhead, or areas of a disc where you can't burn any data. Typically, you lose 15MB of a CD's 700MB capacity each time you burn a new session, so you have that much less space to use for data on the disc. Creator 8 makes this process transparent to the user, but don't be surprised when your disc starts to seem smaller than it's supposed to be.

- **Finalize or close**—When you *finalize* a disc, it means that you are finished with the disc and an end sequence is burned onto the last track. After a disc is finalized or closed, you are no longer able to write to the disc unless it is a rewritable disc.

- **Media types CD-RW and DVD-RW versus CD-R and DVD-R**—There are two basic media types for recordable CDs or DVDs. A CD-R or DVD-R disc is a record-only disc. After you have finalized a CD-R or DVD-R, you can no longer burn data onto it. A CD-RW disc, however, allows you to erase the contents of the disc and rewrite data on top of it even after it has been finalized. Recordable DVDs come in two formats: DVD-R/RW and DVD+R/RW. Having two formats used to be a big problem for DVD users but it isn't any more. The + and – discs are functionally the same; if you bought your burner in the past three years it will almost certainly burn both the + and – formats. They both have the same capacity, and you can burn all the same content to both formats. Nearly all DVD players and DVD-ROM drives can read both formats without difficulty.

102

About Data Disc File Systems

Figuring out what data disc file system to use can be the most confusing concept in burning data discs. Unfortunately, there is not just one standard file system to use when burning discs. The following list describes the most common file systems with an explanation of what they are for:

- **ISO9660**—This is the original format and works on virtually every CD-ROM drive made in Windows, Linux, Mac, and DOS. This format is limited to the 8.3 naming convention, meaning that the file names can only have eight alphanumeric (numbers or letters) characters in them (the .3 stands for the 3-letter file extension, such as **.doc**, **.wav**, or **.jpg**).

- **Joliet**—This is the most common format now and the one you will likely want to use. It supports up to 64 characters, including spaces and several special characters such as the apostrophe. It works on almost all CD-ROM drives on Windows and Linux.

- **UDF102**—This is a newer format that provides for more flexible names up to 128 characters. You need to use this format if you are burning files larger than 1GB in size to a DVD-R/RW or DVD+R/RW disc.

102

About Drag to Disc

Drag to Disc is an icon that was installed on your Windows desktop as Easy Media Creator was being installed on your system. It is extremely easy to use, so familiarize yourself with it because it can save you much time.

First, you need to have a recordable disc in your CD or DVD burner. You can create a data disc by simply dragging files from Windows Explorer or **Media Manager** and dropping them on the **Drag to Disc** icon. When a file is dropped on the **Drag to Disc** icon, it is immediately burned to the recordable disc. When you eject the disc, you are given the option to finalize it.

▶ TIPS

Some CD-ROM drives do not recognize a CD if it has more than one track on it or if it is not finalized. If you plan to share the burned CD with others or use it on a different computer, finalize it.

CD-RW discs wear out. If you are using the CD-RW disc frequently, make sure you have an additional backup of any vital data stored on the CD-RW. Because CD-R discs are so cheap (30–50 cents a disc or often much less), it's almost always better to use CD-R. They're less expensive and more durable, they burn faster, and they're much more widely compatible.

103 Copy a CD or DVD

✔ BEFORE YOU BEGIN	→ SEE ALSO
102 About Creating Data Discs	**107** Create a Disc Image from a CD
	108 Give Your Disc Image Its Own Drive Letter

One of the most common uses for Easy Media Creator is to copy CDs and DVDs. The copy feature is simply a method to take the contents of a CD or DVD and put it on a new CD or DVD.

One reason to copy a disc is to have a backup if the CD or DVD gets damaged. Another use for the disc copy feature is to share CDs or DVDs that you have created with movies, photos, or other content with friends and family.

You cannot use **Disc Copier** to duplicate copyright-protected DVDs.

► **TIP**

If you have two CD/DVD drives in the computer, use a different drive for the source and destination. That way you can copy the entire contents of a CD or DVD to a blank disc directly without having to copy it to the computer hard drive and then burn it to a disc. This speeds up the disc copy process.

103

1 Open Disc Copier

You can open **Disc Copier** by selecting the **Home** menu in the Roxio Creator Suite **Home** page. From the **Home** menu, select **Applications** and then select **Disc Copier** from the **Applications** submenu.

2 Select CD & DVD Copy

From within Disc Copier, click the **CD & DVD Copy** button to bring up the copy options page.

3 Select Source and Destination Drives

Next, select the source and destination drives from the drop-down menus.

4 Set Advanced Options

Click the **Advanced** button to bring up the advanced options if you want to change the copy settings. You have the option on the advanced page to set the burn speed at which your drive will copy the disc. You can also specify the number of copies to burn. If you specify multiple copies, you are prompted to put a blank disc in for each copy.

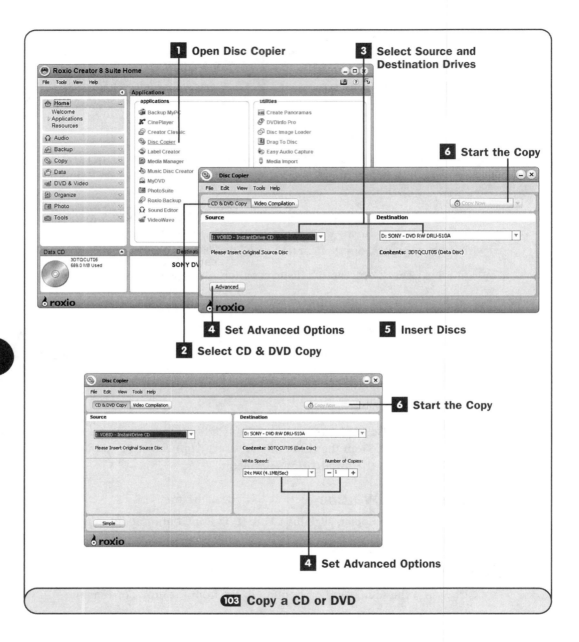

1 Open Disc Copier

3 Select Source and Destination Drives

6 Start the Copy

4 Set Advanced Options

5 Insert Discs

2 Select CD & DVD Copy

6 Start the Copy

4 Set Advanced Options

103 Copy a CD or DVD

5 Insert Discs

Insert the CD/DVD into the source drive and a blank disc that matches the size of the source disc into the destination drive.

6 Start the Copy

Click the **Copy Now** button to copy the disc.

▶ **TIP**

If the source drive or your system is having trouble keeping up with the burner and you are receiving errors when burning, you might want to adjust the speed. Often adjusting the speed to a lower setting makes the burn successful.

---

104 Copy Data Files to a Disc

✔ BEFORE YOU BEGIN	→ SEE ALSO
102 About Creating Data Discs	**105** Create a Data Disc Using Creator Classic
	106 Create a Mixed Audio/Data CD
	107 Create a Disc Image from a CD
	108 Give Your Disc Image Its Own Drive Letter

104

Creating data discs is a great way to preserve a backup copy of files that are important to you. These files can range from music, photos, or movies to bank records, emails, or other documents. You might also want to create data discs with files that you want to share with others or use at a different location.

You can use the **Data Disc** application in Easy Media Creator to create a data project, add files to it, and burn them onto a CD or DVD.

1 Start New Data Disc Project

To begin a new **Data Disc** project, select **Data Disc** from the **Data** menu in the Roxio Creator Suite **Home** page.

2 Insert Disc

After the new **Data Disc** project is opened, you need to insert a blank disc into the burner. This ensures that the estimated free space is reported properly as you add data to the project.

3 Add Data Files Manually Or...

After you have inserted the blank disc into the burner, you can add data files to the project by clicking the **Add Data** button and selecting **Add File** or **Add Folders** from the drop-down menu to bring up a file dialog box.

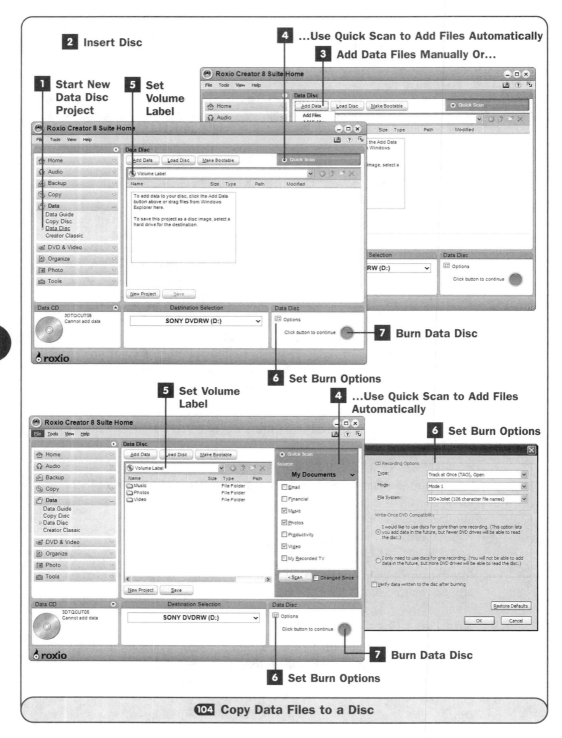

If you select **Add Files**, only the files you select are added to the projects. If you select **Add Folders**, all files and subfolders that exist in the selected folders are added.

Use the file dialog box to select files or folders to add to the project.

■4 …Use Quick Scan to Add Files Automatically

You can also use the **Quick Scan** feature to automatically add files to your project. The **Quick Scan** feature is an extremely useful tool that allows you to add all files of specific types to a project. This saves much time if you only want to add movies, photos, or videos to the data project because you do not need to select them individually.

To use the **Quick Scan** feature, first expand it by clicking the button next to **Quick Scan**. After the view has expanded, you need to click the down arrow in the **Source** option and select **Browse** to bring up a file dialog box. Use the file dialog box to find the folder in which you want **Quick Scan** to search for files and click **OK**.

After you have specified the location to search for files, check the boxes next to the file types for which you want to scan. By holding the mouse over the type name, such as email, you see a list of file extensions. **Quick Scan** adds files with these extensions to the project during the scan.

You can also check the **Changed Since** box if you want to specify an expiration date on the scan. **Quick Scan** only picks up files that have been changed after that date. You can use this feature to do an incremental archive of files since the last time you archived.

After you have finished setting the **Quick Scan** options, click the **Scan** button. New folders with the name of each file type you scanned for are added to the project. Any files found during the scan, including the folders that contain them, are added to the project in their respective file type folder.

■5 Set Volume Label

You should set a volume label that helps you keep track of what is on the disc. For example, you might want to use the date for a volume label if you are updating an archive of data. The name may be up to 11 characters, but cannot use any of these characters: \, /, :, ;, *, ?, ", <, >, |, +, =, ., ,, [, or].

■6 Set Burn Options

After you have set the volume options, you can set the burn options by clicking on **Options** to bring up the **Option** dialog box. Then select **Data** in the **Options** list to set the session type, mode, and file system to use on the disc.

104

7 Burn Data Disc

After you have set the burn options, start the burn process by clicking on the **Burn** button.

---

105 **Create a Data Disc Using Creator Classic**

✔ BEFORE YOU BEGIN	→ SEE ALSO
102 About Creating Data Discs	106 Create a Mixed Audio/Data CD
104 Copy Data Files to a Disc	107 Create a Disc Image from a CD
	108 Give Your Disc Image Its Own Drive Letter

105

Creating data discs is a great way to preserve a backup copy of files that are important to you. Data discs can include files that range from music, photos, or movies to bank records, emails, or other documents. You might also want to create data discs with files you want to share with others or transfer to another computer.

Use the **Creator Classic** application in Easy Media Creator to create a data project, add files to it, and burn them onto a CD or DVD. Although the **Creator Classic** application is a little bit more difficult to use than the **Data Disc** utility, it also has more features, such as the ability to encrypt the disc.

1 Open Creator Classic

You can open **Creator Classic** in two ways, depending on which is easiest for you. If you have the Roxio Creator Suite **Home** page up, select **Data** and then select **Creator Classic** from the **Data** submenu. You can also open **Creator Classic** by selecting **Programs**, **Easy Media Creator 8**, **Data**, **Creator Classic** from the **Start** menu in Windows.

2 Select Disc Size/Insert Disc

After **Creator Classic** is opened, you need to insert a blank disc into the burner or at least set the disc size. This ensures that the estimated free space is reported properly as you add data to the project. To set the disc size, select the size from the **Disc Size** drop-down menu.

3 Add Data Files and Folders to Project

After you have set the disc size, you can add data files to the project using the **Select Source** area of the **Creator Classic** page. The **Select Source** area is essentially the same thing as **Media Manager**. It allows you to browse the computer to find files to add to the data project.

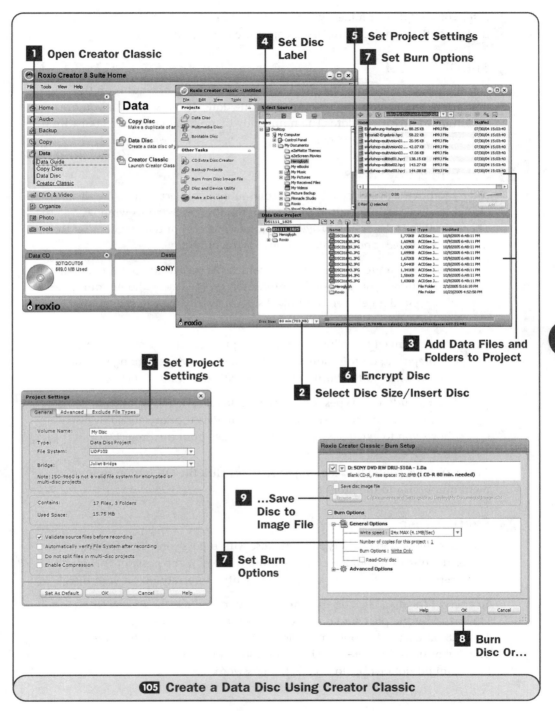

1 Open Creator Classic

4 Set Disc Label

5 Set Project Settings

7 Set Burn Options

3 Add Data Files and Folders to Project

5 Set Project Settings

6 Encrypt Disc

2 Select Disc Size/Insert Disc

9 ...Save Disc to Image File

7 Set Burn Options

8 Burn Disc Or...

After you find files or folders you want to add to the project, drag them down and place them in the **Data Disc Project** area using the mouse.

4 Set Disc Label

You should set a disc label that will help you keep track of what is on the disc. For example, you might want to use the date for a disc label if you are updating an archive of data. The name may be up to 11 characters, but cannot use any of these characters: \, /, :, ;, *, ?, ", <, >, |, +, =, ., ,, [, or].

5 Set Project Settings

After you have set the disc label, you configure the project options by clicking on the **Project Settings** button to bring up the **Project Settings** window. There are three tabs on the **Project Settings** window that allow you to set the general, advanced, and exclude options for the project:

- The **General** tab allows you to set which file system to use on the disc. It also allows you to enable compression on the disc, validate source files, split files between multiple discs, and verify the file system after the burn.

- The **Advanced** tab allows you to enter publishing information if you are preparing a professional disc. It also allows you to change the date of all the files to the burn date or a specific date that you choose.

- The **Exclude File Types** tab allows you to exclude file types from being added to the project even if they are in folders that are added. It also allows you to exclude system or hidden files from the project.

After you have configured the project settings, click the **OK** button to save them and return to the project.

6 Encrypt Disc

You have the option of encrypting the disc with a password. This feature makes the disc unreadable except by those that know the password. This can be a useful feature if you are storing confidential information on your disc.

To encrypt the disc, click on the **Encrypt** button and use the **Encryption** dialog box to set the password and specify whether to use 128-bit encryption. The 128-bit encryption option provides a higher level of security to the disc. The downside is that some applications, especially those outside the United States, might not be able to decode the password.

105

7 Set Burn Options

After you have finished setting the project options, click the **Burn** button to bring up the **Burn Setup** window. The **Burn Setup** window allows you to specify which drive to use when burning the data project to disc, as well as the write speed, number of copies, and several advanced features.

Select the destination drive from the drive list and then set any option you would like in the **Burn Options** area.

8 Burn Disc Or...

After you have set the burn options, click the **OK** button to burn the data to disc.

9 ...Save Disc to Image File

From the **Burn Setup** window you also have the option to save the data project to a disc image instead of a blank disc. This option allows you to keep a copy of the disc to be archived, burned later, or mounted as an *emulated drive*.

105

► KEY TERM

Emulated drive—A logical drive that acts like a physical disk drive in the computer. Drive letters can be assigned to it and it shows up in Windows Explorer.

To save the data project as a disc image, check the **Save disc image file** option and then click the **Browse** button to bring up the file dialog box. Use the file dialog box to specify a destination location, a filename, and the disc image file type. Then click **Save** to close the file dialog and click **OK** to save the disc image.

► TIPS

You can make the data disc bootable by clicking on **Bootable Disc** and loading and using the dialog box to load a boot image from a floppy disk. If you make a disc bootable, you can boot the computer from the CD you create.

You do not need to specify that you need multiple discs for the project. **Creator Classic** automatically recognizes if the data exceeds the size of the disc and you see multiple discs in the **Estimated Project Size** indicator.

106   Create a Mixed Audio/Data CD

✔ BEFORE YOU BEGIN	→ SEE ALSO
102 About Creating Data Discs	105 Create a Data Disc Using Creator Classic

You can use Easy Media Creator to create a *mixed-mode disc* with both audio and video files on it. Mixed-mode CDs are useful if you have a project that uses both audio and data files.

For example, if you want to preserve the memory of a child at a certain age, you can add photos or video of the child to the data portion of the CD and record the child's voice singing or talking on the audio portion of the CD.

► KEY TERM

Mixed-mode disc—A disc that includes both audio and data tracks that can be read by a computer.

106

► NOTE

Mixed-mode CDs are used in computer CD-ROM drives and recorders only. They cannot be played in home or car stereo CD players.

1 Open Enhanced CD Project

First, open **Creator Classic** by selecting the **Home** menu from the Roxio Creator Suite **Home** page. Select **Data** and then select **Creator Classic** from the **Data** submenu. After **Creator Classic** is open, click on **CD Extra Disc Creator** to start a new **CD Extra Disc Creator** project.

2 Select Mixed Mode

From the **CD Extra Disc Creator** project window, click on **Mixed-Mode CD** to start a new mixed-mode CD project. You see two tracks appear in the **Mixed-Mode CD Project** window. The data track is labeled as an 11-digit number with an underscore character in the middle. The audio track is labeled **Audio Project**.

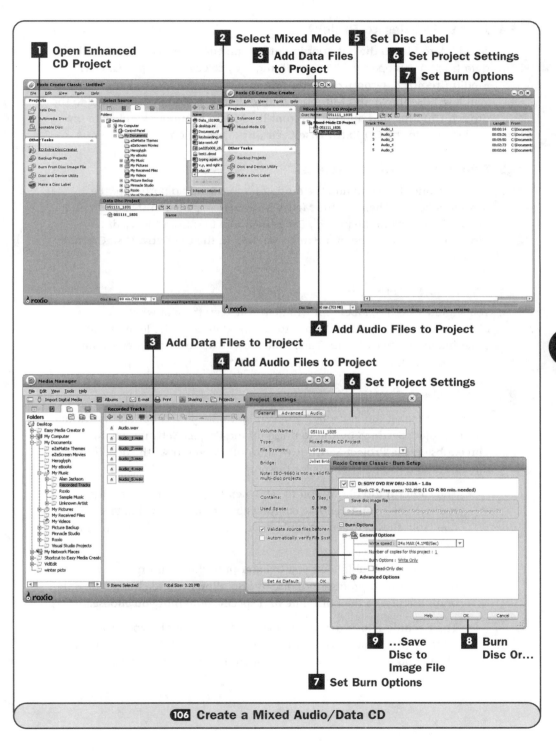

106 Create a Mixed Audio/Data CD

3 Add Data Files to Project

To add data files to the data portion of the mixed-mode CD, first select the data track. Then open the **Media Manager** by selecting **Programs, Easy Media Creator 8, Organize, Media Manager** from the **Start** menu in Windows. Use the **Media Manager** to find data files and folders to add to the project. Drag the files and folders from the **Media Manager** window to the file list area in the **CD Extra Disc Creator** project window.

4 Add Audio Files to Project

Select the audio track to add the audio files to the audio portion of the mixed-mode CD. Then use the **Media Manager**—opened in step 3—to find audio files to add to the project. Drag the audio files from the **Media Manager** window to the audio track list area in the **CD Extra Disc Creator** project window.

5 Set Disc Label

You should set a disc label that will help you keep track of what is on the disc. For example, you might want to use the date as a disc label if you are updating an archive of data. The name may be up to 11 characters, but cannot use any of these characters: \, /, :, ;, *, ?, ", <, >, |, +, =, ., ,, [, or].

6 Set Project Settings

After you have set the disc label, you configure the project options by clicking on the **Project Settings** button to bring up the **Project Settings** window. Three tabs on the **Project Settings** window allow you to set the general, advanced, and exclude options for the project:

- The **General** tab allows you to set which file system to use on the disc. It also allows you to enable compression on the disc, validate source files, split files between multiple discs, and verify the file system after the burn.

- The **Advanced** tab allows you to enter publishing information if you are preparing a professional disc. It also allows you to change the date of all the files to the burn date or a specific date that you choose.

- The **Exclude File Types** tab allows you to exclude file types from being added to the project even if they are in folders that are added. It also allows you to exclude system or hidden files from the project.

106

7 Set Burn Options

After you have finished setting the project options, click the **Burn** button to bring up the **Burn Setup** window. The **Burn Setup** window allows you to specify which drive to use when burning the data project to disc, as well as the write speed, number of copies, and several advanced features.

Select the destination drive from the drive list and then set any option you would like in the **Burn Options** area.

8 Burn Disc Or...

After you have set the burn options, click the **OK** button to burn the data to disc.

9 ...Save Disc to Image File

From the **Burn Setup** window you also have the option to save the data project to a disc image instead of a blank disc. This option allows you to keep a copy of the disc to be archived, burned later, or mounted as an emulated drive.

To save the data project as a disc image, check the **Save disc image file** option and then click the **Browse** button to bring up the file dialog box. Use the file dialog box to specify a destination location, a filename, and the disc image file type. Then click **Save** to close the file dialog and click **OK** to save the disc image.

107

---

107   **Create a Disc Image from a CD**

✔ BEFORE YOU BEGIN	→ SEE ALSO
102 About Creating Data Discs	**103** Copy a CD or DVD
	108 Give Your Disc Image Its Own Drive Letter

Disc images are extremely useful because they take the contents of an entire CD and turn them into a single image file. Image files can be used in a variety of ways. They can be burned directly to a blank disc, turning it into a copy of the original CD. They can also be archived and transferred from one computer to another just like any other file. You can also use the **Load Disc Image** utility to mount a disc image as a virtual drive in the computer.

This task discusses how to use the **Save Image** utility to copy the entire contents of a CD into a disc image file.

1 Launch Save Image to Hard Drive

Launch the **Save Image to Hard Drive Wizard** from the Roxio Creator Suite **Home** page by selecting **Save Image** from the **Copy** menu.

2 Insert Disc

After you have opened the **Save Image to Hard Drive** project, insert the CD or DVD you want to image into a drive.

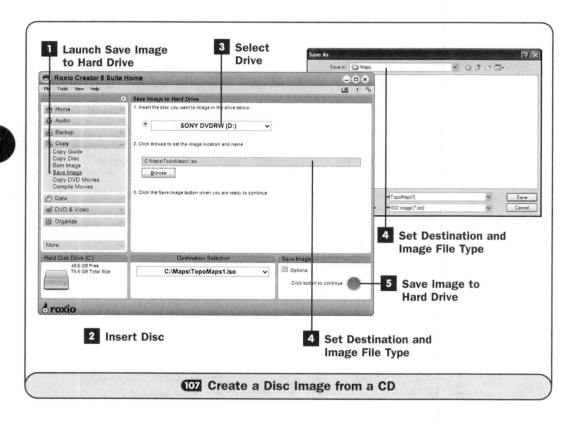

107

107 Create a Disc Image from a CD

3 **Select Drive**

After the disc has been inserted into a drive, select the drive from the source drop-down menu.

4 **Set Destination and Image File Type**

After you have selected the source drive, click the **Browse** button to bring up a file dialog box. Use the file dialog box to specify a destination location, a filename, and the disc image file type.

5 **Save Image to Hard Drive**

After you have specified the destination for the image file, click the **Save** button to save the image to disc.

---

108 **Give Your Disc Image Its Own Drive Letter**

✔ BEFORE YOU BEGIN	→ SEE ALSO
102 About Creating Data Discs	**104** Copy Data Files to a Disc
107 Create a Disc Image from a CD	**105** Create a Data Disc Using Creator Classic
	106 Create a Mixed Audio/Data CD

108

The capability to load a disc image as a virtual computer drive not only saves time, but it also reduces the wear and tear on frequently used CDs. The **Disc Image Loader** utility allows you to assign computer drive letters to a disc image file.

After the drive letter is assigned, the image can behave exactly the way that a regular CD-ROM drive would. You can browse the contents and access it from applications. You can add and delete emulated drives to support several disk images loaded at the same time.

▶ **NOTE**

If you delete the last emulated drive, Windows needs to reboot afterwards.

With hard drives becoming so much bigger than CDs, it makes a lot of sense to simply store commonly used CDs on the hard drive so you don't have the constant worry of scratching or losing them.

For example, many of the clip art packages you can buy today come with numerous CDs. Instead of having to keep track of the CDs and shuffle them in and out of the CD-ROM drive, you can image the discs and load the image files instead.

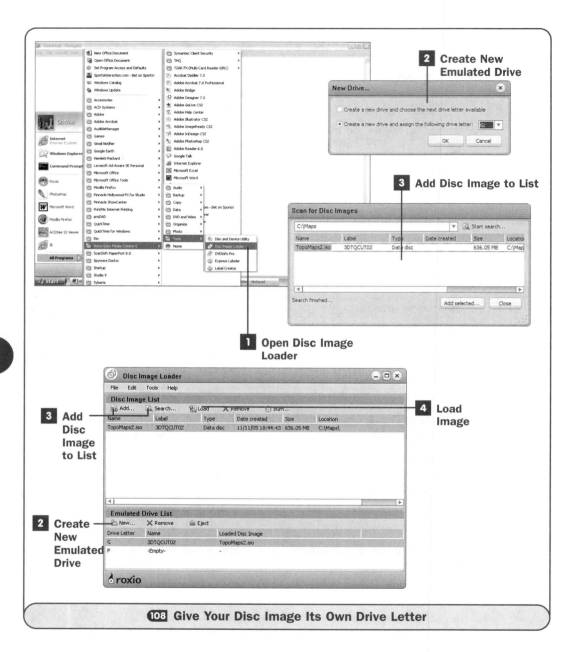

108 **Give Your Disc Image Its Own Drive Letter**

▶ **NOTE**

If **AutoPlay** is enabled on your computer, your disc image file might automatically start playing as soon as it is loaded into an emulated drive. Refer to your Windows documentation for more information about how to disable the **AutoPlay** feature.

This task discusses using the **Disc Image Loader** to load disc images as an emulated drive on the computer.

1 Open Disc Image Loader

Open the **Disc Image Loader** by selecting **Programs, Easy Media Creator 8, Tools, Disc Image Loader** from the **Start** menu in Windows.

▶ **NOTE**

As **Disc Image Loader** starts, it checks to see if there are any currently emulated drives or image files already specified. If you haven't already created an emulated disk or added disc images, you are asked if you want to add them. You can click the **Cancel** button on these questions if you don't want to add them right away.

2 Create New Emulated Drive

After **Disc Image Loader** has started, you can add a new emulated drive by clicking on the **New** button to bring up the **New Drive** dialog box. Then select the option to use the next available drive letter, or assign a specific drive letter to the image and click **OK**.

You might need to assign a specific drive letter to the image in several cases. For example, if you are running an application from the disc image, it might only run from a specific drive letter.

108

3 Add Disc Image to List

After you have created a new emulated drive, you need to add the image to the **Disc Image List** if it is not already there. To add a specific disc image, click the **Add** button and use the file dialog box to find the disc image. Then click the **Open** button to add it to the list.

You can also search for images and add them to the list automatically by clicking on the **Search** button to bring up the **Scan for Disc Images** dialog box. In the **Scan for Disc Images** dialog box, select a disk drive and click the **Start Search** button. Any images that are found are displayed in the image list. After the search has completed, select the images you want to add and click the **Add Selected** button.

4 Load Image

After you have added the disc image to the list, you can load it by either selecting it and clicking the **Load** button or dragging it down to a drive in the **Emulated Drive List** area.

▶ **TIPS**

You can change the image loaded on an emulated drive by selecting the drive in the **Emulated Drive List** area and clicking the **Eject** button. After the disc image is unloaded, drag the new image onto the emulated drive.

You can create a hot key to load a specific disc image file by right-clicking on a disc image in the **Disc Image List** and selecting **Properties**. From the **Properties** windows, select the **Enter Hot Key** text box and press the key sequence you want to use. Then anytime you want that disc image loaded, all you have to do is hit the hot key sequence.

108

14

Backing Up Data

IN THIS CHAPTER:

The capability to back up data has become more important to even the most basic home computers in recent years. Equipment and software for home users has become inexpensive as well as greatly advanced. Computers are being used for photos, music, video, banking, scrapbooking, and a myriad of other things.

In the past, most home users relied on the copy method to back up files that were important to them. The copy method is a simple copy from a hard drive to floppies, zip drives, recordable CDs, or another hard drive. The copy method works, but is not very flexible and it is difficult to keep track of what has been backed up and when.

Roxio Easy Media Creator 8 contains two applications, **Roxio Backup** and **Roxio Retrieve**, to help you back up and retrieve your data. **Roxio Backup** is a utility that allows you to create backup projects that perform backups of specific files. You can create as many backup projects as you like and tailor them to fit your specific needs.

---

109   **About Backups**

109

> → **SEE ALSO**
> ───
> **110** Create and Schedule a Backup
> **111** Perform a Data Restore

The purpose of this task is to help you understand some of the concepts you will run into when backing up data. This task helps you understand what types of media you can use for *backups*, the types of backups and backup schedules, the different options you can set when backing up files, and what files and folders are created on the backup media.

▶ KEY TERM

Backup—A selection of files that are copied from their original location and stored in a new location, providing a reserve copy in case the original files are lost or damaged.

About Backup Media

There are two basic media types to which **Roxio Backup** backs up files: CD/DVD and hard disks. Each media type has its advantages and can be used for specific purposes. You need to understand the differences between the two types of media backups to make the most out of your backups.

The following list describes the two types of backup media and their advantages and disadvantages:

- **CD/DVD**—Backing up to CD/DVD media has the benefit of creating a portable backup. You can back up the data and then take the disc with you wherever you go. It also has the advantage that the backup would be unaffected by a system crash or virus attack that wiped out the computer hard drive. The disadvantage is that a CD/DVD disc is much more limited on space than a hard drive and more easily damaged.

- **Hard drive**—Backing up to the hard drive is faster and has the advantage of considerably more space than CD/DVDs. However, a hard drive backup is limited to the hard disk on which it was backed up. When that hard drive is active on the computer, it is susceptible to viruses. However, if you want to back up a large amount of data and do not want to have to use multiple CD/DVDs, the hard drive is definitely the way to go.

▶ **TIP**

The best of both worlds is to get an external hard drive. They connect to the USB or FireWire port, making them completely portable and they are almost as fast as an internal hard drive.

109

Types of Backups

When you use the copy method to back up files, there is only one method: copying from source to destination. **Roxio Backup**, however, provides some different types of backups that allow you to make much better use of your disc space through incremental backups and better use of your time through automatic scheduling.

The following describes the two types of backups and two types of schedules that are provided in **Roxio Backup**:

- **Full backup**—Full backup means that every file included in the backup is backed up each time. This is the easiest way to manage backups. However, it takes a lot more disc space and time.

- **Incremental backup**—Incremental backup means that only the files that have changed since the last backup are backed up. This is much faster and requires less disc space, but it is harder to keep track of which backup version a file might have been backed up to.

- **Manual**—Manual backup means that you must deliberately start the backup every time you want it to run. This is the best option for backups that must be performed on demand.

- **Automatic**—Automatic backups are scheduled to run on periodic intervals. You should use automatic backups for files you want backed up on a daily, weekly, or monthly basis.

About Backup Options

Now that you understand the types of backups you can perform, you need to understand the advanced options you can set for a backup. These options help you tailor the backup process to best meet your needs by compressing the files to save room, encrypting the files to provide security, or verifying the files to ensure consistency.

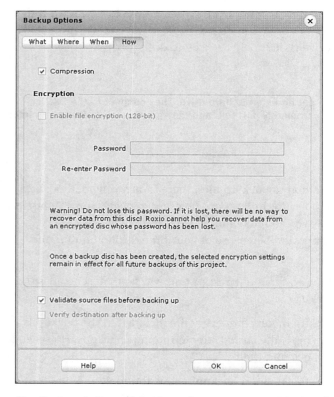

109

The Backup Options dialog box allows you to control what files are backed up, where file backups are stored, when to start a backup, and how to back up files.

The following describes the options that are available for backups:

- **Compression**—Using the *compression* setting for backups compresses the files so you can fit more data on the disc. However, compressing the files slows down the backup and retrieval process.

▶ KEY TERM

Compression—Collapsing the free space inside files so they require a smaller amount of storage space.

- **Encryption**—Using the *encryption* setting allows you to assign a password to the backup. That password must be entered before files can be retrieved from the backup. This is very useful if you want to back up confidential documents such as bank or tax records.

▶ KEY TERM

Encryption—Using a numeric algorithm to control access to files by requiring a password to access them.

- **Source verification**—When the source verification option is set, the source files are verified before the backup takes place. This takes more time, but it is better to verify the source than to have the backup stop in the middle of a burn because of a problem with one of the source files.

- **Destination verification**—When the destination verification option is set, the destination files are scanned after the backup takes place. If the destination files do not match the source files, you are notified. If the data you are backing up is very important, it would be a good idea to set this option.

109

About the Backup File System

This section discusses the file system that is created when you perform a backup using **Roxio Backup**. If you are an advanced user, understanding the file system helps you access the files in the backup without having to use **Roxio Retrieve**. The following are three main folders that make up the Roxio Backup file system:

- **Root**—The root of the backup file system is the root of the CD/DVD disc if you back up to disc, or the destination folder you specify when you back up to hard drive. If you are backing up to disc, the root has two files in it, an autoplay file to automatically start **Roxio Retrieve** and the Launch_ Retrieve.exe application that launches **Roxio Retrieve**. If you are backing up to hard drive, the root only has the Launch_Retrieve.exe application in it.

- **$ROXIO$**—Under the root folder is the $ROXIO$ folder that contains the **Roxio Retrieve** application files. You never need to do anything with this folder.

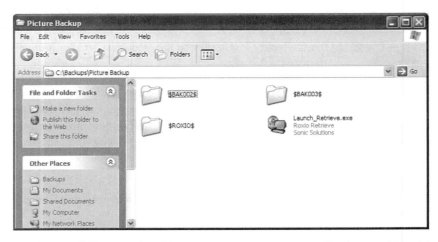

The backup folder contains the Launch_Retrieve.exe *application used to retrieve backed up files, a* $ROXIO$ *folder with application files, as well as* $BAK###$ *folders with the backup data in them.*

- **$BAK###$**—Each time you perform a backup, a **$BAK###$** (**###** is a three-digit number) folder is created in the root folder. Inside the **$BAK###$** folder, a **D_###** folder is created for each hard drive involved in the backup. The files and folders that are backed up are under the **D_###** folders.

110

110 Create and Schedule a Backup

✔ BEFORE YOU BEGIN	→ SEE ALSO
109 About Backups	**111** Perform a Data Restore

The **Roxio Backup** utility allows you to create customized backup projects to back up specific files and folders that you want to preserve. You can create several backup projects to back up different sets of data. For example, you can create a different backup project for banking than for your photos.

Keeping different backup projects for different files helps you manage them better and makes it easier to find files you need to retrieve later.

This task helps you create a backup project, define what files should be backed up, where they will be backed up to, when to perform the backup, and how to back them up.

1 Launch Roxio Backup

Launch **Roxio Backup** by selecting **File Backup** from the **Backup** menu of the Easy Media Creator **Home** page.

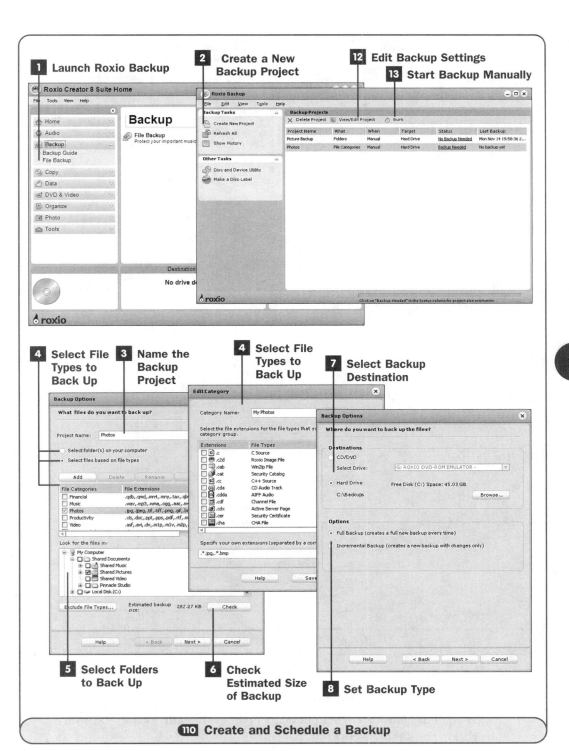

1 Launch Roxio Backup

2 Create a New Backup Project

12 Edit Backup Settings

13 Start Backup Manually

4 Select File Types to Back Up

3 Name the Backup Project

4 Select File Types to Back Up

7 Select Backup Destination

5 Select Folders to Back Up

6 Check Estimated Size of Backup

8 Set Backup Type

110 Create and Schedule a Backup

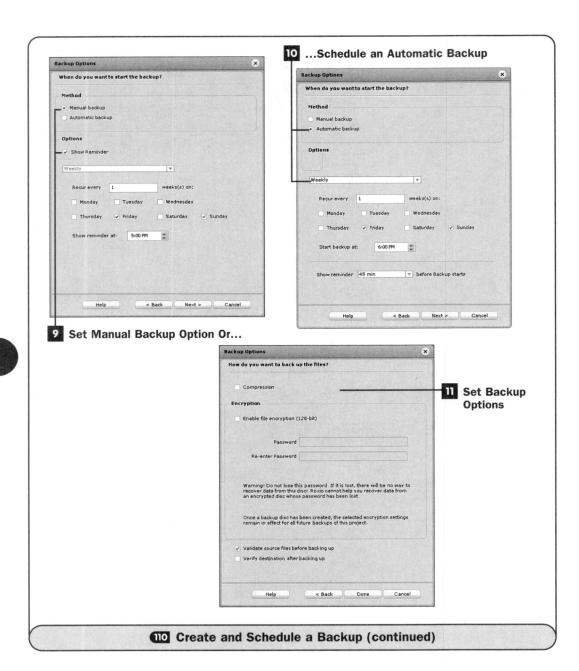

10 ...Schedule an Automatic Backup

9 Set Manual Backup Option Or...

11 Set Backup Options

110 Create and Schedule a Backup (continued)

2 **Create a New Backup Project**

After you have launched **Roxio Backup**, open the **Backup Project Assistant** by clicking on **Create New Project**.

3 Name the Backup Project

After the **Backup Project Assistant** starts, type a name for the project in the **Project Name** field. It is important to use a meaningful name here because you need to use that name to identify the project when retrieving files later.

4 Select File Types to Back Up

Roxio Backup defaults to the **Select folder(s) on your computer** option. When this option is selected, every file in the folders you will select in step 5 will be included in the backup.

You can also limit the backup to specific categories of files by selecting the **Select files based on file types** option. When you select this option, a file category list appears. Each category lists the *file extensions* that will be included in the backup. To add a category to the backup, select the check box next to the category name.

▶ **KEY TERM**

File extension—A set of characters (typically 3 characters) after the last . in a filename that denotes what type of data is contained in the file.

You can create a customized category by clicking on the **Add** button to bring up the **Edit Category** dialog box. In the **Edit Category** dialog box, you need to set the name and then either select file extensions from the list or type in your own extensions, separated by a comma, in the text box provided.

▶ **NOTE**

You can also exclude files types from the backup by clicking on the **Exclude File Types** button and selecting files types to exclude. Files with the extensions that are excluded are not backed up.

5 Select Folders to Back Up

After you are finished setting the file types option, if necessary, use the files system tree to select the check boxes next to folders you want to back up.

6 Check Estimated Size of Backup

After you have added the folders you want to back up, check the estimated size of the backup by clicking on the **Check** button. This displays the estimated size of the backup to the left of the **Check** button. It is always a good idea to check the size of the backup so you know if it will fit on the destination disc or hard drive that you want to use.

110

After you have checked the size of the backup, click the **Next** button to continue.

7 Select Backup Destination

After you have selected what to back up, you need to configure where the files will be backed up to. First select either the **CD/DVD** option or the **Hard Drive** option. If you select the **CD/DVD** option, select the CD/DVD burner from the drop-down list. If you selected the **Hard Drive** option, click the **Browse** button to select a folder in which to store the backup. A folder with the project name is created in this folder when the first backup takes place.

8 Set Backup Type

After you have selected the backup destination, set the backup type to **Full Backup** or **Incremental Backup**. Then click the **Next** button to schedule the backup.

9 Set Manual Backup Option Or...

You can configure the backup method to manual by selecting **Manual backup**. If you select **Manual backup**, you must start the backup manually from **Roxio Backup** each time. This is the best option for a few scenarios. One scenario is if you want to back up files immediately after you change them. Another scenario is if you rarely change the files and only want to perform a backup when you do change them.

▶ **TIP**

You can still remind yourself to back up this project even if you choose the manual method by selecting the **Show Reminder** check box and configuring a daily, weekly, or monthly reminder schedule.

10 ...Schedule an Automatic Backup

You can also schedule the backup to occur automatically on a recurring schedule by selecting the **Automatic backup** option. When you select the **Automatic backup** option, the options area of the page changes and you need to configure the backup to occur on a daily, weekly, or monthly basis by selecting **Daily**, **Weekly**, or **Monthly** from the drop-down list. For each option you can select specific day settings. You can also set the time the backup occurs.

You can also schedule a reminder to be sent to you a specific number of minutes before the backup occurs by selecting a time from the **Show reminder at** drop-down list. If you select **0 min** from the list, no reminder is sent.

110

After you have scheduled the backup, click the **Next** button to configure the backup options.

▶ TIPS

You should schedule a reminder for automatic backups so the backup doesn't start while you are doing something important on the computer for two reasons. First, the computer performance is slowed considerably and second, having open files might interfere with the backup.

You might want to schedule the backup in the middle of the night to ensure that no one is using the computer.

🔟 Set Backup Options

Set the backup options you want to use when creating the backup by selecting the check box next to them. On the **Backup Options** screen, you can enable file compression, encryption with a password, source verification, and destination verification.

After you have finished selecting the backup options, click the **Done** button to save the project and return to **Roxio Backup**.

▶ TIP

Verify source files before backing up is selected by default and should remain selected. It doesn't take much extra time and saves you headaches later.

🔟 Edit Backup Settings

You can edit a backup project at any time in **Roxio Backup** by selecting the project from the **Backup Projects** list and clicking on the **View/Edit Project** button in the taskbar to bring up the **Options** dialog box. All of the options discussed in steps 3–11 are accessible by clicking on the **What**, **Where**, **When**, and **How** buttons.

🔟 Start Backup Manually

You can start a backup manually at any time, even on projects scheduled to back up automatically, by selecting the project from the **Backup Projects** list and clicking on the **Burn** button.

▶ TIP

You can see the history of a backup by clicking on the Show History button. The history report shows the date/time, the number of discs, and the project size of all backups that have occurred. You can also select a specific backup from the drop-down list to see a report of only one backup.

111 Perform a Data Restore

✔ BEFORE YOU BEGIN

109 About Backups
110 Create and Schedule a Backup

The **Roxio Retrieve** utility enables you to retrieve files that you backed up using the **Roxio Backup** utility to either their original location or to a new location. You might need to retrieve the files for numerous reasons. A few examples are if a file is deleted or corrupted, you want to install the files on a new computer, or you want to look at older files in a project.

The **Roxio Retrieve** utility is a stand-alone utility that is copied onto the backup media. This means you do not need to have Easy Media Creator installed on the computer where you are retrieving the data.

1 Open Roxio Retrieve

If you backed up your files to CD/DVD, **Roxio Retrieve** should be launched when you insert the disc into your computer. If the autoplay feature is disabled on your system or if you backed up to the hard disk, open **Roxio Retrieve** by using Windows Explorer to navigate to the folder where that backup was created and double-click on the `Launch_Retrieve.exe` file.

2 Select Backup Version

After you have opened **Roxio Retrieve**, you can select any of the past backups from the **Backup History** drop-down list. The **Backup History** list includes a different version for every backup that has taken place on the CD/DVD or hard disk. This feature can be useful if you need to restore a file that might not be among the most recently backed up versions.

3 Select Files to Retrieve Or...

After you have selected the backup version, use the folder tree to find the file(s) you want to retrieve and select the check box next to the file/folder name. When you have selected all the files you want to retrieve, click the **Retrieve** button to bring up the **Retrieve** dialog box.

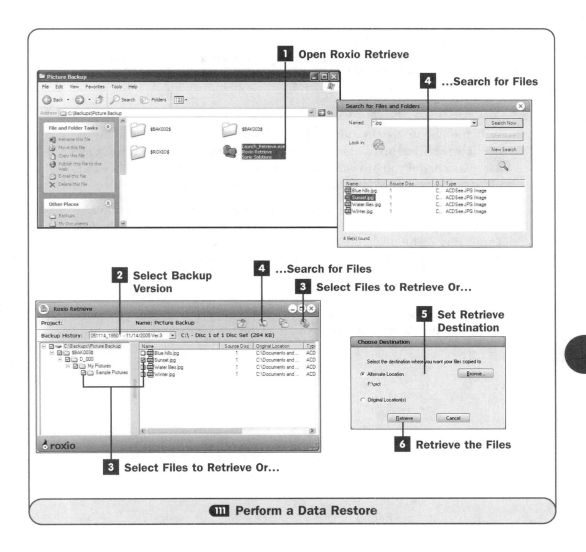

1 Open Roxio Retrieve

4 ...Search for Files

2 Select Backup Version

4 ...Search for Files

3 Select Files to Retrieve Or...

5 Set Retrieve Destination

6 Retrieve the Files

3 Select Files to Retrieve Or...

111 Perform a Data Restore

4 ...Search for Files

You can also search for files to retrieve by clicking on the **Search** button to bring up the **Search for Files and Folders** dialog box. After the **Search for Files and Folders** dialog box is open, enter a filename in the **Named** text box and click the **Search Now** button to find the file(s). If a file is found in the backup, it is added to the files list.

After you have found the file you want to retrieve, right-click on the file in the list and select **Retrieve** to bring up the **Choose Destination** dialog box.

▶ **TIP**

The search feature supports wildcard characters to help you search for files. For example, to find all files that begin with "Sum," you can enter **Sum*.*** in the name field.

5 **Set Retrieve Destination**

From the **Choose Destination** dialog box you can retrieve the file to the location it was backed up from by selecting **Original Location(s)**. You want to use this option if you just want the correct file back where it was—for example, if a document became corrupt or was accidentally deleted.

You can also specify a different location by selecting **Alternate Location**. Click on the **Browse** button to specify a location to which to restore the files. This is very useful if you are backing up from one computer and retrieving to another, or if you just want to restore to a different location.

6 **Retrieve the Files**

After you have selected the destination, click the **Retrieve** button to retrieve the files. If the file already exists, you are prompted whether to overwrite it.

111

Index

SYMBOLS

NUMBERS

A

B

C

F

G

J – K – L

Q – R

U – V

X – Y – Z

Key Terms

Don't let unfamiliar terms discourage you from learning all you can about Roxio Easy Media Creator 8. If you don't completely understand what one of these words means, flip to the indicated page, read the full definition there, and find techniques related to that term.

Alignment   *How an object is lined up in relation to other objects, or how text is lined up in relation to its text box.*   **Page 188**

Aspect ratio   *The width to height ratio to which a video is formatted.*   **219**

AVI DV   *The largest and highest quality video file format. Captured on a MiniDV tape as a DV file and imported into the computer as an AVI file.*   **254**

Backup   *A selection of files that are copied from their original location and stored in a new location, providing a reserve copy in case the original files are lost.*   **376**

Balance   *The volume of the right channel relative to the volume of the left channel of audio.*   **71**

Canvas   *The total working area that an image file is capable of using.*   **149**

Capture   *To convert audio, photos, and video to files that can be read and duplicated by your computer.*   **28**

Chroma key   *A transparency effect based on color, or the exact color that is used for the transparency effect.*   **323**

Color panel   *A still frame in a video production or slideshow that is created by choosing a solid color for the background. It can be used to break up portions of the production or as a menu. A color panel has all the attributes of a still shot. It's also called a blank slide.*   **285**

Compression   *Collapsing the free space inside files so they require a smaller amount of storage space.*   **379**

Convert   *To change a file from one format to another.*   **57**

Crop   *To delete the unselected portion of a file.*   **68**

Cutout   *An area of an image that has been cut from a larger area.*   **174**

Data disc   *A CD or DVD with files on it that can be read using a CD or DVD drive in a computer.*   **354**

Disc image   *The contents of an entire CD or DVD that has been turned into a single image file.*   **354**

DPI (dots per inch)   *A term used to quantify the digital dots per actual inch of an image. For instance, 300 dpi means that a printed image has 300×300 (90,000) dots per square inch. The higher the dpi is, the higher the quality of the printed image is.*   **Page 132**

Emulated drive   *A logical drive that acts like a physical disk drive in the computer. Drive letters can be assigned to it and it shows up in Windows Explorer.*   **365**

Encryption   *Using a numeric algorithm to control access to files by requiring a password to access them.*   **379**

Exposure   *The amount of light a photo is exposed to as it is being taken, usually determined by the aperture of the lens.*   **144**

File extension   *A set of characters (typically 3 characters) after the last . in a filename that denotes what type of data is contained in the file.*   **383**

FireWire   *The common cable format used for transferring video from one device to another.*   **252**

Frame rate   *The number of frames that appear in every second of video.*   **273**

Horizontal scaling   *Adjusts the width of text in a project based on a scale of 1% to 100%.*   **188**

Import   *To place a file on the computer. You can import by digitizing an external source such as audio, video, or a photo, or you can import files from another digital source, such as an external hard drive or a network.*   **124**

Internal track   *A text or a special effect that is linked to a specific video or photo file.*   **276**

Jukebox disc   *A music CD that is made up of MP3 files and folders. It can hold a lot more than a conventional CD and the folders become playlists.*   **91**

Key frame   *A frame within a video that sets a definition for the frames around it.*   **241**

Layer   *A separate component within a larger project that can be manipulated independently of the other components of the project.*   **73**